BUILDING A CULTURE FOR SUSTAINABILITY

BUILDING A CULTURE FOR SUSTAINABILITY

People, Planet, and Profits in a New Green Economy

JEANA WIRTENBERG

Foreword by Andrew Winston

 PRAEGER

AN IMPRINT OF ABC-CLIO, LLC
Santa Barbara, California • Denver, Colorado • Oxford, England

Copyright 2014 by ABC-CLIO, LLC

Library of Congress Cataloging-in-Publication Data

Wirtenberg, Jeana.
    Building a culture for sustainability : people, planet, and profits in a new green economy / Jeana Wirtenberg ; foreword by Andrew Winston.
        p. cm.
    Includes bibliographical references and index.
    ISBN 978-1-4408-0376-5 (hard copy : alk. paper) — ISBN 978-1-4408-0377-2 (ebook)   1. Sustainability—Case studies.   2. Social responsibility of business—Case studies.   I. Title.
    HC79.E5W5655   2014
    658.4'083—dc23   2013041579

ISBN: 978-1-4408-0376-5
EISBN: 978-1-4408-0377-2

18 17 16 15 14   1 2 3 4 5

This book is also available on the World Wide Web as an eBook.
Visit www.abc-clio.com for details.

Praeger
An Imprint of ABC-CLIO, LLC

ABC-CLIO, LLC
130 Cremona Drive, P.O. Box 1911
Santa Barbara, California 93116-1911

This book is printed on acid-free paper ∞

Manufactured in the United States of America

To our dear sweet mother Pearl Cecile Wirtenberg, who will remain in our hearts forever. Mom showed us the way to live a sustainable life.

Contents

viii Contents

Foreword

The world is facing a number of enormous challenges and threats to our continued prosperity. The mega-forces bearing down on society and business can be daunting: climate change and extreme weather; resource constraints and rising commodity prices as we add billions of middle-class consumers; growing inequality around the world; a new, radical transparency driven in part by technology and a new level of connectivity.

Any one of these mega-challenges alone is enough to justify rethinking how we live our lives and how all our institutions operate. These issues affect all of us, but the business community in particular will be at the center of solving these challenges, which are all included (sometimes awkwardly) in the buckets called "sustainability" and the "triple bottom line."

To take on big issues, we need a major shift in how companies operate, what I'm calling "The Big Pivot," which means shifting our priorities from short-term earnings focus to solving the world's biggest problems and using capitalism, markets, and competition to do it profitably.

But to move companies down a different path, we need examples of success, tactical best practices, and not a small amount of hope. Jeana Wirtenberg's *Building a Culture for Sustainability* is offering all three of these important elements. Wirtenberg suggests her own kind of pivot, what she calls a "profound transformation, from a singular focus on profitability to an integrated triple bottom line."

Wirtenberg's approach is to capture all that needs to change at companies under the banner of "culture," a notoriously hard thing to define. One model of culture that I've found useful comes from Edgar Schein at MIT who boils down what an organization stands for into three levels, from tangible actions and behaviors ("artifacts") through the stated values to the more deeply held beliefs and "assumptions."

Given the scale of our challenges and the depth of change we need to truly drive sustainability into an organization, we might logically conclude that we need to get down to that third level. But how do you do that? How do you even know if you've succeeded in changing beliefs?

Well, I think you can tell, in part, what a company believes by looking at those higher levels, the actual policies and initiatives that companies put in place. More importantly, recent research on how to change behaviors and make new habits in your life suggests that you act the way you want to be before you really believe it (e.g., get up in the morning and run enough times in a row, and you're a runner). I think an organization can change what it believes by deciding, deliberately and strategically, to change the more visible policies.

This book is filled with deeply researched case studies that give us many examples of how leading companies act differently to build a culture for sustainability. You'll see organizations taking a full, holistic (one of Wirtenberg's favorite words) view of their business. These leaders are making broad thinking a part of the corporate culture and systematically creating more sustainable supply chains, operations, and products and services for their customers.

Many of the best practices here will seem logical, such as chemical giant BASF's work to integrate sustainability into everyone's goals and into leadership development—or Ingersoll Rand's "One STEP Forward" program that builds awareness of global challenges and how employee actions at work and home matter. These are straightforward culture-building examples, but not always easy to do well.

And there are deeper, subtler ways that companies operate which fall under this book's broad culture banner as well. Consider how companies make investment decisions. In the conclusion to this book, Wirtenberg highlights a few issues that are cross-cutting themes and challenges, including how to measure the return on investment (ROI) of sustainability initiatives.

This theme spoke to me because it's at the heart of our problems. I believe that ROI is broken. Companies are good at understanding the "I" part—how much something will cost—but not very good at measuring the full value of "R." What's the value of building deeper relationships with customers by helping them solve their sustainability challenges? How about the value of attracting and retaining the best people who want to work for a company that shares their values? Or protecting a license to operate that local communities provide to companies that they want to live with?

These are all measures of the value that building a culture for sustainability brings to an organization. The leaders will create better places to work, certainly, but also become more innovative and better partners to their customers. So finding ways to shift the way we think about ROI is a tactical, strategic, and cultural issue, which brings me back to the whole idea of culture. It's so amorphous because it's really the sum of everything an organization does.

As many have commented—and Wirtenberg quotes one BASF executive saying—"culture is what everybody does when no one is looking." But in a world of radical transparency, where every action your employees or your suppliers take is open to scrutiny, everyone *is* looking now. So companies need to build a culture for sustainability because it's the right thing to do, because all of the major stakeholders (including their customers and employees) are watching, and because it's profitable.

Often managers say they don't know where to start on this complicated journey toward sustainability. They need examples of how it's done. Companies, and the managers that make up those organizations and create their company's culture, would do well to learn from the great examples laid out here.

Andrew Winston
Founder, Winston Eco-Strategies
Co-author of *Green to Gold,* and
author of *The Big Pivot*
September 2013

Preface

This book is about hope and possibility for the generations to come. With humility and profound gratitude to the hundreds of people I have come to know along this journey, many of whom are represented in this book, and to the millions more who are committing to creating a sustainable future for us all—and with full awareness of the mega-trends and enormous challenges confronting humanity and our precious earth—I stand for the possibility that *we can and will* find a way to be and have *enough . . . for all . . . forever.*

Core Sustainability Concepts

Systems thinking	Socio-economic justice	Intergenerational responsibility

Enough . . .	. . . for all . . .	. . . forever.

Figure 0.1   © 2013 Bob Willard. Used with permission.

Purpose of This Book

This book is designed to provide a practical, straightforward, applied guide to successfully building a culture for sustainability in the global marketplace for firms of all types, from those just starting their journey to sustainability to those already on the journey who are seeking to accelerate and deepen their positive impacts on people, reduce their environmental footprint, and enhance their financial bottom line in the short, medium, and long term.

The book presents in-depth "best practice" case studies of nine mid-size through large global companies that are leaders in sustainability and corporate social responsibility and includes the "whats" and the "hows" of each enterprise's path to sustainability. These unique stories are viewed through the eyes of the participating leaders, managers, and individual contributors.

The case studies represent different approaches and a diverse cross section of industries and sectors—consumer products, manufacturing, business-to-business, pharmaceutical, chemistry, hospitality, telecommunications, and professional services—and functions. They offer unique experiences to help readers appreciate, emotionally as well as intellectually, what it feels like for employees to work in a company that gives meaning to their work lives by enabling them to contribute simultaneously to creating a better society, saving the planet, and increasing their company's financial and economic value. Myriad practical examples of innovative and exciting initiatives show readers how to engage the hearts and minds of employees and highlight the remarkable results that can be achieved from a triple-bottom-line approach (people, planet, and profits). This book

- Introduces a lens through which to view a firm's culture for sustainability
- Helps companies learn from each other's experience through best practices and through what didn't work
- Offers proven methods that can be customized to a company's unique needs for creating work environments in which employees are fully involved in, and enthusiastic about, their work
- Elucidates the importance of employee engagement in developing and implementing a sustainable culture
- Shows the reader how to recognize potential employee engagement opportunities and interventions for sustainability

- Provides deep appreciation of emerging green/sustainable business trends, best practices, and the business environments and cultures that support them
- Helps the reader identify the strengths and weaknesses of his or her firm as these relate to building a sustainable culture for the short, medium, and long term

Methods Used in Creating This Book

Here I briefly describe how this book came to be. As discussed in the acknowledgments, my work with the Institute for Sustainable Enterprise (ISE) at Fairleigh Dickinson University (www.fdu.edu/ise) gave me the opportunity to work with and come to know almost all the companies whose cases are included here, most of which have joined ISE as Corporate Partners.

In 2009, the ISE Corporate Partners started a series of Corporate Partner Roundtables, which I codesign and facilitate and which are continuing to this day. Five roundtables on the topic "Creating a Culture for Sustainability" (http://view.fdu.edu/default.aspx?id=8553) were held between September 2010 and June 2011. The companies' stories and the quality and authenticity of the dialogue across companies impressed and inspired me so much that, in September 2011, when ABC-CLIO Praeger invited me to write a book on sustainability, I decided to share them with the rest of the world.

When I had identified the companies and they had agreed to participate, I created an interview protocol and asked each company to identify up to a dozen leaders, managers, and individual contributors, based on criteria I'd developed, for me to interview. I conducted one-on-one interviews with more than 70 individuals in 2012 and 2013. I taped and transcribed each so that I could be certain of the interviewees' exact words and the nuances in their voices. Many of them gave me access to internal documents, which I perused. I also conducted my own secondary research, involving hundreds of documents, books, and articles.

After accumulating and reviewing all the information I could on each company, I went over it again to determine what to focus on in each chapter and to find elements that best represented each company's unique approach and the story of its implementation: the most illuminating quotes, best practices, strategies, results, and conundrums. During the writing process, I went back to the companies (sometimes several times) for clarification, updates, answers to questions that arose, and assurances that I had accurately reflected their programs, accomplishments, challenges, and commitments.

Over the two years that I worked on this book, there were, not surprisingly, many significant twists and turns. For example, I had selected 10 companies to profile, but an acquisition of one of the companies stopped my interviews midway and ultimately prevented me from including it. In more than half the companies, key people I had interviewed left and went elsewhere. In one case, it was the CEO who moved on.

In the conclusion, chapter 11, I provide some caveats and limitations to help contextualize the best practices and a table in the appendix that readers can use to quickly find examples of best practices in specific categories arranged by key stakeholders—people, community, customers, planet, supply chain, shareholders. Second, I present the essential elements of a culture for sustainability. Third, I distill the key lessons learned by these companies and the challenges they, and others aspiring to join the journey to sustainability, face now and will continue to face long into the future. Fourth, I provide my own recommendations for the sustainability-inspired habits that will be necessary to produce the kind of deep change that will help put us on a course to a truly sustainable world.

Who Should Read This Book

The book is designed primarily for business leaders and managers, organizational development professionals, consultants, and practitioners who are looking for ways to achieve better triple-bottom-line results by creating a culture for sustainability.

The book will also be of great interest to professors and students in business, human resources, and sustainability-related fields. It can be a course adoption for upper-division undergraduate and graduate students, part of a core curriculum, and a provocative resource for teaching and research in sustainable business, organizational behavior, human resources, environmental psychology, social issues, organizational development, and more.

The book will also interest a thoughtful general audience—consumers, suppliers, shareholders, stakeholders, and the like—concerned with issues surrounding sustainability.

How to Read This Book: Key Features

The book has a number of features to help readers get the most out of the in-depth case studies. Each chapter includes:

- Best practices from the highly successful global company profiled
- A "lessons learned" section
- Sidebars with tips and examples that can be used by any type of business
- Compelling insets, quotes, and examples from employees who have participated in a wide variety of employee engagement activities
- Frameworks and tools that readers can use to analyze and assess the progress of their individual companies and customize to their specific situations
- Resources that enable readers to identify and contact helpful outside sources

In these ways and others, the book is designed to be a valuable guide into a sustainable future with enough, for all, forever.

Acknowledgments

I wish I had the space to acknowledge by name the hundreds of people who have contributed to my thinking and the dozens of people and organizations who helped in tangible and intangible ways to make this book possible. Scores of thought leaders inspired and fueled my vision. I will name two here who touched my life in ways they will never know: Ray Anderson transformed his own company, Interface Inc., and in the process became a role model for sustainable business. And C.K. Prahalad, a groundbreaking strategist who showed how corporations could increase the standard of living of those at the "bottom of the pyramid" and benefit financially from that work at the same time.

I would like to thank the Institute for Sustainable Enterprise (ISE) at Fairleigh Dickinson University, especially the Corporate Partners, who provided the impetus and foundation for much of the material in this book. It was through their generous sharing of an inside view of their best practices, challenges, and lessons learned at our "Building a Culture for Sustainability" series of Executive Roundtables that I found the inspiration, context, and eventually the content for much of this book. I would like to express my deep appreciation to ISE's principals and research fellows Joel Harmon, Kent Fairfield, Dan Twomey, Matt Polsky, Bill Russell, Gerard Farias, and Jonathan Cloud for their thought leadership, vision, and collaboration, and to Maura Pniewski for her invaluable support which helps make all our work possible.

I want to acknowledge the nine companies that allowed me into their facilities to conduct my research and the gracious people at each company who helped me organize and conduct my interviews: Barry Dambach at Alcatel-Lucent, Laurie Roy at Alcoa, Scott Sandman at BASF, Jyoti Agarwal at Bureau Veritas, Matt Wasserman at Church & Dwight;

Christopher Tessier at Ingersoll Rand, Oonagh Puglisi at Pfizer, Roni Croucher at Sanofi, and Faith Taylor and Nicole Gaglio at Wyndham Worldwide. I am especially grateful to the 70-plus people from around the world whom I interviewed at these nine companies. Each is named in his or her respective chapter, so I won't repeat them all here.

I am grateful beyond words to my phenomenal editor George-Thérèse Dickenson, who patiently coached, coaxed, and encouraged me to make this book an authentic expression of everything I have learned and want to communicate to the world. I could not have done this without her selfless and unwavering commitment to capturing the nuanced meaning of my words and her masterful attention to the minutest details of sentence structure and grammar.

To stay focused as I wrote this book, I had to put many things aside, and I would not have been able to do this without colleagues who are as understanding and supportive as mine. I am especially grateful to Transitioning to Green principals William G. Russell, Linda M. Kelley, and Bill Scalzitti, who individually and collectively demonstrate the rarest combinations: they are not only brilliant and inspirational, but also grounded and practical, knowledgeable and wise, and generous to a fault. I also want to acknowledge my extraordinary, insightful, and well-grounded business partner Tom Drucker and our fantastic, efficient assistant, Ryan Bryant.

I am eternally grateful to my best friend Rose Ann Alspektor who has always been there for me. I hope that I can do the same for her as we move forward on our life journeys.

Also I must acknowledge my loving family. I am enormously grateful to my mother Pearl, whose constant caring and concern for my well-being kept me nourished spiritually and physically, even as her own health began to wane. Mom was the quintessential embodiment of sustainability: she believed in simplicity, was never ostentatious, and always did what is right. She was intensely curious and inquiring about everything—people, business, and the world. She was a gentle soul, generous, gracious, and incredibly smart, yet always humble.

I am grateful for the support and caring of my siblings: my wonderful and brilliant brother Alfred I. Wirtenberg and sister-in-law Margaret Wirtenberg who cheered me on through every step and helped in myriad small and big ways to keep me going; my brother Philip Wirtenberg who always helps broaden my perspective, keeping me honest, open-minded, and on my toes; and my sister Sharon Wirtenberg whose unconditional love and understanding through good times and bad means the world to me.

Finally, I want to acknowledge my loving husband Bill, who supports me in fulfilling my dreams and is there for me in the abundant times of joy, and the scarce times of sadness. Together with our fabulous sons, Justin and Spencer, my entire family helps keep me centered, alive, and happy every day of my life.

CHAPTER 1

Building Bridges to a Sustainable Future: Understanding and Creating a Culture for Sustainability

Whether they realize it or not, companies today must choose between two fundamentally different paths: the path of yesterday and unsustainability, and the path of a prosperous and sustainable future for themselves, society, and the planet. We are all immersed in the same profound transformation, from a singular focus on *profitability* to an integrated *triple bottom line:* a holistic approach that simultaneously unleashes the talent, creativity, and innovation of *people,* takes care of our *planet,* and produces a *prosperous* future for the generations to come. This triple-bottom-line focus on *people, planet,* and *profits* has been talked about for years, ever since John Elkington coined the term in his book *Cannibals with Forks* in 1998.[1]

Like all companies, the nine profiled in this book need to operate inside the current economic reality, which rewards short-term profits and puts shareholders above all else. Yet these companies consciously choose a sustainable path for themselves, their people, and the planet. Why? And how do they do it? What goes into the choices and decisions they make every day regarding how to run their businesses? What challenges do they face? What lessons have they learned?

This book tells the rich and authentic stories of why and how these nine successful global companies, from a wide cross section of industries and sectors, are making the transition to the triple bottom line in the emerging green economy. I describe how they are contributing to, and benefiting from, this transition. I share their struggles, their challenges, their successes, and the lessons they are learning on the journey to sustainability.

My intention in writing this book is to provide inspiration and practical ideas for people in all organizations—small, medium, and large companies; nonprofits; and public and educational institutions. I invite each person reading this book to say aloud, "If they can do it, so can I!" Take note of ideas that may be a fit for your organization, or even kernels of ideas on which you can build a foundation for your own journey to sustainability.

Setting the Context: The Urgent Need for Systemic and Holistic Change

There is no doubt that today we are experiencing global economic, ecological, and socioeconomic justice problems[2]—financial crises, social unrest, and environmental disasters. Systems thinking tells us that these upheavals are inextricably intertwined. They point to a fundamental lack of sustainability and the urgent need for systemic and holistic change. The time for this change is now, and I choose to be optimistic and believe that the needed changes are not only possible, but already occurring.

Critical is a shift in how organizations are led, are managed, and operate, moving from the single-bottom-line measure of profit to the triple-bottom-line focus on people, planet, and profit. When I speak about sustainability throughout this book, I am referring to much more than going green or engaging in eco-friendly practices; I am speaking about a fundamental and profound redefinition of the purpose, way of being, and way of operating of every function and facet of an organization.

The voices and actions of the nine diverse companies breathe life into this redefinition as they put the triple bottom line into practice, embedding it as an intrinsic part of their vision, mission, purpose, policies, practices, systems, and processes. They engage their employees in co-creating a sustainable future for themselves and us all, and in this book, readers will experience the ways in which each company is making its own unique contribution to sustainability, fueled by the passion, hearts, and minds—and just plain common sense—of these employees. Readers will find a multitude of examples of how each of the companies' people are discovering and implementing sustainable business practices and responding to the marketplace with products and services that meet the needs of tomorrow as well as today.

Envisioning a Sustainable World, 2050

I begin with my personal dream. It is of a world built on the foundation of a caring and green economy, where people live in peace and harmony, with universal literacy, and a resilient and regenerative infrastructure. In my vision, the world circa 2050 is flourishing economically, and the people are flourishing psychologically, emotionally, socially, spiritually, and physically. The world, and its multiplicity of cultures, embraces inclusivity, respect, and diversity. Its people and its leaders are now on a new course, the path to being truly sustainable forever. In this world, every female and male child has full access to education; the digital divide has disappeared, and everyone is connected to everyone else instantaneously; hundreds of thousands of local communities are self-sustaining through new forms of commerce; cradle-to-cradle use of natural resources (renewable, reusable, zero waste) is ubiquitous; sustainable design principles guide building practices; corporations have redefined themselves as existing to serve societal needs, are committed to the health and well-being of every person on the planet, and prosper financially, creating good jobs, serving their customers' and communities' needs, and continually expanding local, regional, and global economies. I fully recognize that my dream of a world of possibilities, sufficiency, and sustainability exists in a world plagued by seemingly insurmountable problems and challenging megatrends.

Megatrends 2013–2050

How can we meet the basic needs of food, water, energy, housing, and education for the 7 billion people we have now in 2013, let alone for the 9 billion people who will inhabit the earth in 2050? Richard Wells, in "To Build Long Term Sustainability, Envision the Future First," has identified eight trending global realities that he believes will most significantly affect the future of firms and nations in the decades to come. Each of the nine companies in this book is focused on at least one, and often several, of these eight megatrends:

- **Growth of the middle class.** Although definitions of "middle class" vary, projections of trends are in agreement. The middle class in emerging nations is expanding rapidly, and that expansion carries with it rising expectations for an improved quality of life.
- **A resource crunch.** As a growing proportion of the world's poor adopts middle-class lifestyles and consumption patterns, energy, water, food, and other basic commodities will become increasingly scarce.
- **Persistent inequality.** Despite the growth of the middle class, global poverty will not soon diminish. Societies and businesses will be faced

with persistent, and possibly growing, divisions between their poorest segments and their middle and upper socioeconomic strata. These divisions will be the sources of both "base of the pyramid" business opportunities and of social instability and volatility.

- **Major demographic changes.** For Europe, Russia, and Japan, aging populations rapidly are becoming a dominant demographic reality; China and the United States are not far behind. Latin America can reap a "demographic dividend" for one or two decades, but it too must prepare for an aging of its population. For the Middle East, Africa, and parts of Asia, the challenge is the opposite extreme—over half the population of many countries in these regions is 25 or younger and lacks adequate employment opportunities.

- **Urbanization.** Rural populations will continue to migrate to cities in search of economic opportunities, creating demand for new infrastructure, water, and resources. Growth will take place primarily in emerging mid-sized cities and new megacities.

- **Growing human health vulnerability.** An aging, more sedentary population with changing diets will be vulnerable to chronic diseases such as obesity, diabetes, and cancer; a globally more mobile and interconnected world will be more vulnerable to pandemics and antibiotic-resistant bacteria.

- **Increasing environmental vulnerability.** Water scarcity, pollution, waste, and biodiversity loss will diminish the natural buffers that ecological services provide against natural and artificial perturbations. Climate change will have a systemic multiplier effect that, in addition to its own direct impact, will amplify the impact of health, urbanization, water scarcity, and biodiversity loss, and diminish the resiliency of natural systems.

- **Growing connectivity.** In just the past half decade, we have witnessed an astonishing surge in the effect (both positive and negative) of social media and its concurrent empowerment of individuals. The coming of Big Data, cloud computing, machine-to-machine communications, and artificial intelligence will compound and magnify this trend.[3]

It is unclear at this time how these megatrends will play out and how they will affect businesses and the people on the planet. While no one has a crystal ball, scenarios help us describe potential future realities based on the incomplete information we have today. They are stories of future existence developed by looking at current trends and foreseeing various paths that could be taken. They are not absolute, but they show us that we *can* guide the future in a more positive direction. The choice is ours. We are at a critical juncture, and there is little time left. All businesses, as well as shareholders, customers, stakeholders, and the citizens of nations, regions, and cities, must choose sustainability and take control of what we have collectively created. This book distills and represents some of the best thinking and recommendations for how we can and must go about doing that.

Building a Culture for Sustainability

Even though 93 percent of CEOs consider sustainability important to their company's success, most do not know how to embed it into their company.[4] I propose that culture is the missing link here; it is key to accomplishing the shift to a sustainable future in organizations. And for this reason, I chose to focus on organizational culture in this book.

In *The Sustainable Enterprise Fieldbook: When It All Comes Together,* my colleagues and I described *organizational culture* as "the shared values, beliefs, and work styles that define what is important to a specific organization," and note that it "influences acceptable behaviors and practices."[5]

What does a culture for sustainability look like and how do companies get there? As we will see in the chapters to come, each company defines a culture for sustainability in its own way. Yet there are common threads running through each of these companies' definitions (which I identify and synthesize into an overall vision of a culture for sustainability in the book's conclusion, chapter 11). Here are a few examples from the following chapters to help readers see the magnitude, depth, breadth, and scope of this book.

Alcatel-Lucent's (chapter 2) approach to sustainability is anchored in three fundamental elements: economic prosperity, environmental quality, and social integrity. It creates a grand vision and makes sustainability a business imperative. Many inventions from its world-renowned Bell Labs have been breakthroughs for sustainability. The company's sustainability initiatives inspire and mobilize employees to "get it" and "implement it," by embedding environmental responsibility into the way they think and operate, reducing environmental impact through innovative applications of communications solutions. Employees are not only reducing environmental impact but also slashing total costs through holistic, end-to-end network approaches that drive an eco-sustainable communications transformation.

Alcoa Howmet Dover's (chapter 3) culture for sustainability is created through a *shared vision* of a new reality with no landfilling waste, pollution, or injuries. Standing in that future state vision, the company helps its people personally connect to that vision, inspiring and focusing employees' energies in an aligned and unified direction.

Undergirding Alcoa's shared vision is its commitment to being a values-driven company with a zero-tolerance culture. Perhaps what stands out most about Alcoa's commitment to a culture for sustainability is that it encompasses not only its employees, but all the stakeholders and communities in which its facilities are located.

With the stated purpose "We create chemistry for a sustainable future," BASF (chapter 4) is committed to protecting the planet's natural resources while creating greener and cleaner products and solutions that meet the needs of the future. BASF accomplishes this by preparing its employees for the work of tomorrow; building greater awareness to shift the mind-sets of its employees, customers, and other stakeholders; getting close to its customers; finding solutions to intractable problems; and igniting contagious passion. Key is BASF's systems approach to creating a culture for innovation and sustainability throughout the company. And undergirding BASF's systems approach is its "Verbund" concept, which permeates every function, facet, and operation of the organization.

Bureau Veritas (chapter 5), a world leader in testing, inspection, and certification services, leads by example and is adamant about having an internal culture for sustainability that is visible to its clients. Motivated by a firmly held belief that their actions can positively improve the ecosystem and minimize environmental impacts, its employees engage their families in taking on environmental challenges that affect industries around the world.

Church & Dwight (chapter 6) embeds a culture for sustainability in its employees' mind-sets, encouraging thinking and acting sustainably in employees' everyday behavior and practices. The company respects and learns from failure, and reports the bad with the good. When two brothers-in-law sat in a small kitchen in 1846 with their baking soda product—which became the basis of the iconic Arm & Hammer brand—they created what has become an enduring heritage of sustainability for Church & Dwight. Through sustainable development and product stewardship, the company embodies its dedication to operating responsibly (in the design, development, and manufacture of its products) and advancing human health, environmental quality, social well-being, and economic growth.

Ingersoll Rand (chapter 7) continues its legacy of solving big problems and making a transformational impact on a global scale with its sustainable products and services. It is committed to addressing formidable global challenges such as climate change and energy efficiency—seeing the former as "a global threat to future social, environmental, and business performance" and the latter as key to a less-energy-intensive way to support growth in the United States and in developing markets. The company is committed to fully integrating sustainability into the way it does business and into how everyone in the company approaches the work that they do every day. The company not only instills a sustainability mind-set internally, but also seeks to help its customers become more sustainable themselves by creating value with minimal negative environmental impact.

Pfizer's Global Health Fellows Program (GHF)—an initiative within Pfizer, one of the largest and most diversified companies in the global health-care industry—leverages the skills of Pfizer's employees to strengthen access to, quality of, and efficiency in health-care delivery across the globe and enhance the employees' skills and experiences. GHF, described in detail in chapter 8, helps build a culture for sustainability through employee engagement and leadership development.

Sanofi (chapter 9) translates the triple bottom line by putting the patient and the person at the center of its 12 strategic corporate social responsibility (CSR) priorities, which are organized around four pillars: patient, people, ethics, and planet. The company wraps its culture for sustainability around a passion to help people. It has evolved from environmentalism to social consciousness to innovation, providing access to medicines, reducing health-care costs, and fostering a culture of innovation.

Wyndham Worldwide (chapter 10), widely recognized as one of the greenest big companies in America, makes CSR and sustainability a way of working that embodies its vision, expresses its values, celebrates its diversity, and supports work–life balance. Understanding that its business activities affect the earth and its resources, it is committed to developing environmental best practices in its programs, products, and services. The company works actively to persuade its employees, suppliers, owners, and local communities to minimize their environmental impact, reduce energy consumption, track performance, reduce water use, minimize waste, implement sustainable procurement practices, and participate in local-community environmental activities. It makes the business case front and center, embeds sustainability in its values and strategic priorities, creates small wins that generate long-term success, and wraps it with fun.

How Do We Get There?

The good news, as evidenced in every chapter of this book, is that culture is fungible. It can change, and business leaders and managers can help shift the balance to sustainable mind-sets and behaviors by influencing their own and other's belief systems. More good news is that companies don't need to resort to top-down command and control, coercion, or even peer pressure. People already care about these issues. Companies just need to offer the enabling environment, encouragement, and reinforcement for people to contribute what already resides within them. I wrote this book to provide pathways for organizations of every size, sector, and industry to do just that.

CHAPTER 2

Alcatel-Lucent: Transforming Communications for the Twenty-First Century

Leave the beaten track occasionally and drive into the woods. You will be certain to find something that you have never seen before.
—Alexander Graham Bell

Walking into the lobby of Alcatel-Lucent's Murray Hill offices in New Jersey, the first thing one sees is an imposing bust of Alexander Graham Bell, the inventor of the telephone, and beneath it, his prophetic words. Off to the side of the lobby is a staggering array of inventions representing hundreds of patents from Bell Labs scientists. As innovative as these technologies and processes were when they were introduced, many of them—such as the transistor—have ubiquitously penetrated our everyday lives to such an extent that they are now taken for granted, and it seems unimaginable that we ever lived without them. It is striking how far we have come in telecommunications in the century and a half since Bell's birth, and yet our sights are keenly set on how much further we can go. The potential of telecommunications to transform people's lives in a sustainable way, not only in the developed world but also in the most remote areas of the globe is almost inconceivable, and yet its realization may be within our collective reach and just around the corner.

Today, Alcatel-Lucent is a global telecommunications company with some 76,000 employees doing business in approximately 130 countries. The company focuses on communications technology, products, and services, as well as on research and development in its world-famous

Bell Labs. And now sustainability is one of the key areas of focus within the company and has been integrated end to end, including into the innovation engine of Bell Labs.

The chapter describes how the company defines sustainability, the ways in which sustainability is evolving at Alcatel-Lucent, and how it is being integrated into the fabric of the company's overall core strategy. It shows how the company is saving money through holistic, end-to-end network approaches that drive an eco-sustainable communications transformation. In addition, this chapter captures specific examples and stories of how Alcatel-Lucent's sustainability initiatives inspire and mobilize employees to "get it" and "implement it," by embedding environmental responsibility into the way they think and operate, reducing environmental impact through the innovative application of communications solutions.

Defining Sustainability at Alcatel-Lucent

Alcatel-Lucent's approach to sustainability is structured around three fundamental elements: economic prosperity, environmental quality, and social integrity. The company sees corporate responsibility (CR) as the overall umbrella and defines sustainability within that context as "meeting the needs of our company in a way that ensures our ability to survive and thrive in perpetuity." It takes a holistic (end-to-end) life-cycle approach to telecom networks, delivering sustainability in all stages: development, use, and end of life. The focus is on "building smarter, more efficient telecom networks; creating eco-enabling telecom applications; embedding eco-responsibility into the way we think and operate; and creating an eco-conscious culture within the company." It takes a multidisciplinary, triple-bottom-line (people, planet, and profits) approach to sustainability.[1]

Alcatel-Lucent starts with a broad and far-reaching outside-in look at global sustainability issues and trends to determine where and how the company can make the greatest impact. In 2011, it conducted its first formal materiality assessment to identify and validate key areas of focus for its sustainability initiatives. It reviewed over 40 sustainability issues affecting its industry, ranging from customer expectations, risk management, the environment, employees, and ethics and governance to products, services, supply chain, community, and philanthropy. Each of the issues was analyzed by more than 50 Alcatel-Lucent executives and sustainability experts involved in key functions including finance, R&D, operations, legal, Human Resources (HR), compliance, sales, marketing, procurement, communication, public affairs, and philanthropy. Top customers also had the opportunity to share their views.

As a result of this extensive analysis, Alcatel-Lucent identified five overarching focal areas, encompassing 20 specific sustainability issues that represented the most significant impact on its business and were of the greatest concern to its key stakeholders: product innovation and environment; its people; digital inclusion; ethics, compliance, and business; and supply chain. Although the company has a clear prioritization and focus on these issues, its 2011 CR report makes clear that it "must and will continue to manage or monitor the full range of Corporate Responsibility issues and expectations facing our company and industry, and work to improve our strategy and management systems over time."[2]

Here I highlight a few of the many breakthroughs that Alcatel-Lucent and Bell Labs have made in their efforts to respond to the sustainability issues they have identified. These examples demonstrate how brilliant minds working together toward a single goal, in the context of a common purpose, can reinvent the future for all in ways we cannot even imagine.

Bell Labs: From Inventions to Breakthroughs for Sustainability

Solar Technology

More than 60 years after Bell Labs invented solar panels, in the 1950s, solar technology still has not been widely adopted or implemented in the developed world, but thanks to an innovation by Alcatel-Lucent, hybrid solar-wind systems are being used throughout the developing world to power base stations in remote areas that have no local electricity grid. Base stations in these remote areas would normally run off diesel generators 100 percent of the time. With the hybrid power system, they typically use the diesel generator only about 5 percent of the time, increasing the quality of the service and dramatically reducing the amount of CO_2 emissions. The company has already deployed about a thousand such hybrid base stations, providing connectivity for the first time to large sections of the Middle East and Africa. Through this technology, Alcatel-Lucent can bring educational opportunities to millions of people around the world who have never had such access, making significant strides in solving the intractable problem known as the digital divide.

Green Touch

Green Touch, a global consortium of telecommunications companies organized by Bell Labs, is stimulating a new phase of worldwide innovation and collaboration. It focuses the collective energy of companies across the globe on the higher purpose of developing an energy-efficient global telecommunications network. Green Touch has set an audacious goal of finding ways to make the network "a thousand times more energy efficient" by 2015. According to Barry Dambach, senior director, Environment, Health, and Safety (EHS) and Sustainability at Alcatel-Lucent, based on *GeSI SMARTer 2020: The Role of ICT in Driving a Sustainable Future* (gesi.org/smarter2020), about 2 percent of CO_2 emissions comes from the information communications technology (ICT) industry, including from end-user devices, telecommunications networks, and data centers. The ICT is a key player in greenhouse gas (GHG) abatement solutions in a world that continues to increase its need for connectivity and real-time data traffic. GeSI estimates that the ICT-enabled abatement solutions could be seven times its own emissions in addressing climate change.

"Green Touch is a noncompetitive, consortium of some of the best minds in the world coming together to solve a global problem," said Barry Dambach. Recognizing that Green Touch is the vehicle by which the industry can establish its whole strategy and approach, Alcatel-Lucent sees a plethora of opportunities for companies to develop products that align with the overall strategy. According to Dambach, "That's where the competitive part comes in."[3]

lightRadio

Alcatel-Lucent significantly strengthened its commitment to sustainability in 2011 with its launch of the breakthrough green technology solution known as lightRadio. This exciting new application of Alcatel-Lucent's disruptive innovation with a focus on energy efficiency "streamlines and radically simplifies mobile networks while shrinking their carbon footprint by more than 50%."[4] lightRadio enables wireless operators to deploy small cell sites quickly and at a significantly lower cost than was previously possible. These distributed cell sites, invented by Bell Labs, are little bigger than Rubik's cubes and obviate the need for huge cell towers. They need a local energy source, but can be run from solar, wind, and other renewable sources.

Photo 2.1   Photo of lightRadio. (© 2011 Sandra Cornet-Vernet Lehongre. Used with permission.)

Getting Smart: Smart Grid, Smart House

Still another collaborative effort is a strategic industry group focusing on how energy can be used much more wisely. Commonly called smart grid or smart house, this entails, for example, connected meters that automatically turn lights off when no one is home, and devices and software that give parents the ability to monitor children at home from their offices. Smart technologies already are having widespread application in the hospitality industry as exemplified by Wyndham Worldwide (see chapter 10). Applications of these smart technologies in hotels affect the entire customer experience, allowing customers to, for instance, set up room temperatures at various hours of the day, tell their room what time to turn lights on and off, or even set up golf games and other leisure-time appointments remotely.

Building a Culture for Sustainability

What Does a Culture for Sustainability Look Like?

Alcatel-Lucent's mission "to realize the potential of a digitalized world"[5] permeates everything the company does and every action of every individual within it. A culture of and for sustainability at Alcatel-Lucent is one in which all employees get this *and* implement it, top-down and bottom-up. The company asks, What if a corporation thought of itself as a global citizen first? And employees answer: They see themselves as such citizens, and their local actions reflect a global commitment.

During my interview with the then–head of Sustainability at Alcatel-Lucent, Richard Goode, he explained that "a culture for sustainability at Alcatel-Lucent means everybody can say our goal is digital inclusion. We're going to connect the unconnected world. We're going to make sure the 2 billion people with no access to communication services for health care, for life, for education, for learning have all that in the next 20 years."[6] (At the time he was head of Sustainability at Alcatel-Lucent; he is now at Ernst & Young.)

In such a culture, employees include sustainability concepts in their daily routines in the office and at home. They incorporate sustainability thinking into every job function they perform, whether in procurement, facilities, product development, network design, marketing, finance, or HR. Employees find meaning, passion, and inspiration in the company's global mission and at the same time each individual performs every element of her job every day with an awareness of the importance of minimizing her impact on the environment—conserving water and energy, reducing GHG emissions, and so on—and being relevant to her local community.

How to Get There

The ultimate challenge for Alcatel-Lucent is how to do all this while simultaneously driving toward a stronger business culture. This requires inextricably linking sustainability to such business objectives as cost, quality, and on-time delivery. The winning formula for Alcatel-Lucent's culture then is to *both* find ways to meet business objectives *and* do it in a way that is sustainable.

In this culture, the HR function plays a particularly critical role and leaders are working to embed sustainability in all HR systems, processes, and tools. This includes embedding sustainability in job descriptions, leadership development, performance management tools and metrics, and management and employee training. Last but not least, each function includes sustainability in its objectives.[7]

Alcatel-Lucent is taking seven major steps to continue building such a culture for sustainability. Each of these is briefly described below.

Creating a Grand Vision

Alcatel-Lucent starts with a grand vision: "to realize the potential of a connected world." This requires ensuring the company has access to the natural resources, raw materials, energy supply, and suppliers it needs in such a way that it can make a profit and serve its customers. The company firmly believes that "bridging the digital divide can only be achieved with a reliable, eco-sustainable and affordable infrastructure . . . that is capable of reaching key populations, and robust enough to accommodate a variety of compelling and useful applications." This belief informs its core strategy and is embodied in "direct actions with public stakeholders to promote the benefits of digital inclusion."[8]

Making the Business Case: Sustainability
Is a Business Imperative

CR and sustainability are clearly seen as business imperatives by Alcatel-Lucent—so much so that, according to head of Corporate Responsibility and Sustainability Christine Diamente, CEO Ben Verwaayen makes this point at every opportunity and in the most compelling language: "It's an absolute necessity for our industry." "This is make or break." "If we're not green and energy efficient, we're out of business." He recognizes that today's rapidly changing world asks much of companies, that they can be significant positive forces in guiding the changes, and that in order to continue to be viable forces and to survive, they must put a strong emphasis on responsible citizenship. A quote of Verwaayen's that Dambach included in a 2011 presentation sums this up nicely: "The world is evolving at a rapid pace. Because corporations have an important role to play in that changing global reality, Alcatel-Lucent considers Corporate Responsibility a business imperative."[9]

Diamente is also adamant about this and told me during an interview at the company's North American headquarters, in Murray Hill, New Jersey, that sustainability is "a competitor differentiator, a customer requirement, and an industry necessity."

Starting at the Top

For Alcatel-Lucent sustainability starts at the top with senior management and leadership commitment. CEO Verwaayen is passionate about sustainability, makes it a business priority, and has embedded it in the company's strategy. He speaks about it internally and externally. He even blogs on green issues. Externally, he is very active in the climate taskforce at the prestigious World Economic Forum (WEF), where he is also a board member. The WEF, one of the foremost platforms for dialogue on today's global issues, comprises a wide cross section of institutions including corporations, public authorities, civil society, religious faith groups, and so forth. Verwaayen also chairs the Energy and Climate Change Taskforce at the Confederation of British Industry (CBI) association, a working group of the United Kingdom's top CEOs on climate change. This is a responsibility that dates back to his previous role as head of the British operator BT.

Embedding Sustainability in the Organization's DNA

In 2011, Verwaayen challenged the organization to embed CR and sustainability into Alcatel-Lucent's DNA with the conviction that it must be in every activity of the company and deeply embraced by every employee.[10] It speaks to the way Alcatel-Lucent is governed, incorporating both a top-down and a bottom-up approach.

Setting Priorities and Making Commitments

To create its culture of sustainability, Alcatel-Lucent has established three overarching priorities and three core values-based commitments. The priorities speak to the environment, people, and the global challenge of digital inclusion (see sidebar "Alcatel-Lucent's Corporate Responsibility Priorities").

The values are (1) to take a zero-tolerance stand on corruption and breaches of integrity; (2) to collaborate and do business only with partners and suppliers who share and support Alcatel-Lucent's values; and (3) to act with pride and passion as global citizens, actively engaging as a company and volunteering as individuals in the communities in which the company is present.[11]

In June 2011, Alcatel-Lucent announced 50 targets to further demonstrate its commitment to CR as a business imperative. These included targets in the areas of philanthropy, carbon footprint, product energy efficiency, supply chain, human resources, and operations, among others. In 2008, it committed to reducing its absolute carbon footprint from its operations by 50 percent by 2020 (against its 2008 baseline); as of the beginning of 2012, it had already reduced it by 22.4 percent.

ALCATEL-LUCENT'S CORPORATE RESPONSIBILITY PRIORITIES

Environment

Lead the industry in developing and deploying globally recognized innovation in eco-sustainable communications technologies.

Our People

Invest in our people and talents while reflecting the diversity of the markets we serve and the communities in which we operate.

Digital Inclusion

Realize the potential of a connected world and digital inclusion by developing and deploying affordable communication solutions that will increase access to education and socioeconomic development in the world's citizens in a sustainable manner.

Source: Alcatel-Lucent Corporate Responsibility Report 2011, 4. Used with permission.

Communicating with Authenticity and Transparency

The people whom I interviewed insisted that transparency is critical. On a yearly basis, the company reports what it has achieved and openly admits what it hasn't. They strongly believe that a company has to be able to admit it still has a lot of work to do.

Managing by fact is an essential element of the sustainability mind-set at Alcatel-Lucent. It begins with a willingness to measure and be transparent about the things that are really important. To this end, every year the company publishes its sustainability activities according to the Global Reporting Initiative (GRI) A+ Level of transparency and the United Nations Global Compact Advanced Level. In addition, it participates in key sustainability indexes, which provide the best and highest frameworks for a good business sustainability strategy.

This allows Alcatel-Lucent to home in on the issues external stakeholders care about. The company learns from asking—and answering—such questions as, What are the Dow Jones Sustainability Index (DJSI) scorers asking about? The old adage "What gets measured gets managed" rings true here. The company recognized that its data will be far from perfect the first year and advises that companies new to sustainability be prepared for this and not let it hold them up. No organization will get more accurate data until it gets started. In fact, Alcatel-Lucent had a practice year before it established its carbon footprint baseline.

Recognizing Accomplishments and
Disclosing Areas for Improvement

While maintaining its commitment to transparency and authenticity in its communications, Alcatel-Lucent has been the recipient of many awards and distinctions. In 2011, it ranked first among communications technology companies in the DJSI (www.sustainability-index.com), topping a list of 14 organizations assessed by DJSI's rating agency, Sustainable Asset Management (SAM). The assessment was translated into scores along the three dimensions of the triple bottom line (economic, environmental, and social). In 2012, DJSI ranked it as Technology Supersector Leader, above other companies in the communications technology, semiconductor, hardware, and software sectors.

In the spirit of transparency, Alcatel-Lucent responds each year to the Carbon Disclosure Project (CDP) (www.cdproject.net). The CDP represents approximately 550 investor groups with combined assets of $71 trillion as of 2011. Its mission, as stated by Alcatel-Lucent, is to "accelerate solutions to climate change by putting relevant information at the heart of business, policy and investment decisions."[12] The CDP provides companies with a disclosure score and a performance band.

In 2011, Alcatel-Lucent's report to the CDP resulted in a score of 89 out of 100 possible points, putting it on the CDP's Carbon Performance Leadership Index in the "A" band. This score reflects the degree of action an organization has taken on climate change and is evidence of its ability to translate its commitments into action and results.

Connecting with Diversity of Employees
around the World

A commitment to diversity is paramount at Alcatel-Lucent. The company considers this commitment a way to "future proof" the organization in a world in which the long-term stability and success of a business will require its being not only tolerant of, but welcoming to, different genders, cultures, generations, and the like.

StrongHer

One program the company considers extremely successful is StrongHer. The women of Alcatel-Lucent created this bottom-up affinity group in 2011 to support one another on issues related to gender diversity. Strong-Her organizes local events and by 2013 had grown to include 900 members (16 percent of whom are men) and more than 1,000 followers around the world (the "followers" remain informed about the group but don't actively contribute). Started in Paris by Elisabeth Eude—senior strategist in corporate strategy (and described as a maverick by Diamente[13])—and a few of her colleagues from different organizations and functions (e.g., corporate finance and strategy) within Alcatel-Lucent, StrongHer has spread to 48 countries. Hundreds of employees participated in the first anniversary celebration through videoconferencing and social media.[14] Eude told me that StrongHer is structured, organized, and coordinated by a board of six women founders together with leaders of local "antennae" (typically two to six people) in 15 countries.

Local StrongHer antennae gather input on potential topics using the Engage intranet channel (described later in this chapter under Best Practices) and, based on level of interest, sponsor a variety of events. Recent programs have included local networking sessions with discussions or guest speakers on such themes as reacting to sexism in the workplace, using timesaving activities to better organize one's day, and increasing self-awareness and personal development using the Myers-Briggs Type Indicator (MBTI, www.myersbriggs.org). Articles and videos may be posted on the Engage intranet, and people come to the live sessions prepared to discuss them. One group sponsored a program on developing one's reputation on social media. Guest speakers have included an HR representative who explained Alcatel-Lucent's talent development process, and female executive role models, such as Diamente, have given motivating and inspirational presentations.

Often StrongHer local activities intersect with volunteerism and corporate social responsibility activities. For example, local groups raised money for local charities by sponsoring a foot race in France, a garage sale in Egypt, and a clothing collection for a girls' orphanage in Morocco.

When I asked Eude why she is so active in StrongHer in addition to her fulltime job, she explained, "It's like a hobby, and I am very passionate about it."[15] She told me about a recent StrongHer blog focused on the day-to-day struggles of a working mother at the company. The mother received numerous expressions of empathy and online support from StrongHer members and said, "What helped me get through a very challenging day is this vibrant community where I can find so much incredible support."

StrongHer is an extraordinary example of how culture change happens from the bottom up and the top down. The CEO and management gave the signal, but it was the employees who came up with the idea and made it happen.

Hiring and Working across Generations

To remain sustainable over the long haul, Alcatel-Lucent will need to attract and retain the best talent, continually bringing in and engaging a pool of bright, innovative, and engaged young adults. As with many other companies, it is finding that the millennial generation is far more interested in what the company is doing regarding green and socially responsible goals—such as how it is reducing its carbon footprint—than previous generations were.

Moreover, Alcatel-Lucent has a growing number of younger employees who are particularly tech-savvy. It has found that shorter and more frequent communication works best for this generation. In addition, responding to this generation's ease with the online world, the company has made improvements to its internal search engine so its employees can readily find internal information.

"ConnectEd" to Youth

From a global social responsibility perspective, in 2011, the Alcatel-Lucent Foundation partnered with World Education, Inc. (www.worlded .org/WEIInternet) to create the global signature program ConnectEd. This program supports the United Nation's Millennium Development Goals to have universal primary education for all by 2015. ConnectEd addresses those factors that limit the life and work options of disadvantaged youth, particularly girls and women. It focuses on technology as a way to transform educational, work, and life outcomes. Alcatel-Lucent employees actively participate in ConnectEd activities by using their expertise to support implementation, serve as role models, mentor, and advise the young participants. ConnectEd is currently training 13,500 children over three years (through March 2014) to bring them into the digital economy. The program is working with marginalized communities in seven countries: Australia, Brazil, Cambodia, China, Egypt, France, and India.

Photo 2.2   ConnectEd schoolgirls. (© 2011 Sandra Cornet-Vernet Lehongre. Used with permission.)

Work–Life Balance

A major diversity-related issue at Alcatel-Lucent is work–life balance. The company has found that flexible work arrangements and the wise use of technology can contribute to reduced employee stress levels, enhanced employee productivity, reduced costs, and diminished environmental impact. To demonstrate its support for flexible work arrangements, the company has put teleworking policies in place in every region and almost all countries in which it has a significant employee presence. It has a dedicated global website with recommended resources for improving work–life balance, including tips on how to be a more effective home worker and how to improve time-management skills. On average, Alcatel-Lucent employees worldwide work one day per week at home.

From a global perspective, Alcatel-Lucent was able to work with unions in Europe to craft a collective company agreement on teleworking for its locations in France, Belgium, Spain, Italy, and Germany. The agreement states that all employees may telework, provided an organizational analysis of his or her job activities determines that they are amenable to work from home and a mutual agreement exists between the employee, her manager, and HR.[16]

Alcatel-Lucent encourages employees to consider whether they really need to be at work from this time to this time and to ask themselves, "What do I really need to do to get the job done?" In this manner, the company manages by objectives and not by the clock. For global employee Christine Diamente, there is nothing magical about sitting in the corporate office every day. Technology enables her to do her work effectively and efficiently from home or wherever she is in the world. At the same time teleworking greatly reduces her carbon footprint.[17]

Best Practices

While Alcatel-Lucent is well along on the way to building a culture for sustainability, it openly acknowledges that it still has many challenges and obstacles. Before I review some of the challenges the company is confronting and how it is addressing them, I highlight four best practices that it is using to engage the hearts and minds of employees and other stakeholders: the Engage internal social media discussion platform; Alcatel-Lucent's collaborative approach to stakeholders and coopetition; the ways the company is tying sustainability to innovation; and its commitment to fully integrating sustainability into the company's strategy. My hope is that these best practices can inspire or contribute to other companies who are not as far along on the journey to sustainability. We only have so much time, so let's all learn what we can from one another.

"Engage": Maximizing Communication through Social Media

Alcatel-Lucent has leveraged internal communications and social media through an award-winning new discussion forum known as Engage. Engage is an internal social networking platform that reaches out to employees across generations and countries around the world. Its purpose is "to enable employees throughout the company to share, collaborate and exchange best practices, leveraging each other's expertise and talents."[18] Engage has been adopted by over 57,000 employees in all 130 countries in which Alcatel-Lucent operates.

In its first year, Corporate Communications presented Alcatel-Lucent's sustainability priorities to the company via Engage, eliciting more than 4,000 responses from employees about how to improve the company's sustainability performance. Every one of these comments was read and a summary was presented to the company's top 200 leaders at the company's annual management meeting. Importantly, the employee feedback from Engage was incorporated into the Corporate Responsibility Action Plan. In this way, Corporate Communications was able to go back to the employees and tell them specifically how their input was used and how the company was responding to their concerns.

In addition to being a vehicle through which the company can show its responsiveness to employee concerns, Engage provides a means by which the company can regularly post accomplishments and good news. Alcatel-Lucent has learned that sharing accomplishments—however small—on an ongoing basis is more motivating than chiding employees about what hasn't been done. Also, through Engage, employees can get automatic notification of new posts in areas of interest to them.

Collaborating across Stakeholders and Industries

Alcatel-Lucent believes that no one company can implement sustainability alone. There are many examples of Alcatel-Lucent's participating in cross-stakeholder collaboration as a means of achieving its ambitious sustainability goals; most notable is the Green Touch consortium mentioned previously. Another example is a joint project in which Alcatel-Lucent and Toyota created a "next generation" car, fully connected and interacting with the Internet.

Other examples involve collaboratively generating shared data. The ICT industry has found that it is much more efficient and sustainable for organizations to gather data jointly than to each work alone to generate essentially the same data. Historically, there has been a high level of collaboration across the entire industry, and this continues to evolve; much information that was considered proprietary 15 years ago is now shared. In some cases, such data collection has turned into a shared service business for which the companies performing the data collection are being compensated.

Alcatel-Lucent has found great value in joining sustainability groups not only within its industry, but across industries as well. One of these is the Institute for Sustainable Enterprise at Fairleigh Dickinson University, which runs Corporate Partner Roundtables on sustainability-related subjects. The real value of these cross-industry groups is seeing what other companies are doing and developing relationships and offline discussions with other members of the group.

Tying Sustainability to Innovation

Innovation is the engine of sustainable growth at Alcatel-Lucent. And innovation based on sustainability principles could not possibly take root without a strong culture that supports idea generation. To invite and welcome new ideas, Bell Labs runs the Entrepreneur Bootcamp. It puts out a call for idea generation, runs contests open to employees, and presents the new ideas to an internal board. If an employee's idea is one of the five selected and supported in North America, the employee is provided with support from an employee with an MBA to further develop the idea from a business perspective. Alcatel-Lucent also provides financial backing to incubate the idea and bring it into reality. The thinking behind the Entrepreneur Bootcamp is to demonstrate the social impact of the potential product or service and to publicize it in a way that brings awareness to how Alcatel-Lucent's innovations are improving people's lives.

Integrating Sustainability Fully into Company Strategy

Alcatel-Lucent believes that the investment community will consider it a plus if an enterprise embeds sustainability into its long-term innovation strategy and perspective. This is seen as an indication that the organization is on the cutting edge. Alcatel-Lucent has observed great enthusiasm for its sustainability strategy on the part of the investment community.

Challenges

Like other global corporations, Alcatel-Lucent experiences many daunting business, environmental, and people challenges along the road to accomplishing its noble and audacious goals. And as we have seen, the company strongly believes that as a global corporation, it has a responsibility to help address and resolve the world's great challenges. These include many of the defining challenges of the twenty-first century, such as climate change, transformation to a digital economy and the digital inclusion dilemma, education and illiteracy, poverty, and so on. The company also believes that the ICT industry is well-positioned to play a critical role in ensuring that isolated communities are connected and experience economic growth and social cohesion—all the while doing it green.

In this context, I highlight a few of Alcatel-Lucent's most significant challenges in building a culture for sustainability and show how the company is working to overcome them. These include "stuck in the middle";

overwhelming workloads and competing priorities for managers' limited time and attention; "short-termism"; the difficulty of demonstrating the return on investment (ROI) for sustainability; and the necessity for HR to step up to the role of advocate and enabler of change. In my work with numerous companies, including several represented in this book, I have observed many of these same challenges, so they are hardly unique. My hope is that others can relate to these challenges and learn valuable lessons as they go about building their own cultures for sustainability.

Stuck in the Middle

One of the most difficult challenges at Alcatel-Lucent is the lack of "sustainability in the middle." Clearly CEO Verwaayen is passionate about and highly visible on the subject of sustainability. Sustainability experts and directors such as Christine Diamente and Barry Dambach are also not only passionate but extremely knowledgeable and capable. Employees and top management "get it." The challenge is that it has not yet permeated middle management nor has it been included in their goals and objectives. For Goode, this is a particularly critical challenge: "People say buy-in from the top is the most important thing, but I disagree. You also need buy-in from the folks in the middle, or you won't be successful. You will go ahead but then get stuck . . . 'stuck in the middle.'"[19]

Given these managers are under enormous pressure to get things done every day, they have little or no time to think about integrating sustainability into their day-to-day work. Several people I interviewed at Alcatel-Lucent suggested that this problem could be addressed by finding ways to integrate sustainability into what these middle managers are already responsible for doing, so it is not perceived as being yet another "bolt-on or add-on thing to do." They all agreed that is more effective to show middle managers how sustainability helps them work better, faster, and cheaper. For example, the best way to focus a logistics person on sustainability might be to find an intensity measure of grams of CO_2 per ton mile shipped and to integrate that metric into her existing goals. That way, it's right in line with her functional specialization and fits seamlessly into things she is already focused on managing.

Competing Priorities: Too Much on My Plate

With the enormous challenges and heavy workloads employees face, sustainability cannot be seen as *one more thing* to add to an already overflowing plate. People become tired of the initiative of the month and experience a phenomenon known as initiative fatigue. Again, this can be avoided by embedding sustainability into everyone's job so that it becomes a way of thinking and doing business and not a separate thing someone does when and if he has time.

Dealing with Short-Termism

One of the greatest challenges companies face in their search for the secrets to surviving and thriving over the long haul is what I call short-termism. This is the phenomenon in which everything seems to pull managers to put the "urgent" ahead of the "important" and to lose the long-term sustainability perspective in the search for short-term results.

Alcatel-Lucent confronts this directly, setting long-term goals in the context of global megatrends and challenges, often looking five or ten years or even decades ahead. The company establishes baselines and sets specific targets and goals for the medium and short term, with measureable targets and milestones all along the way. But at the same time, it must comply with short-term reporting requirements imposed by the global financial markets. Keeping its eye on the long term while addressing the short-term is a formidable challenge for Alcatel-Lucent, like many other companies whose focus is on long-term sustainability.

Demonstrating the Return on Investment

At Alcatel-Lucent it is important to make a really strong business case for sustainability when proposing a specific initiative. Executives usually analyze such proposals from a cost perspective because that's what resonates most with them. This presents a challenge and an opportunity: quantifying sustainability-related cost savings and using the resulting savings to fund new initiatives. "My personal battle cry is 'follow the carbon, find the money,'" said Goode.[20]

Human Resources: Stepping Up as Advocate and Enabler of Change

HR can generate an "employee multiplier effect" through employee engagement initiatives. Yet at Alcatel-Lucent, HR hasn't fully integrated sustainability into its work and needs to play a much larger role. Areas in which HR needs to provide help include leadership and management development and training in sustainability-related functional areas (e.g., sustainable supply chain, green accounting, etc.). HR needs to make sustainability part of the orientation at Alcatel-Lucent. And the sustainability leaders I interviewed want HR to become an advocate for embedding sustainability in everyone's goals and objectives.

Online learning and e-learning offer a great opportunity for training employees at Alcatel-Lucent. One successful e-learning program that has already been implemented can become a model for subsequent programs. A one-hour, fully scripted e-learning session from Alcatel-Lucent's course catalog shows employees what a carbon footprint is, how to calculate one, and what the company is doing to reduce its own footprint.

Lessons Learned

As Alcatel-Lucent reflects on the lessons learned from its journey to sustainability so far, a few things stand out, which I summarize here. Again, my hope is that other companies, both large and small, will learn from these lessons so they can advance more rapidly on their own journey to sustainability.

- Create a shared focus on solving a global problem—such as the dilemma of the digital divide.
- Make use of frameworks and tools that have already been proven and that work (see Frameworks, Tools, and Resources, the next section). For example, read and understand the Greenhouse Gas Protocol and become an expert in its use.
- Join some of the Internet's sustainability-related groups for discussion and networking with peers (e.g., LinkedIn, GreenBiz).
- Educate yourself and do your homework. There is no shortage of websites, books, magazines, articles. And most colleges have Sustainability 101 courses to start you off.
- Learn about the business. You need to understand business and customers before you can be credible in how you can make a difference in that company.
- Network. This is the best way to learn about sustainability within and across industries.

Frameworks, Tools, and Resources

Participate in Existing Frameworks and Global Standards

Just as there is no shortage of information on just about every aspect of sustainability, there is no shortage of existing comprehensive and high-quality frameworks and global standards for almost any purpose a business may have. There is no need to reinvent the wheel. And always remember that the magic doesn't come from the tool, but what you do with the tool.

Alcatel-Lucent participates in, uses, and recommends several of these, including the following:

- Dow Jones Sustainability Index (DJSI)
- United Nations Global Compact
- Global Reporting Initiative (GRI)
- Carbon Disclosure Project (CDP)
- GeSI
- Greenhouse Gas Protocol (GGP)
- Life-Cycle Analysis (LCA)
- World Resources Institute (WRI)

Using these may require a learning curve and some customization, but the important thing is to just get started!

Use Carbon-Accounting Tools

"If you are not using an enterprise carbon-accounting calculation tool, and you are a Fortune 1000 company or even close, you are putting your company at risk. Spreadsheets to calculate your carbon footprint just don't cut it," said Richard Goode.[21] He recommends managers look at what SAP, HARA, Enviance, and other tools use as executive-decision support systems. These systems allow managers to run many different kinds of analyses that will tell them where their business is using energy and will give them actionable data. The tools enable them to do multivariate analyses that allow them to tell which buildings use more energy per square foot than others and to see where the data does not seem to be accurate for the building's use.

The website www.epa.gov/climatechange/wycd/index.html offers a number of tools for reducing emissions and a calculator for calculating GHG emissions.

Build Sustainability Metrics: Total Cost of Ownership

In making the business case for a green product, people frequently argue that green and more-energy-efficient products cost more than their "nongreen/unsustainable" counterparts. This view is based on a fallacy because it often doesn't consider the costs associated with the actual *use* of the product. For example, if management is going to replace a machine when it breaks, they might as well put in the most-energy-efficient machine possible. If they buy the very cheapest replacement, based only on first costs, they will often end up paying much more in the long run. If they can show total cost of ownership (TCO) is less with an energy-efficient machine, and have aligned it with their company's ROI requirements, why would they not buy it? So the trick is to put in the most-energy-efficient machine and simultaneously make the business case for it. An expanding trend is for companies to increase the acceptable payback number of years associated with green projects to support the integration of sustainability into facility operations.

So we see that TCO is an important measurement framework and tool for supporting advancements and investments in sustainability. Looking at the TCO, rather than just the purchase cost, provides richer data that will help make the case for investing wisely and sustainably.

Conclusion

Today, Alcatel-Lucent continues on its journey toward building a culture for sustainability with passion, authenticity, transparency, and velocity. So far, it is not only producing breakthrough technologies toward its vision of realizing the potential of a connected world, such as Green Touch and lightRadio, but it is also finding ways to significantly reduce the company's impact on the environment. For example, between 2008 and 2011, Alcatel-Lucent reduced the carbon footprint produced by its operations by 22.4 percent. Between 2009 and 2011, the company reduced its percentage of waste landfilled from 36 percent to 25 percent. Alcatel-Lucent knows it has a long way to go, but the company is finding more and more ways to move ahead with the engagement of the hearts and minds of some 76,000 employees in approximately 130 countries around the world.

Postscript

In early 2013, CEO Ben Verwaayen resigned and Michel Combes became the new CEO of Alcatel-Lucent. I had the opportunity to follow up with Christine Diamente to see how she thought this change may affect Alcatel-Lucent's commitment to sustainability. Diamente said,

> At Alcatel-Lucent, corporate responsibility and sustainability is a business imperative, and we have the luxury that it is a priority at

the top, but it is also driven bottom up. And as we pass on to a new CEO, this will be an important legacy. StrongHer is an example of how sustainability is really in the DNA of our employee base. . . . Of course sustainability has to have leverage and sponsorship at the top, but when you get that critical mass, and it's driven bottom up and across the DNA of the organization so that it is part of the way we do business, that makes it very, very powerful.[22]

CHAPTER 3

Alcoa: Connecting People to Communities

We're either going to change the people, or we're going to change the people. I've said that over and over again. And over the years we've done that.

—Steve Fromkin, 2012

From his very first interview at the company in 1996, Steve Fromkin, environmental, health, and safety manager at Alcoa Howmet's Dover, New Jersey, facility, found a kindred spirit in then–plant manager the late Jim Johnson. Fromkin saw that Johnson and he shared a common vision that the entire Howmet (now Alcoa Howmet) Dover plant could become sustainable. They envisioned facilities that produced no landfilling waste and no discharge of pollutants into drains or into the air and in which all employees worked safely and went home every night to their families in one piece, healthy and uninjured. They were committed to bringing about fundamental changes in disposal practices and ultimately transforming the plant's legacy and reducing its footprint. This chapter describes how this cultural transformation was accomplished at Alcoa Howmet Dover over the 17 years that followed, bringing two men's noble vision from a pipedream to a reality.

Alcoa Howmet, now owned by Alcoa, Inc., is a global leader in airfoil and structural castings and primarily serves the aerospace and industrial markets. Producing such products involves significant potential environmental impacts and safety hazards for its people. The company began manufacturing operations in 1949. The Dover plant spans 127 acres with four manufacturing facilities and has approximately 1,000 employees.

In 1996, the year Steve Fromkin joined the plant, it produced 800 tons per year of landfill waste. Fromkin and Johnson knew they needed to engage all the people in the plant, exciting them about their vision, if they were going to have a chance of accomplishing their formidable goals. They started by forming three teams focused on waste minimization ("waste to cash"), pollution prevention, and environmental conservation. In those days, they didn't use the term *sustainability;* they didn't start referring to their endeavors as sustainable and green until late 2000. "We didn't know what to call it. We just knew it was the right thing to do," Fromkin told me in an interview.[1] They had defined Alcoa Howmet Dover's first steps and taken actions to start moving it forward on its journey to sustainability.

Besides its being "the right thing to do," there was another compelling reason for the Dover plant to embrace these bold goals. Northern New Jersey is one of the most difficult places for manufacturing in the United States. Fromkin and Johnson knew they needed to find ways to turn their commitment to sustainability into a competitive advantage. They set upon learning how to conserve their resources, turn waste into cash, and reduce costs by increasing energy efficiency. "Quantitatively we couldn't put a dollar figure to it, but we knew we could take waste and turn it into a revenue stream," said Fromkin.

This chapter describes how far Alcoa Howmet has come on its journey to sustainability, where it is now, and how it got there. I describe the current vision of a culture for sustainability that brings forth the passion, full participation, and engagement of all the people. I highlight some of the key processes it used, along with best practices around employee engagement, and frameworks, resources, and tools, zooming in on some of the local programs at Alcoa Howmet Dover and zooming out to some of the programs offered by the parent company, Alcoa, Inc., which provides its facilities across the globe with a large portfolio of sustainability-related initiatives. I present the lessons learned as seen through the eyes of the leaders and managers, so that others—small, medium, and large enterprises—can benefit. Because Alcoa Howmet, like all companies, is still on its own journey to sustainability, I highlight major challenges and opportunities, and where possible, how they are being addressed.

Global Sustainability Approaches for Driving Dramatic Results

Alcoa Howmet was acquired in 2000 by Alcoa, the world's largest integrated aluminum company with some 61,000 employees in more than

200 locations in 30 countries and more than \$23.7 billion in 2012 revenue. Alcoa's lost workday injury rate is one-tenth that of the average U.S. manufacturing workplace,[2] and Alcoa is widely considered one of the world's most sustainable companies.[3]

Founded in 1888 by Charles Martin Hall, who invented the aluminum smelting process in 1886, Alcoa has been the aluminum industry leader for 125 years. It is the largest producer of aluminum in the world and the leader in aluminum technology and innovation. Alcoa is the only aluminum company covering every stage of aluminum production—upstream, midstream, and downstream.

Alcoa considers aluminum a "miracle metal." From an environmental sustainability perspective, aluminum has "infinite recyclability, as fully 75 percent of all aluminum ever produced is still in use today," said Laurie Roy, Human Resources (HR) director, Alcoa Power and Propulsion, during our interview.[4] Roy described how Alcoa is constantly finding innovative applications for aluminum—in, for instance, traveling buses, siding, and new products that may minimize environmental impacts. According to the information provided by Alcoa during our interview, aluminum makes cars and trucks more fuel efficient: a pound of aluminum in a vehicle can lessen the amount of greenhouse gases it releases into the atmosphere by 20 pounds over its lifetime. Aluminum also makes electronic gadgets cooler, makes air and space travel possible, and is one of history's most popular, most-recyclable beverage containers. According to Alcoa at a Glance, "More than one trillion cans have been recycled in the U.S. since Alcoa pioneered the industry in 1972."[5]

Alcoa is especially notable for the highly successful partnerships it creates with nongovernmental organizations (NGOs) and local communities around sustainability issues. Through workshops and other methods, it works closely with customers, management,

Photo 3.1   Aluminum has infinite recyclability. (© 2013 Alcoa, Inc. Used with permission.)

employees, communities, and other stakeholders on sustainability initiatives that generate strategies and implement action plans.

Building a Culture for Sustainability

This section describes what a culture for sustainability looks like at Alcoa and Alcoa Howmet today through the eyes of the Alcoa Howmet employees I interviewed and presents five essential enablers that I culled from the interviews and related research: creating a shared vision, being a values-driven company, creating a zero-tolerance culture, staring at the elephant, and following a process.

What Does a Culture for Sustainability Look Like?

Describing a culture for sustainability, Roy focused on three distinguishing characteristics, which were reinforced by everyone I interviewed, regarding how the company operates: (1) raising awareness, (2) personally connecting, and (3) acting consistently. "All employees are aware of what sustainability means for us personally," she said, "and for our organization and the communities in which we operate. It means we care about that. We all act and behave in a way that is consistent with that in the workplace and in our lives."[6]

How to Get There

Building a culture for sustainability takes time and comprises many small, and not so small, steps. Many of the Alcoans I interviewed think that looking intensely at the company to determine where it is and where it needs to go, creating a process, and then following the steps of that process, repeating and revising them if necessary is critical. "It's not a home run," Fromkin said. "Like baseball, you score runs through a lot of singles here, a single and a stolen base there. Rarely do you get the grand slam. There are multiple iterations till you get there, so over time you get better till you get to where you want to be."[7]

Laura Carpenter, plant manager at Alcoa Howmet's facility in La Porte, Indiana, told me about one such "single" and how she learned from this small step:

> We decided to heed Pew's comments about buying local food, so we held a luncheon for our employees with food from local farmers. We brought in local farmers with sweet corn and apples and

caramel from local orchards. This way we supported the local economy and saved greenhouse gases. Everyone loved it. I didn't realize how important it is for people to go local; it was a very good feeling. When we were asked to do it again, man, it was cool.[8]

Creating a Shared Vision

Steve Fromkin and Jim Johnson shared a vision of a possibility, even when it seemed remote and they weren't sure how it could be achieved. They took a stand for a new reality (i.e., one with no landfilling waste, pollution, or injuries) for their facility and then stood firmly in that future-state vision. Over the years that followed, they found ways for people to personally connect to that vision. And they provided specific and measurable opportunities for people to take actions that would help move the organization toward that vision and ultimately make it a reality.

Simply put, they created what is known as a shared vision—"a collective state of mind that unifies, inspires, and focuses effort. Shared vision is a clear picture of future success that is widely owned and personally felt." Such a vision is not a vague aspiration, but is "everyone gazing out on the horizon, and through their different views, seeing the same thing." The organization's future success is not constrained by the realities of today. The picture of the future helps break through people's comfort zones and preconceived notions of what is achievable. And it is not just top-down but is communicated in such a way that people are able to participate fully and contribute their own perspectives to the vision so it becomes widely embraced throughout the organization. The vision connects to people's hearts and their heads, evoking creative energy and building momentum and enthusiasm.[9]

Being a Values-Driven Company

Everyone I spoke with at the company described Alcoa as values based or values driven. As Roy said, "We are a values-based company. For us excellence goes well beyond productivity. For us excellence means we are great corporate citizens and an inclusive workforce, valuing all the differences that we have and actually doing what we say. We are living our values." These employees deeply believe that Alcoa will be more successful if everything they do is aligned with the core values to which Roy was referring: integrity; respect; environment, health, and safety (EHS); innovation; and excellence.

Every manager is required to attend "Alcoa University," a weeklong recalibration to ensure managers have a deep understanding of the company's values. Believing that managers already have a good understanding of the company's financials, Alcoa made the strategic decision to focus managers' attention on its values and on what drives the Alcoa value system.

Sustainability is an integral part of these. It is described as important as, if not more important than, results. "I see more plant and operations managers lose their jobs for values than results," said Fromkin.[10]

Creating a Zero-Tolerance Culture

Although the kind of work Alcoa does (e.g., mining, refining, manufacturing, operations) can be dangerous, the company established a standard of zero tolerance for fatalities. Fromkin has been working steadfastly on this for 10 years, holding Alcoa Howmet Dover's managers accountable for leading these initiatives.

Staring at the Elephant

Given the enormity of sustainability challenges facing many organizations today, it is easy to become overwhelmed and even paralyzed. As Fromkin pointed out, investing some time early on "staring at the elephant" helps bring clarity and focus to the organization's efforts. The important thing is to pick a few projects that will help move your organization toward the vision it has created. Alcoa Howmet stared at the elephant and then created a process to move the company into action with velocity and commitment.

Following a Process: Measuring Aspects and Impacts

How did the leaders and managers accomplish this? Alcoa Howmet crafted a process that began with identifying and rating major "aspects," such as risk liabilities and compliance, and "impacts," such as the amount of silver that was being discharged.

Ultimately, the plant managers—working with their technical teams (e.g., facilities engineers, maintenance engineers, and technical engineers)—rated every aspect and all their impact. Then they created and selected those projects that would have the greatest return on investment. This involved choosing one or two conservation projects, one or two waste-minimization projects (targeting, e.g., potassium hydroxide and silver, the largest contributors to its hazardous waste stream), and one or two pollution projects (targeting, e.g., particulate emissions into the atmosphere).

By implementing a clearly defined process with the input of its engineers and technical workers, Alcoa Howmet was able to make measurable improvements in all three areas in the first year.

Best Practices

Here I highlight five best business practices for building a culture for sustainability: becoming environmental stewards, igniting employee engagement through volunteerism, recognizing progress, catalyzing community and stakeholder involvement, and creating accountability through metrics and measurement.

Becoming Environmental Stewards

As stewards of the environment, Alcoa has much to be proud of—thanks to the employees. Here are a few of Alcoa Howmet Dover's quantifiable achievements as of March 2011:

- 48 waste streams recycled or reused
- 75 percent reduction in water use
- Elimination of direct discharge of thermal wastewater into Rockaway River
- 100 percent reduction in soluble concentration of silver, other metals, suspended solids, hydrocarbons in process wastewater
- 80 percent reduction in fugitive particulate air emissions
- 82 percent reduction in generated hazardous waste
- 75 percent reduction in regulated landfill disposal
- 40 percent reduction in overall landfill waste disposal
- 15 percent reduction in electricity use

Collectively, these reductions translate into over $1.5 million in annual savings, and approximately $8 million in savings since 1999.[11]

In terms of waste minimization, Fromkin pointed out that Alcoa Howmet Dover has reduced its yearly average of 800 tons of waste to regulated landfill disposal to 30 tons/year. It has set an ambitious goal to bring that down to *zero* within the next eight years and, according to Fromkin, is on track to meet this stretch goal, despite the fact that all "low-hanging fruit" has been plucked. "We have some pretty difficult challenges ahead of us now," said Fromkin, but he remains steadfast in his commitment to the goal and laid out the following ways in which the plant is moving toward it.[12]

Composting

Alcoa Howmet Dover is composting all its cafeteria waste, people's lunches, and paper. It uses cups and plates that are compostable. It is the first Alcoa facility worldwide to compost.

Particulates

It took 10 years, but by 2012 Alcoa Howmet Dover had eliminated all release of particulates by replacing the manufacturing equipment with high-tech, state-of-the-art equipment. The total cost was more than $10 million, which was spread out over the 10 years it took to achieve this.

Water

Alcoa Howmet Dover reduced its water use and consumption by almost 75 percent, from an average of 40 million gallons per year of water consumed in the mid-1990s to approximately 12 million gallons of water per year by 2012. Remarkably, at the same time, Alcoa Howmet Dover's overall production significantly increased.

How was Alcoa Howmet Dover able to simultaneously increase production and reduce its water consumption? It took a wide variety of initiatives, for example, replacing 11 open-loop cooling towers with closed-loop cooling towers, putting flow restrictions on much of its equipment, and switching to low-volume faucets in bathrooms.

Some of these endeavors required changes in equipment, but equally important, they required changing people's mind-sets and habits, so that, for instance, people are aware of the negative effects of unnecessarily leaving faucets on. Fromkin told me that the average hose uses six to eight gallons of water every minute.

Igniting Employee Engagement through Volunteerism

Alcoa sees volunteerism as a powerful contributor to employee engagement. "We believe it makes people more productive and produces better business results when people feel they are making a difference," said Roy.[13] She added that "volunteerism is huge" at the company, and the numbers bear that out: in 2012, Alcoans volunteered more than 800,000 hours—the equivalent of 385 people working full time for a year.

The Alcoa Foundation (www.AlcoaFoundation.com) focuses on two core themes: improving the environment and preparing individuals for careers in science, technology, engineering, and mathematics (STEM) and in manufacturing. In addition to financial and product donations, the company and the foundation also invest in programs to promote employee volunteerism around the world. Some of Alcoa's signature engagement programs are Worldwide Month of Service, Bravo!, ACTION (Alcoans Coming Together in Our Neighborhoods), Green Works, Earthwatch Institute fellowships, Make an Impact, and Alcoans in Motion (AIM).

Getting people together to make a difference on behalf of others less fortunate serves as an excellent opportunity to build team esprit de corps. "What better way to do a team-building activity than doing something to make a difference? Outside you start to see each other as people with common interests and hobbies. It makes managers more approachable and breaks down issues among their people. As teams come together to work with a nonprofit, they realize their issues are petty in the big scheme of things," said Roy.

In our interview, Roy shared the touching example of a team who volunteered their services in a homeless shelter. She told me it not only helped the people find ways to work more effectively together but also helped make everyone "more appreciative of what we do have."

Roy described how volunteer and nonprofit experiences increase employees' pride in the organization and help them become ambassadors who are proud to work for Alcoa. Programs such as these demonstrate to employees that the company is not just about work; it *cares* about the communities in which it operates. Alcoa is simultaneously and synergistically making an investment in the community in two critical ways: by making available human and financial resources. Roy believes that "this helps set Alcoa aside from other organizations. We're out there. We're giving back. Our leaders are partnering to help others in the community."

Worldwide Month of Service

Alcoa's Month of Service forms the centerpiece of Alcoa's volunteerism programs. In October 2012, Alcoa achieved a new milestone when a majority—60 percent, or 34,000—of Alcoa's employees participated in the program worldwide. Collectively, they volunteered in more than 1,050 events across 24 countries and partnered with more than 2,050 nonprofit organizations. In the process, more than 265,000 aluminum cans were recycled, 36,000 children were assisted, 13,000 meals were donated and 151,000 hours of service were donated.[14]

Bravo!

If an employee performs 50 or more hours of community service in a year, Alcoa Foundation will make a $250 Bravo! grant to the organization where the service was performed. Nearly 7,000 grants are awarded on behalf of Alcoa employees who participate in Bravo! each year, volunteering 525,000 hours, which is comparable to 252 people working full time for a year. The foundation awards more than $1.75 million in Bravo! grants to nonprofits in 17 countries each year.[15] Roy told me that because Alcoa was celebrating its tenth anniversary of the Bravo! grant in 2012, it "tripled down" and gave the award three times in that year.[16]

ACTION

Through ACTION, employees identify a nonprofit's genuine need and work on the ground to fulfill that need.[17] The Alcoa volunteers' participation may result in the targeted nonprofits being eligible for a $1,500 to $3,000 grant. The Alcoa Foundation donates $1,500 when four or more employees volunteer at least 20 hours and $3,000 when eight or more employees volunteer at least 40 hours. To encourage local ownership and accountability, each Alcoa location is given an ACTION allocation, and Alcoa Foundation's local representative coordinates all ACTION events and applies for the grants. Each year, more than 12,000 Alcoans participate in more than 700 ACTION projects, volunteering 50,000 hours and raising in excess of $1.75 million for nonprofits.[18]

The ACTION grants fund projects ranging from those that dovetail with Alcoa's environmental stewardship goals (e.g., tree planting or river-bank cleanup) to charities that focus on issues affecting employees' personal lives (e.g., autism and childhood diseases). They have included building ramps for handicapped access; repairing a tile floor that was rotting in a homeless shelter; and providing and serving picnic lunches in a summer camp for people with disabilities. Sometimes the work is performed solely by Alcoans; in other cases, members of the nonprofit work alongside Alcoa employees.

Green Works

Alcoa mobilizes its employees and communities to reduce, recycle, and replenish through its Green Works program, which celebrates "environmental holidays." About 20,000 employees in 20 countries volunteered under this program in 2012, resulting in the planting of more than 60,000 trees; the rehabilitation of 100 rivers, parks, and recreation areas; and the recycling of more than 45,500 pounds of electronics equipment.[19]

Earthwatch Institute Partnership

One of the highlights of Alcoa's approach to engaging employees and local communities is its ongoing partnership with Earthwatch Institute (www.earthwatch.org), which involves significant employee participation both in weeklong fellowships in field locations around the world and after they've returned.[20] Each year employee fellows are selected to become "citizen scientist" volunteers who work with professional scientists to help shape local, regional, and global environmental policies on such issues as climate change, ecosystem services, and fresh water preservation. In 2012, 25 Alcoa employees from 12 countries worked alongside Earthwatch scientists, participating in research projects and learning about environmental science.

The employee and community fellows conduct hands-on research, develop targeted learning materials, and do real-time blogging, including posting information about their ongoing activities. After their weeklong "expedition," employees become environmental ambassadors, sharing the

Photo 3.2 Jianguang Guo, from Kunshan, China, and Sue English, from Wagerup Refinery, Australia, on a 2012 Earthwatch expedition to China's Gutianshan Forest. (© 2012 Alcoa Foundation. Used with permission.)

knowledge they learned with their coworkers and communities. Over the past 10 years, 169 employees from 21 countries contributed more than 10,500 hours collecting scientific data. In 2012, the program was offered in three languages (English, Mandarin, and Portuguese), garnering participation from employees from North America, Asia, and South America.[21]

Make an Impact

Make an Impact began in Alcoa Australia in 2006 to increase employee awareness about ways to simultaneously improve energy efficiency and save money. The Alcoa Foundation brought the program to the United States in 2008 through a partnership with the Pew Center on Global Climate Change (now the Center for Climate and Energy Solutions; www.c2es.org). The program has been launched in 30 U.S. cities and has identified more than 40 million pounds of carbon savings, equivalent to 2 million gallons of gasoline. In 2012, the program expanded to Brazil. In one of its U.S.–based projects alone, Change Our 2tomorrow (CO2) Schools' Challenge, participants from eight competing schools identified 10.7 million pounds of carbon savings.[22]

The objective of the school challenge was to get as many people as possible—students, parents, grandparents, and friends—to use the Center for Climate and Energy Solutions' carbon calculator (alcoa.c2es.org/footprint/home). As the projects evolved, schools began to use not only this tool but also the center's tips for simple things to do to save energy and become more sustainable.

Carpenter and her HR manager, Tera Grinnell, persuaded two middle schools in the area to take up this challenge. And one of the schools, Paul F. Boston Middle School, was named the grand prize winner.[23] It received a $5,000 grant and 850 recycling bins from the Alcoa Foundation for inspiring more than 1,160 students, teachers, and families to use the online carbon calculator to measure the amount of energy wasted in homes.[24]

The school used a portion of the money to plant trees on its property. Alcoa employees were given time off from their jobs, as a part of Alcoa's Month of Service, to work side by side with their children on the ground, planting the trees. In addition the local Make an Impact project managers helped educate the school board, which made the carbon calculator part of the school's science curriculum.

This example demonstrates how four key elements came together to produce outstanding and multifaceted results: (1) an easy-to-use and practical tool for raising awareness (the carbon calculator), (2) engaged leadership and employees, (3) work that connects sectors and boundaries (corporations, nonprofits, and schools), and (4) the embedding of new tools into the school curriculum.

Alcoans in Motion

Alcoans in Motion (AIM) encourages greater physical fitness while raising money for employees' favorite charities. Each Alcoa location is given an allocation for an AIM event, which is then coordinated by a representative from the Alcoa Foundation. Teams of five or more employees are eligible to receive up to $2,500 for the charity of their choice. In 2012, AIM events were held in 16 countries, involving 2,500 employees. Many of the organizations funded were health related, supporting research in cancer, heart disease, and diabetes, among others.

Recognizing Progress

In addition to the volunteer programs offered companywide through Alcoa Foundation, Alcoa Howmet Dover offers several local programs that engage employees in sustainability initiatives by recognizing them for their accomplishments. I describe two of these here.

Applause

In the Applause program, employees are given small tokens of appreciation such as movie tickets and dinner tickets when they accomplish a specific goal. These are often given for sustainability-related accomplishments to reinforce the employee's commitment and contributions to the goals that have been set by local management.

Gotcha!

Alcoa Howmet Dover uses its Gotcha! program for local recognition at the plant and frequently gives out "Gotcha! cards" on the spot. The original goes to the employee and a copy goes to her supervisor. The card recognizes demonstrations of Alcoa's values, which are highlighted and then checked off on the Gotcha! card: integrity, EHS, respect, innovation, and excellence.

Catalyzing Community and Stakeholder Engagement

Alcoa is committed to building ongoing, transparent engagement with all its stakeholders. "We need to engage our communities as well as our employees," said Roy. "We really believe we can all make a difference together."[25]

The company develops and implements complementary and synergistic stakeholder-engagement processes at both the global and local levels. The global signature programs typically involve partnerships with NGOs and nonprofits such as the Nature Conservancy, Engineers Without Borders, World Resources Institute, and Institute of International Education.

At the local level, Alcoa works to understand the issues and concerns of the communities in which it operates and energetically develops opportunities for open dialogue and honest, fact-based discussions. It does this primarily through the implementation of the Alcoa Community Framework and community advisory boards (CABs).

Alcoa Community Framework and Community Advisory Boards

Each Alcoa operating facility implements the Alcoa Community Framework, a comprehensive tool designed to help location managers assess community needs, develop public strategy plans, and strengthen relationships with key constituents. As part of this approach, Alcoa establishes CABs composed of plant leadership and influential people outside the company who provide guidance on community issues, present opportunities, and help resolve concerns when they arise. By directly engaging the community—encouraging members to offer suggestions, ask questions about the plant's policies and actions, voice their opinions and concerns—and listening to them, Alcoa gains a "social license" to operate there.

The framework also provides a tool for sharing best practices and learnings across Alcoa locations. (For specifics on the Community Framework, see Frameworks, Tools, and Resources.)

Keystone Institute for Teacher Education

The Keystone Institute for Teacher Education, a nonprofit supported by Alcoa Foundation since 1997, provides 30 middle-school teachers each year with the training and curriculum to investigate current environmental issues with their students, increasing environmental literacy. The teachers attend a weeklong field-training program in Colorado where they conduct hands-on experiments. Through this program, Alcoa has equipped 190 teachers in 76 Alcoa communities.

Creating Accountability with Metrics

Alcoa is very metrics and measurement driven.[26] As Roy said during our interview, "If you're not measuring it, how do you know if you're making progress?"[27] Steve Fromkin spoke about how Alcoa Howmet Dover is taking specific steps to meet 2020 goals and regional targets for landfill, energy, and water. Although the goals are typically long term, the company sets targets, metrics, and measurements of major milestones along the way.[28]

A3 Process

An Alcoa Howmet best practice in metrics is known as the A3 process. Its objective is to identify those levers that are the most critical to achieving a particular goal so that plants may avoid measures that just waste time and diffuse energy.

The first step in the A3 process is to take the time to truly assess the problem. This is often overlooked in companies as people rush to come up with solutions to what often turn out to be the wrong problems.

The purpose of this step is to objectively understand the current condition. This is accomplished by observing the process as it is today and usually requires engaging the workforce, especially people on the front lines who are closest to the work itself. It means asking good questions and spending time really listening to employees. A culture for sustainability doesn't look for blame or point fingers but rather inquires, explores, and discovers what is and is not effective and working.

The second step in the A3 process is to identify "where we want to be in relationship to a specific next phase in time." This is often referred to as envisioning the "to be" state.

The third step is to craft an action plan to help move the organization from its current condition to the desired to be state.

Appropriate measurements such as responses to the questions below can be captured at different levels and at each phase of the A3 process.

Level 1—Did I go through an assessment and do I have a plan?
Level 2—Did I roll out and execute my plan?
Level 3—Did I assess current metrics after implementing my plan?
Level 4—Will the change I made be sustained?
Level 5—Am I getting the desired outcomes?

The only way to know the condition has truly been changed is to test it with observable data and new observations. Were employee meetings held? Did the employees hear the key messages? Were the messages effective?

Investing in People to Build an Engaged Workforce: Human Resources

Over the years, the role of HR has changed dramatically. Several years ago Alcoa transformed its own HR department. HR's primary role became that of a business partner, and transactional activities moved into a shared-services function. HR was challenged to embrace the role of a valued business partner. At Alcoa, HR helps coordinate and facilitate the CAB, implement the Community Framework, and reinforce the link between the Alcoa Foundation and the community.

As this transformation began to take hold at Alcoa, it became clear that one of the most significant ways that HR adds value is by investing in people to build an engaged workforce. Talent management became key, specifically with regard to the acquisition, retention, and development of the people who will lead Alcoa into the future. Because sustainability is so central to Alcoa's future, it was embedded in Alcoa's talent-management strategy at all levels (supervisory, leadership, new employees, orientation, and executive development).

HR developed "Alcoa—Our Story," a high-level overview of the company for all new employees. To build better business acumen, modules on understanding sustainability have been added to Alcoa's learning and development platforms.

Four Es and a P

Alcoa's HR department developed and implemented a simple, elegant, and memorable competency model to drive sustainability and employee engagement throughout the company. It is called Four Es and a P. The P stands for *passion*, which is instrumental to capturing the minds and hearts of the employees at Alcoa. Passion is generated from Alcoa's values-driven culture and fueled by its enduring commitment to sustainability and the community. The Es stand for *edge, energy, energize,* and *execute.*

In addition to these high-level competencies, there are many examples of subcompetencies—such as change orientation, strategic orientation, trustworthy relationships with teams and community—that are used by HR to help build a culture for sustainability. These all can help achieve or diminish the success of sustainability initiatives.

These competencies and subcompetencies are used in Alcoa's learning and performance-management platforms to educate and reinforce employees about desired behaviors to create a culture of and for sustainability at Alcoa.

Challenges

Changing Mind-Sets and Behavior

Like most companies committed to sustainability from a people, planet, and profits perspective, Alcoa faces many challenges from every direction. In terms of the Alcoa Howmet Dover employees, Fromkin told me that the "majority of people are on board and want it. Seventy-five percent understand it, buy into it, and it automatically resonates with them; they get it. Then there's still around 25 percent who just don't get it. They are a real challenge. You end up spending the majority of your time trying to change the minority of people." He added, "These are difficult nuts to crack because you need to change people's habits."[29]

Can you, and if so, just how do you change that mind-set? According to Fromkin, the key is to hold first-line supervisors and managers accountable; make it an expectation. All the leaders in the company, Roy said, have a performance-management requirement to participate in the community.[30]

STEM

A second challenge for Alcoa is ensuring that technical talent is available to drive the level of innovation and scientific excellence required to build a sustainable future. The STEM education gap and shortage of talent in the United States is widely touted and is experienced by not only Alcoa but also most of the companies featured in this book. The ability to attract and retain young people from these technical fields will be essential if Alcoa is to maintain its competitiveness.

Through a partnership with the Manufacturing Institute, Alcoa Foundation is working with Alcoa locations and community colleges to close the skills gap in advanced manufacturing by developing curriculums and certifications to train individuals for available jobs. In 2012, nearly 1,400 students, many of whom were U.S. veterans, received industry certifications at 15 community colleges. Best practices from these efforts were shared with participants from around the world.

Lessons Learned

As Alcoa reflects on the lessons learned from its journey to sustainability so far, a few things stand out. I present these so that small, medium, and large enterprises can use them to jump-start and then build their own cultures for sustainability.

- Recognize it takes time and it's a journey. It can be a fun journey as we all learn how to be more sustainable.
- Think about how you engage your workforce. Be sure to involve your employees and the community in your success every step of the way.
- Build awareness through ongoing employee education. Try exciting employees' attention through "toolbox talks" where everyone stands for a short meeting on a specific sustainability topic.
- Remember as a leader your job is not to have all the answers but to elicit them from your people. Inspire and involve your employees in finding answers and solving problems.
- Install a process and a make a plan. The process starts with making a commitment, setting milestones and targets, and having a plan.
- Start somewhere! Don't think you can't take this on because you don't know where to begin.
- Have a 10-year plan. Pick one or two projects per year in each key area to focus on for your company.
- Don't try to eat the whole elephant. Focus on small wins that add up. For example, instead of trying to install solar everywhere, install five panels. Put in high-efficiency ovens. Every year it accumulates.
- Stick with your commitment no matter what. Know that there will be challenges, but you can't let obstacles derail you.
- Inspire people to help create a better work environment. People want to come to work and do a good job. Recognize that sometimes life gets in the way. Help people cope with these situations when they arise.
- Learn from others. Ask larger companies to help mentor you. Consult with other companies such as Alcoa. Nonprofits and others are eager to help. Seek out and make use of helpful tools. There are lots of free resources available. Useful websites and organizations are sprouting up all the time.
- Measure everything.

Frameworks, Tools, and Resources

Alcoa Community Framework

Alcoa's commitment to stakeholder engagement is one of the hallmarks of its commitment to sustainability and corporate citizenship. And the

Alcoa Community Framework provides the principal methodology for managing stakeholder engagement at the local level.

The Alcoa Community Framework articulates Alcoa's expectations for open, fact-based, and transparent dialogue with its stakeholders and offers a means for achieving this. It provides explicit behaviorally based standards for interacting with stakeholders; specific, clear, and consistent standards and expectations for location leaders; a process for identifying stakeholder groups; and best practices for ensuring the effectiveness of the entire stakeholder-engagement process.

The Community Framework comprises eight strategic levers to guide broad strategic engagement at the local level wherever Alcoa operates:

Community Assessment and Public Strategy Plan. The Community Assessment and Public Strategy Plan is the foundation for all of Alcoa's Community Framework activities. It is designed to help local leaders and employees develop a fact-based understanding of the surrounding community and issues to which Alcoa needs to pay attention. This information provides valuable input for the development of a community-based strategic plan that addresses business and community priorities and potential perceived or real risks that can or are affecting Alcoa in that particular community.

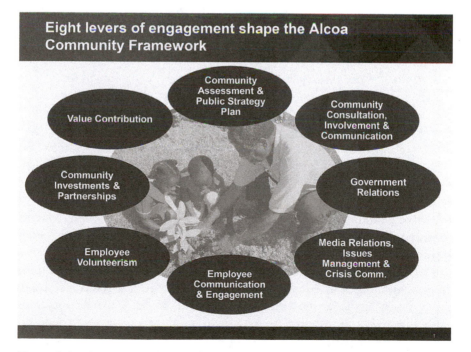

Figure 3.1   © 2013 Alcoa Foundation.

Government Relations. Alcoa considers relationships with government stakeholders critical to its ability to educate its influencers about its business and to inform policies that impact its operations. Alcoa expects each of its locations to understand key issues that affect its business and to be able to speak about these articulately and persuasively to political officials.

Community Consultation, Involvement, and Communication. Alcoa believes that maintaining regular contact with key community leaders and organizations can help ensure its business is well understood by the communities in which it operates. At the same time, such ongoing contact helps Alcoa understand the challenges faced by these communities. The company seeks to create an environment for open and honest, fact-based, two-way communications through its participation in associations, NGOs, and forums that are convened by Alcoa and external groups. These forums provide important opportunities for sharing information and raising and resolving issues as they emerge.

Community Investment, Partnerships, and Collaboration. Alcoa takes a collaborative approach with the intention of providing mutual benefits to all its partners. It believes in strong community partnerships and investing its resources to strengthen the sustainability of the local communities in which it operates. It does so by focusing on specific measurable outcomes that benefit the local communities wherever the company has a presence. At the same time, Alcoa tries to capitalize on its core competencies as a mining, manufacturing, and engineering company.

Employee Communication and Engagement. As we have seen, Alcoa highly values and promotes an actively engaged workforce that understands its business and adds value to the company's bottom line. The company believes that engaged and well-informed employees can serve as ambassadors for Alcoa in the communities in which it operates. This is the philosophy that underlies many of the programs and best practices reviewed throughout this chapter.

Employee Volunteerism. As we have also seen, mobilizing employees to actively volunteer in their local communities results in many benefits to reputational capital, building goodwill for the company that goes beyond Alcoa's financial and economic contributions.

Media Relations, Issues Management, and Crisis Communications. Alcoa encourages its locations to nurture stakeholder relationships of every ilk, in particular the media. Alcoa's media policies provide locations with guidance and resources to help them build a strategic and proactive media relations plan.

Value Contribution. The Alcoa Community Framework is designed holistically so that, by simultaneously creating and strengthening goodwill and enhancing its business, all community relations activities are beneficial to the community and to the company's partners, employees, and the company itself.

For each of the eight levers, there are four levels of evaluation (red, yellow, blue, and green) ranging from underdeveloped (red) to robust (green). A survey tool helps plants identify key stakeholders and prioritize the local community's issues. After conducting an initial community assessment, the local team crafts a public strategy plan that will form the basis of the rest of its activities, including engagement with stakeholders and community investment planning supported with Alcoa Foundation funds. At the end of each year, each facility conducts a self-assessment of its compliance with the plan based on the eight framework elements. These ratings are then aggregated in a Location Compliance Scorecard.[31]

An annual community assessment helps the local team increase its understanding of the facility and the community and determine how it can best demonstrate responsible corporate citizenship. This annual assessment incorporates internal and external perceptions about Alcoa, business priorities, role in the community, and local needs.

The Alcoa Community Framework also supports effective engagement with other critical stakeholders, including the public, government, media, and employees.

As well as the assessments, the Community Framework provides a variety of other tools—location-specific newsletters, town hall meetings, plant walkthroughs, suggestion systems, recognition systems, family days, community days, and more—designed to help locations build effective relationships with all their stakeholders.

Center for Climate and Energy Solutions

Alcoa has developed a partnership with the Center for Climate and Energy Solutions, as demonstrated by the Make an Impact program discussed earlier in this chapter. Alcoa considers the center's website an important, rich, and invaluable resource.[32] During our interview, Carpenter said that she appreciates the center's website because it is written in simple terms, has a wealth of practical information, and makes it easy to find resources.

In particular, Alcoa is using the center's carbon calculator in its challenge to students and schools (alcoa.c2es.org/challenge) in conjunction with the Make an Impact program described earlier in this chapter.

Conclusion

Alcoa's approach to sustainability is holistic and comprehensive. It is a model for supporting a broad cross-section of stakeholders. It builds employee pride, which contributes to employee productivity. Alcoa's values-driven culture is more than words, as the company strives to lead by example through everyday actions.

Alcoa's long-term view and commitment to its people, the community, and the environment—and the actions that embody them—position the company well to attract and retain the next generation of employees. They help build Alcoa's brand and reinforce the perception both inside and outside the company that it is a values-based and values-driven organization.

The story of Alcoa and its Alcoa Howmet Dover plant offer four powerful messages for organizations of all sizes that are committed to building a culture for sustainability. First, inextricably link sustainability to the success of your business; it deepens employee engagement and stimulates innovation.

Second, work steadfastly to instill a sustainable mind-set throughout the organization, but be aware that it won't happen overnight. Touch people's hearts and their heads, as kindred spirits with a common vision can catalyze powerful long-term changes in organizations. Recognize that building a culture for sustainability often represents a fundamental paradigm shift in the culture, so it must be led and managed from that perspective.

Third, to make this cultural transformation stick and produce sustainable results, recognize that it will involve many diverse activities on the ground and in the trenches. Although it may start with some easy-to-accomplish, low-cost initiatives, ultimately it will require implementing new work practices—including new policies and procedures—and then training and holding people accountable to them. Fromkin summed it up poignantly when he said, "Filling up a vat of water and shutting it off is every bit important as making a good-quality product."[33]

Fourth, recognize that safety and environment go hand in hand. If the people who entrust their lives to the company every day are truly cared about, they will rise to the occasion and care about the company as well. People's commitment to their own well-being will be extended to the environment and the communities in which the company operates, creating a virtuous cycle for everyone. As a result, the company and its leaders will change its legacy for generations to come.

CHAPTER 4

BASF: Creating Chemistry for a Sustainable Future

Chemistry is what enables the transition to a sustainable society.
—Robin Rotenberg (2012)

Even from my car—as I was driving up to BASF's North American headquarters—I sensed something special and unique about the company's commitment to sustainability. The lawn looked more natural than those outside most corporate offices. A row of parking spaces close to the U.S. Green Building Council's double-Platinum Leadership in Energy and Environmental Design (LEED)–certified building was reserved for energy-efficient vehicles (though it was filled to the max, so I had to park my own hybrid vehicle elsewhere). I later learned that the building itself is quite literally a showcase for what the chemistry industry can do to foster sustainability in the world, with close to 40 BASF solutions featured in it.

Entering the building, I was drawn into the Innovation Center in the lobby where customers, schoolchildren, and others were learning about sustainability in a fun and creative atmosphere. In the center of the room was a large table with touchscreens. Also on the table were crystal cubes representing different industries and functions. By selecting a cube from dozens lining the wall and placing it in a designated space on the table, a visitor could open a whole new world of possibilities for learning and exploring solutions in sustainable development.

Along the side wall was a screen with scrolling words that told inspirational stories of how BASF has and is making a difference by saving lives, preventing diseases, and creating innovations around the world. The powerful words, "From the earth to the earth. . . . [w]e create chemistry for a sustainable future. But what on earth do we mean by sustainability?" called out to me. Curious, I watched and learned more about what sustainability means to BASF: "Sustainability is about. . . . [p]rotecting our planet's resources. Creating greener, cleaner, better products and solutions that meet the needs of tomorrow's world."

Myriad examples scrolling down these wall panels helped me understand how BASF translates its grand statements into specific solutions for addressing global needs. I learned that BASF has developed a filtration membrane for cleaning contaminated water—a technology that could spare millions from waterborne diseases and provide greater access to safe clean potable water for millions of people around the world. BASF water purifications solutions have already been a critical factor in the virtual eradication of Guinea worm disease, with infection rates having fallen by 99.9 percent. BASF expects this to become the first parasitic disease in history to be completely eradicated. Other illustrations showed how BASF helped create compostable plastic bags and reduced pollution in Beijing by equipping its buses with selective catalytic reduction (SCR catalysts)—a cost-effective way to reduce NO_2 emissions.

I learned about smart forvision, a concept car that is a joint Daimler and BASF project. Among its features are lightweight construction for safety, weight reduction, and electrical-energy efficiency, a roof featuring transparent organic solar panels that power the car's electrical systems, and all-plastic wheels for further weight reduction and fuel efficiency.

Intrigued, I was ready to begin the process of personally interviewing a cross-section of BASF's leaders and managers—in Environment, Health, and Safety (EHS); Corporate Communications; Human Resources (HR); and Sustainability—to learn how the company is making all this possible. A few weeks before my first visit to the company's headquarters, I had had the opportunity to hear a keynote presentation by BASF Corp. Chairman and CEO Hans Engel in which he presented the big picture. This gave me a basic understanding of how all the initiatives I saw on the lobby's walls fit together. Now I was going to get the individual stories.[1]

This chapter describes how BASF defines sustainability by taking a long-term view grounded in a deep understanding of megatrends for 2050. I explain how the company enables its employees to discover solutions to the major challenges facing humanity in the areas of food, energy, transportation, and housing, and describe how BASF has created a broad spectrum of employee-engagement initiatives for building a culture for sustainability. I present a wide range of best practices—including the key roles of HR and Corporate Communications—that are illustrations of how BASF is creating a culture for innovation and sustainability throughout the company. Undergirding BASF's systems approach is its "Verbund" concept, which permeates every function, facet, and operation of the organization. BASF defines *Verbund* as "an interconnected system of relationships generating greater value than the sum of its parts."[2]

I also highlight some of the key challenges BASF is grappling with and discuss how it is addressing them. Finally, I describe some of the major lessons learned and recommend frameworks, tools, and resources from the perspective of the BASF leaders and managers who have been deeply immersed in the company's journey to sustainability for more than 25 years.

Defining Sustainability at BASF

BASF believes that its long-term viability and success as a company is tied to sustainability. And "sustainability means aligning economic success with environmental and social responsibility," said Dr. Kurt Bock, chairman of the board of executive directors. "This will ensure our long-term business success."[3]

Taking a Long-Term View of Megatrends

BASF takes a future-focused, holistic view of sustainability that is grounded in science. According to Engel, demographic challenges are setting the stage for the future of the chemical industry.[4] This dovetails nicely with something then–director of Product Stewardship Ed Madzy told me in our interview: "We see chemistry as the enabling science for the 2050 world of 9 billion people."[5] So demographics are setting the stage for chemistry's future, and the science of chemistry will be crucial to overcoming the obstacles created by the world's exploding population. As it increases—9 billion people are expected to inhabit the earth by 2050—the need for sustainable solutions to help house, feed, move, and power the growing population increases as well. These challenges are compounded by the rising level of affluence of people in both developing and developed countries, especially as people in the developing world race to attain the lifestyles they are exposed to through globalized media.

In addition, extended life expectancies contribute to overpopulation, and a rising standard of living increases consumerism. While eradication of diseases and new drugs have extended the life expectancy of many people around the globe, "by saving lives, you're creating other issues, and you have to come back in balance," said senior vice president of EHS, James Bero.[6]

At the presentation I attended, Engel highlighted four "megatrends" that are driving innovation for sustainable development: a growing and aging world population; urbanization; energy demand and climate protection; and globalization and developing markets.[7] BASF considers each megatrend a global challenge *and* a global opportunity that will open up areas of innovation at BASF in health and nutrition; construction and housing; energy and resources; and mobility and communication.

Responding to Megatrends with Sustainability

Several leaders at BASF told me that because meeting the needs of people continues to place increasing strain on the earth's natural resources, it is more important than ever to respond to these megatrends through the lens of sustainability. Already, use of these resources exceeds the earth's regenerative capacity by one-and-a-half times per year (the equivalent of one-and-a-half earths every year).[8]

According to BASF Sustainability leader, North America, Charlene Wall, BASF's contributions to a more sustainable world are grounded in several critical questions: Regarding transportation and communication, with 2 billion cars expected to be on the road worldwide by 2030, how can we reduce emissions and fuel consumption? Regarding construction and housing, with 60 percent of the world's population expected to live in cities by 2030, which materials are needed to make energy consumption more efficient? Regarding health and nutrition, with 8 billion people expected to be living by 2030, how can we ensure ample food and water supplies for everyone? And regarding energy and climate, with 40 percent more primary energy needed by 2030, how can we contribute to climate protection and energy supply?[9]

With 342 production facilities on five continents and more than 113,000 employees worldwide, BASF creates chemistry to serve all major industries. Increasingly, the company is focusing its innovation on emerging sustainability-oriented industries such as wind and solar power, biotechnology, energy efficiency, sustainable construction, water treatment, and fuel cell technology.

"We drive sustainable solutions" is one of BASF's four interconnected strategic principles defined in its "We create chemistry" global strategy. Sustainable solutions are seen as those that achieve measurable value and achieve an empirical balance between ecology, economy, and social responsibility. Driving sustainable solutions is directly linked to three other strategic pillars that form the foundation of the BASF business model: "We add value as one company; We innovate to make our customers more successful; and We form the best team."[10]

Balancing the Environment, Economics, and Society: A Systems Approach

The basis of its commitment to sustainability is BASF's Verbund systems approach that permeates its internal organization. It is committed not only to creating products for a sustainable future but also to creating a culture for sustainability that encompasses its employees, stakeholders, suppliers, and the communities in which its facilities are located.

I asked Wall, who has been with BASF about 20 years, how such a strong holistic commitment to sustainability evolved at the company. She said that she first came across the term *sustainability* around 2000; before that, through the 1990s, the sustainability focus was largely on the environment. From 2000 to 2010, sustainability at BASF evolved to include more than environmental concerns, and the company developed new lenses and measurement systems that reflected this new understanding.

In 2001, BASF offered its customers a new service in North America: eco-efficiency analysis (EEA) of products and processes. Using a comprehensive, life-cycle approach, BASF's EEA methodology empowers customers and BASF's own businesses to incorporate economics, environmental conservation, and social considerations into the sustainability equation.

In addition to EEA, BASF has developed a number of new measurement systems and frameworks to quantify sustainability based on a holistic, cradle-to-grave view of processes and products, from the sourcing of raw material to the eventual disposal of finished goods. These include SEE Balance, which measures "socio-eco-efficiency" by accounting for environmental, economic, and social impacts, and "SET," which accounts for sustainability eco-efficiency and traceability. Each of these became a sustainability screening tool, a lens through which sustainability impacts and outcomes could be effectively measured and monitored.

BASF's EEA weighs economic and ecological factors and has become widely accepted worldwide by universities, governments, and companies as a tool for accurately measuring the sustainability of products

Figure 4.1   © 2013 BASF. Used with permission.

and processes. More than 400 analyses have been completed by BASF for its customers using this eco-efficiency methodology.

The EEA takes a life-cycle approach, examining the environmental impact of all phases of the life of products—from the consumption of raw materials and all phases of production (including energy consumption, emissions, and end products) through the use phase and the recycling/disposal phase. Life-cycle data is gathered in six environmental categories: raw materials, energy consumption, land use, emissions, toxicity, and risk potential, and is depicted on an ecological fingerprint, a data visualization of the comparison of the elements being evaluated. The data is then weighted and aggregated to obtain an overall environmental impact.[11]

Over the past few years, said Wall, BASF has begun to examine certain industry or value chains more closely.[12] For example, it is looking at agriculture and biodiversity, creating tools such as AgBalance, which is a "holistic method for life cycle assessment in agricultural and food value chain production, including ecological, economic and societal impacts."[13] When I asked how BASF went about doing all this, Wall explained how it took its eco-efficiency engine and began with a stakeholder analysis. Starting with its nutrition business, the company examined its food value chains, taking into account important stakeholder perceptions, such as considerations of animal welfare. Whereas early on BASF's analyses were conducted by sustainability experts, "now we see the first phenomenon of a sustainability expert sitting with a business person to develop something jointly and drilling into the business value chain," said Wall.[14] This represented an important shift that has continued and deepened over time regarding quality, performance, and eco-efficiency as the approach moved from a corporate-sustainability-expert model to one that integrates sustainability into BASF's business and value chain.

This new approach has been used successfully in BASF's construction chemicals business with the company applying BASF's EEA to its products and solutions used in the construction business. It developed Green Sense concrete mixtures, which were used in the construction of One World Trade Center (Freedom Tower) in New York City. In addition to saving water and energy and reducing CO_2 emissions, the Green Sense concrete mixture has resulted in cost savings "based on optimizing the raw materials to produce a very workable, high performance mix."[15] This project alone saved more than "30,000 gallons of fresh water, 8 million kWh of energy, 12 million pounds of CO_2 emissions, and nearly 750,000 pounds of fossil fuel versus a typical concrete mix formulation."[16]

What does this evolution of perspectives on sustainability and tools have to do with building a culture for sustainability at BASF? Wall said the two are analogous. Together they represent a cultural evolution that has occurred as BASF has become a networked matrix organization. The company's overall purpose and strategy, which she describes as being at a 30,000-foot strategic level, is supported by action at ground level. Applying sustainability to specific industries, businesses, and value chains (in a search for ways to integrate sustainability into the heart of the business operations) makes sustainability real for every employee, in every function and every part of the company.

In 2011, BASF launched a new long-term global strategy called "We create chemistry" predicated on the purpose statement "We create chemistry for a sustainable future." As BASF cross-fertilizes sustainability approaches across its diverse businesses, it intentionally seeks to build a network—a living, breathing connection between the sustainability experts and the businesses. As Wall explained it, now employees might say, "I know I have certain products in my portfolio that bring sustainability benefits. I have sustainability tools I can use . . . but in my own value chain assessment and operations, I am looking more closely at what sustainability means in my specific business." And this is causing everyone to ask, "What else can we do to drive this purpose?" Ultimately, this is "channeling energy throughout the entire company so every employee can understand what this means in his daily workplace and daily life."[17]

Building a Culture for Sustainability

The idea of an extended network has permeated every facet of the company, and is critical to its culture for sustainability. This network, exemplified in the concept of Verbund that I mentioned in the introduction to this chapter, generates passion, excites motivation, and provides comfortable opportunities for inquiry and learning. As Wall told me, "We are working to create a Verbund of knowledge around sustainability so everyone feels equipped to talk about it whether talking to their neighbor, their customer, or their child at home, in terms of what it means to BASF and to them as well."[18]

What Does a Culture for Sustainability Look Like?

"Culture is what everybody does when no one is looking," said senior vice president, HR, Judy Zagorski.[19] And she has witnessed BASF's culture for sustainability firsthand in times of challenge and adversity. She recounted several compelling examples of leaders and employees rallying together to find creative solutions to significant financial and human challenges.

When the bottom fell out of the market in late 2008, BASF's leaders and employees collaborated quickly and decisively to drive to reduce operating costs in a way that met the short-term financial challenges, kept employee impact to a minimum, and maintained the company's strategic approach and commitment to long-term growth. BASF engaged people throughout the organization in helping to come up with the solutions. "I give [former North American CEO and current global CEO] Kurt Bock a lot of credit. While a lot of business leaders went right to top-down, slash-and-burn tactics, our leaders demonstrated their commitment to inclusive problem solving and innovation; it was extremely impressive," said Zagorski.[20]

Another example of BASF's culture for sustainability is the inclusive, team-oriented approach it took in preparing for and reacting to Hurricane Sandy in late 2012. This included strong support from BASF colleagues on the Gulf Coast, most of whom had experienced the wrath of Hurricane Katrina in 2005. Several people I spoke with described how everyone bent over backward to reach out, give back, and help one another. "That says more about culture than anything," said Zagorski.[21]

Corporate Communications director Andreas Meier described a culture for sustainability as the sum total of many behaviors that support shared values. "Using sustainable solutions instead of traditional plastics in the cafeteria; using materials and resources efficiently in the office; and making use of feedstock as efficiently and cleanly as possible," he said. "It's the entire system. It's putting electric car plug-ins close to the building and giving them better parking spots. It's all about walking the walk—those little things make the difference."[22]

Changing Mind-Sets

"The vision for the culture [at BASF] is grounded in collaboration and innovation," said Wall during our interview. This is in tune with the "interconnectedness" of Verbund—compounding the value derived from the diverse workforce and broad expertise of the company with a mind-set that is elastic and continually forward-looking.[23]

Zagorski explained that a long-term view of sustainability at BASF has implications for culture change at the company.[24] It means moving from a focus on filling jobs to do the work of today, to developing a workforce that's capable of executing the work of today but more importantly preparing themselves for the work of tomorrow. From a tactical standpoint, this means building very strong foundations in core competencies, development, and training practices, and identification of emerging talent who can be the next generation of leaders for the organization.

Getting Close to Customers

Senior vice president, EHS, James Bero spoke with me about the importance of getting close to customers in order to identify sustainability-related business opportunities. He said, "We believe we'll do a much better job by letting the people who are closest to the customer identify the trends, identify the opportunities, and drive the product development."[25]

He pointed out that in some of its businesses, BASF customers aren't sure exactly what they want or need. This requires BASF's employees' getting even closer, not just to their immediate customers, but to the end consumers as well. Bero advises, "Understand their needs, and then help your customers innovate to find a solution their clients want."[26]

Zagorski explained the cultural shifts necessitated by BASF's strong focus on connecting more closely with markets and customers and approaching innovation from a more "outside-in" solution-based perspective rather than trying to sell internally driven innovations into the marketplace.[27] This required shifting the mind-set and the skill set of BASF's workforce to reflect a better understanding of the market, the megatrends that were affecting its customers and their customers, and putting together solutions from BASF's portfolio of products and technologies that would help meet the challenges of tomorrow.

Finding Solutions to Intractable Problems

BASF finds and hires people who see the megatrends, understand where the company is going, and want to be part of a team that comes up with solutions to big problems. Bero said, "This is the key to solving the problems of the future. We invest and assign staff to the things that we believe will make a difference. We put our money where our mouth is. Employees and potential employees see evidence of this here in our building and hopefully, in everything we do."[28]

Letting Science Decide

As a company deeply grounded in science, informed, empirical, fact-based decision making is the way at BASF. In our interview, Bero emphasized that this can be challenging when dealing with certain elements of the media, politics, and the nongovernmental organization (NGO) community who too often let emotion, rather than concrete scientific fact, guide decision making and opinion.[29]

Wall echoed this observation: "We want to be absolutely sure that any claim we make is 100 percent valid before we say anything about it. Sometimes it's difficult to make your voice heard when someone else who wasn't so thorough is touting their latest 'eco-friendly' product." Even though this can be trying, she said, "what I love about BASF is . . . when we do it, we're going to do it wholeheartedly, authentically, thoroughly, and we're going to do a darn good job. That's my biggest pride point with BASF."[30]

Making the Shift from Functional to Solutions-Driven Strategy

Everyone I spoke with described how BASF does things strategically, taking a phased and long-term approach. Doing things strategically is seen as allowing greater alignment and creating impetus. It results in sustaining people's ideas, the better use of ideas, and more-effective knowledge transfer. Not only does BASF foster a strategic approach, but it also drives a particular kind of strategic approach—one that helps the company home in on solutions.

In our interview, Bero described the evolving role of the central EH&S group as the company makes the shift from a functional to solutions-driven strategy. "Rather than a chief EH&S officer driving sustainability within a company, the businesses have to drive the solutions," said Bero.[31] At the same time, the central group's function is to address issues that affect all the businesses, requiring people with broad understanding.

Integrating Sustainability into Everyone's Goals

Madzy explained that the "next great thing" BASF did was to require that every person in the company have a goal in each of the four strategic pillar areas.[32] Regardless of whether they work, say, on the factory floor, in a laboratory, or in a sales position, they must define sustainability in their own words and work on a goal that improves BASF in those four areas. This means that people have to understand how the job they do every day affects the sustainability of BASF, the sustainability of the industry, the sustainability of the marketplace, and the sustainability of the world.

Madzy went on to explain how this process of goal setting unfolds and how it translates into employee engagement, helping to create and reinforce a culture for sustainability at BASF. "Once you set a target like that it galvanizes the community inside BASF to achieve those goals. Initially there's low-hanging fruit but eventually people start looking under rocks. It engages leadership of the company, technical people, and people get behind it; they read about it, get excited about it, and that's how you get your employee engagement," he said.[33]

Creating Sustainability Champions

One way BASF is working to embed sustainability throughout its vast organization is by creating sustainability champions within the organization to create channels of informal communication and knowledge. These are typically people who have been proactive in sustainability within their business or function.

Igniting Contagious Passion

Among others I spoke with, Bero described the emotional connection people have to trying to do the right thing around sustainability at

BASF. "When the subject is sustainability," he said, "I have to turn volunteers away. There's a real passion. Not everyone has that passion, but it's contagious. You provide a framework, and a few people who are very enthusiastic tend to get others on board."[34] One way they do this is by telling stories. These may be shared in a variety of ways, through the intranet, town hall meetings, and face-to-face.

Madzy said, "I never cease to be amazed at how committed the people in my department [EHS] are to the job that they do. They feel what they're bringing to the table helps make the world a better place."[35] Simply by providing people the chance to use their skills in a vigorous way to help improve the world, BASF excites employees' passion, which they then pass on to others in their field.

Best Practices

Inspiring People through Communications

Like other critical functions at BASF, communications start with a robust strategic plan. This includes "clear objectives, strategy, and tremendous executive support." The highest level in the company clearly supports the sustainability story, how it is told and how it is lived. "If it's not, it's just not going to be seen as important by our greatest ambassadors, who are our employees," said vice president, Corporate Communications, Robin Rotenberg.[36]

At the same time, communications needs to address the somewhat negative image the public has of chemistry and chemical companies. Through ongoing education, BASF shows that chemistry is critical to the sustainability of the world as we know it—that chemistry is needed to feed people, house people, and provide transportation and mobility, especially as the global population is exploding. "Chemistry is what enables the transition to a sustainable society," said Rotenberg.[37]

In these and myriad other ways, Corporate Communications plays a central and catalytic role at BASF, continually infusing messages about sustainability into communications at every level throughout the company. All media channels are deployed to get the message out. These include a weekly e-newsletter and an active sustainability-focused community on BASF's internal social media platform, connect.BASF. Even so, the communications experts I spoke with said it was important not to *overuse* the word *sustainability*. Instead, they recommended describing sustainability without using the word, instead citing meaningful examples of it which BASF refers to as proof points.

We Create Chemistry World Tour

The We Create Chemistry World Tour is a traveling showcase that demonstrates BASF's innovations in sustainability to its employees, customers, and other stakeholders. It was frequently cited by the people I interviewed at BASF as a best practice. The world tour was conceived, managed, and coordinated by Corporate Communications at BASF in 2012. To reach thousands of customers and other external stakeholders, the tour required tremendous effort across the entire organization, particularly in the Corporate Communications department. It featured 20 innovations—each in its own booth—linked to various aspects of sustainability.

Director of Corporate Communications Andreas Meier said that during the tour participants were bursting with energy and enthusiasm.[38] The half-day events, he said, were highly inspirational experiences for participants, employees, and customers alike. More than 5,000 out of 17,000 employees participated in the North American tour. The event itself began with music—a dramatic opening over a dark stage, creating a magical moment when everything lit up at once.[39] Each event was hosted by two executives.

Photo 4.1   We Create Chemistry World Tour North America. smart forvision: A look at the future of electric mobility. (© 2013 BASF. Used with permission.)

Although the event was designed in Germany, it is traveling around the world (it was in Asia at the time of the interviews I conducted) and was presented in six locations in North America: Detroit, Michigan; Florham Park, New Jersey; Charlotte, North Carolina; Toronto, Canada; Houston, Texas; and Mexico City.

At the event, the participants each received an iPod touch, which helped them navigate through the booths, enabled live tweeting, and generated numerous questions. Because of the world tour, Meier said, "almost everybody knows about our purpose statement, and our values, which have sustainability as a core value. It has become part of everyone's DNA, much more than in the past."[40]

Simply Dare!

In 2010, BASF introduced an employee empowerment program called Simply Dare! to clear the way for employees to fast track and implement their innovative ideas, rather than having them languish in an inbox and be forgotten. Innovation champions in each department, called daredevils, facilitate and encourage ideas that simplify work and contribute to each of the four strategic principles. Each department can also compete for an annual prize by voting online for ideas from employees across the company. The program has generated several hundred ideas since its inception, and has fostered collaboration and innovation across the organization.

Leveraging Human Resources

As BASF began to incorporate sustainability into its core central strategy, it realized that HR could play a significant role. Zagorski explained how HR approached this: "We focused first on understanding what the core business strategy was and how it was likely to evolve over the next 10 to 20 years. When you're building a human-capital strategy, you really do have to look far out into the time horizon because you're planting seeds that will take root and flourish over time and ultimately you want to produce the kind of flower that you [will] need in the future."[41]

Three-Prong Global People Strategy

BASF's Human Resources' Global People Strategy is composed of three prongs: excellent people, excellent place to work, and excellent leaders. Zagorski said that this strategy was developed with an eye toward sustainability, which, she said, "is a lens through which as an executive team, we look at our decisions, our policies, and our practices, as well as our own behaviors."[42] Here I highlight a few of the HR best practices loosely organized in the three prongs.

Excellent People: Talent Management

The first prong, excellent people, was designed to implement HR practices that identify and develop talent and emphasize competencies that will differentiate the company in the future. It is driven by the four megatrends and a long-term view of sustainability. These talent-management practices are the foundational elements of a companywide change-management process. "You can put the processes and tools in place, but if people don't use them, there aren't going to be any results," said Zagorski.[43]

A significant step forward at BASF was HR's engaging the entire North America leadership team as part of a business strategy that incorporated human capital for the first time; previously HR had a separate strategy that was intended to deliver on the business goals it received. Now BASF had a business strategy that included HR. "That might sound subtle, but it was a really big shift because we had to get about 50 leaders to take responsibility and ownership for these goals versus seeing that as something that HR was going to do," said Zagorski.[44]

A key aspect of talent management is recruitment, and HR is recruiting differently than in the past. Specifically, it is actively looking at more diverse talent pools in North America, and it brings a larger team—including both business and functional groups and HR—to recruitment events on college campuses. In addition, HR recruits in places where diverse talent resides, such as the Society of Women Engineers, National Black MBA, and Society of Professional Hispanic Engineers.

BASF has a very strong commitment to fueling diversity by building strong, diverse teams that are close to its customers and markets. Chief Diversity Officer for North America Patricia Rossman said, "We want to be a company that reflects the markets we serve, inclusive of all backgrounds."[45] The company seeks to leverage the many different cultures it brings together from around the world, including the diversity of ideas, experiences, and global markets. It understands how these cultural differences can affect BASF's commercial success and its retention of diverse talent, enabling the company to be more innovative and do a better job of meeting the needs of the marketplace.

Excellent Place to Work

The results of an employee survey, an extremely low turnover rate, the interviews I conducted with managers and employees, and other indicators I reviewed suggest that employees consider BASF an excellent place to work. The employees are highly committed to the company and believe in and trust its leadership.

Zagorski stressed HR's commitment to its employees when she said, "The most significant thing we can do as an institution is to provide a place where people can have meaningful work and can continue to develop their skills and contribute. That is one of the reasons we exist as a corporation. What I love about BASF is we never lose sight of that."[46]

Rossman echoed this and also suggested two specific ways to retain talent; she said it is important to ask, "Are you running a group where people are dying to get into it, or dying to get out of [it]? Are you giving people opportunities for visibility and development?"[47]

Like other corporations, BASF faces rising medical costs, but it is committed to providing competitive employee benefits and invited employees to help devise ways to continue offering these even as other companies were slashing them. It conducted a survey of its employees, the Total Rewards Survey, to gather information that became key to the redesign of its compensation and benefits packages. The survey examined what employees value, beyond their paychecks, about working at BASF. The findings were used to develop the You @ BASF program, a new HR website, and the Healthy You wellness campaign.

Healthy You provides employees with incentives to track and monitor their own health, with the help of professional support resources, and realize actual incentives if they improve their health. The program is unique in that the employees share financially in its benefits. BASF provides monetary benefits to an employee if she reduces her risks. BASF gains by having a reduced risk pool. "We're sharing with our employees. It's a win-win," said Zagorski.[48]

Excellent Leaders: Developing Leaders in a VUCA World

BASF takes a comprehensive and holistic approach to leadership development, an approach that the company believes is essential in a world that is volatile, uncertain, complex, and ambiguous (VUCA). BASF's professional-development program (PDP) prepares potential leaders for this world. As Zagorski said, "In a VUCA world, the leaders that are going to be most successful are those who are open, innovative, and adaptable. We are looking at people who have that entrepreneurial drive and that willingness and ability to learn constantly and apply those things to the unsolved challenges of the future."[49]

BASF's PDP offers internships and an accelerated development program across a variety of disciplines, including engineering, PhD chemists, supply chain, finance, HR, and more. In many cases, undergraduates are offered full-time employment with BASF after successful summer internships. The PDP includes an accelerated onboarding to BASF through a series of rotational experiences across different businesses and functions, at least one of which involves international experience. A senior executive mentor is assigned to provide ongoing coaching and development advice throughout the program, and an annual conference—which includes leadership-development training, community service experiences, and networking with top leaders at BASF—is held for all PDP program participants.

Caitlin Harmon, a PDP I spoke with who joined the company in organization development within the HR function, described for me firsthand how valuable the program has been for her: "In such a large, global company, PDP gives us an opportunity to stretch our wings, helps us understand the business, and learn that it's OK to make mistakes. It taught me not to be afraid to ask for more opportunities. The program helps leaders learn how to be leaders, and gives people a sense of loyalty to the company."[50]

A mandatory part of the PDP is the corporate social responsibility (CSR) module, in which participants volunteer on a regular basis in community-based giving with Habitat for Humanity or a project specific to one of BASF's local sites, such as those in the Gulf Coast. Harmon told me that with regard to creating a culture for sustainability, the program is "phenomenal" in that it helps people think about what they're doing every day and how they personally can contribute to greater sustainability.[51]

High-performing people have many career options, and BASF understands that its dedication to sustainability helps differentiate it for these people. Recruits have reported to HR that they accepted BASF's offer because of its sustainability record. Zagorski has seen this in her own work in HR: "People really want to be part of a company that has a purpose that's meaningful. The experience they have every day or every week shows them we don't just talk about this, we live it. We care about them and the communities in which we operate. We care about our customers. Our goal is to reflect that in everything we do." In these ways, BASF has seen how its commitment to sustainability and social responsibility helps it recruit the best people.

Emerging Talent

Like most companies, BASF historically has promoted the best performers. But for the company to be sustainable, it had to shift from concentrating solely on high-performing individuals to focusing also on *emerging talent*—those people who exhibit the ability to develop others and lead high-performing teams. It began to devise means of identifying and accelerating the development of both high-performing and high-potential talent and preparing future leaders for the challenges they would face. An employee-development process was implemented across the organization all the way down to the department level so that the entire company would have a common framework, common language, and common method for developing people, including future leaders and experts.

HR invites some of the emerging talent to development centers where they are exposed to leaders two levels above them from outside their business lines. The leaders give the participants feedback, coaching, and mentoring regarding their leadership behaviors.

In addition to receiving this feedback, participants—who are put together in cohorts with people who are not necessarily from their line organization—conduct business simulations and case studies to sharpen their skills.

Development Centers

The development centers are part of an overall "action learning" philosophy. The idea is to take people out of their normal business environment for only "short bursts" rather than long periods of time as may have been more common in the past. For example, a regional development center might require people to attend a two-day experience, followed by coaching and feedback sessions with a mentor over 12 to 18 months. Other development options include participating in a market or customer focus team, in which people will work with colleagues from across business units and functions to address a growth opportunity in a specific industry or customer segment.

Market Customer Focus Teams

With its action learning model, BASF tries to "anchor in the work that people do and give them space to practice new behaviors."[52] The work Sustainability leader Charlene Wall did as an emerging leader in a team that created compostable snack bags for the Seattle Mariners baseball team in Seattle, Washington, exemplifies market customer focus teams in action. The Seattle Mariners are a member of the Green Sports Alliance (www.greensportsalliance.org). In 2012, the Seattle Mariners pledged to divert 85 percent of its waste from landfills, a tremendous increase from the 12 percent diverted in 2006.[53] A diverse market customer focus team—comprising people from multiple functions and business lines—was formed to find ways to develop eco-efficient packaging for BASF's customers. Given Wall's work in eco-efficiency, she was a good fit. The people on the team continued to perform their regular jobs while also working together to identify solutions for BASF's customers, including the Seattle Mariners, giving team members the opportunity and practice ground to try out new behaviors.

The team fulfilled its mission, leveraging its material technology to create 100 percent compostable snack bags, made from BASF's Ecoflex, initially for the Seattle Mariners (and now marketed as part of BASF's product line), as part of the Mariners' campaign to be 100 percent compostable. According to *Environmental Leader,* "The first 10,000 fans that arrived at Safeco Field to see the Mariners take on the Boston Red Sox received a free bag of peanuts in BASF's prototype packaging, developed with its biopolymer technology." The Mariners vice president of operations described this flexible packaging as "the holy grail of greening our waste stream."[54]

Managing Culture Change

Each step in the intensification of its culture for sustainability brings BASF new issues to address. And each of these issues is a chance for an affirmative form of change, one that encourages positive elements already present in BASF and its community to surface and become stronger. Or, as Zagorski said in our interview, "It's not about changing who we are . . . it's about becoming an even better version of who we are."[55]

Core Spotlight Behaviors

BASF is reinforcing its culture for sustainability through its competency model, known as core spotlight behaviors. As part of the "We create chemistry" strategy, BASF places particular emphasis on key specific and actionable spotlight behaviors that complement BASF's core values: being creative, open, responsible, and entrepreneurial. The competencies are clearly articulated at a behavioral level and are presented in a way that makes them easy to understand and use. For instance, HR provides a library of examples of each competency at all job levels.

Knowledge Transfer: Transitions at Work

Although BASF has a very high retention level, like many companies, it is facing the retirement of many long-term employees who have gained valuable experience and knowledge over the years. So the transfer of explicit and tacit knowledge has become a critical success factor for the company's sustainability. BASF is already thinking ahead to 2020, the point at which the demographics presage a large uptick in its turnover.

To address this, BASF is introducing several new programs, one of which is Transitions at Work. A unique aspect of this program is Retirement Notification Pay. Under this feature, people are offered a financial incentive to inform BASF of their retirement plans sooner than they otherwise would. This notification, with a lead time of 6 to 12 months, enables BASF to put into place such knowledge-transfer processes as job sharing, mentoring, and job shadowing. This allows BASF to maintain its customer relationships, without missing a beat, by replacing people in positions in a sustainable way and transferring the necessary knowledge before the retiree leaves the company.

The program was piloted in 2011 in a manufacturing plant and was rolled out in other manufacturing plants in 2012. It is particularly unique in that it is entirely self-funded through the savings it brings to the company. Rather than hiring contractors to do the work—a very costly alternative—or making quick fixes when someone retires, the program enables BASF to take some of the risk out of the equation and develop a more sustainable solution for talent.

Metrics that Matter: Materiality Assessment

"Materiality assessment" is an important component of how BASF homes in on metrics that matter. This assessment is a process whereby BASF interviews internal and external stakeholders, asking them to provide input to determine the most important sustainability issues.

Senior vice president, EHS, James Bero said he is a believer in "what gets measured gets managed."[56] He thinks the data should help you determine where you are now and give you a tool to tell you where you're getting better. For example, water consumption is a key area BASF is focusing on, starting with reducing the water consumption in its plants. Because of this focus, BASF has cut its consumption of municipal water for operations by 3 million gallons, according to Bero. "As a science-based company, BASF operates in the realm of hard data, measurement and empirical fact," said director, Marketing Communications North America, William Pagano. "Advancing sustainability requires reliable, scientifically sound methods of evaluating sustainability."[57]

As discussed earlier in this chapter, BASF is a standard bearer relative to life-cycle analysis (LCA) and EEA. EEA is defined by the National Science Foundation as "a method for quantifying and evaluating the environmental and economic performance of products and process alternatives. The analysis evaluates the economic and environmental impacts of a product or a process through its anticipated life cycle. The term *eco-efficiency* was coined in 1992 by the World Business Council for Sustainable Development (WBCSD), which defined it as "creating more goods and services while consuming fewer resources and generating less waste and pollution."[58]

In 2010, BASF interviewed 300 stakeholders for its materiality assessment, including customers, government representatives, academics, NGOs, and employees. It asked for feedback on the relevance of different issues to the stakeholders and on the impact to or relevance for BASF. This type of process brings to the fore issues that might be important for BASF to consider; for instance, through the 2010 process, the issue of water consumption surfaced as a key issue for BASF. Once the materiality assessment is completed, BASF examines what it is already doing to address the issues and what else it can do. Then BASF sets corporate goals and metrics and publishes related performance data on its website and in its annual report.

Challenges

In my view, BASF is on the leading edge in building a culture for sustainability. Yet, like other global corporations, it faces daunting challenges in its quest to embed sustainable mind-sets and behaviors throughout the company. "The challenge is being really clear about what sustainability means and how we are going to live it. An ongoing challenge is to constantly align everything that we do, what we say, how we act, with that core purpose," said Zagorski.[59]

Here I present six key challenges BASF is facing and discuss how it is addressing them. The challenges are managing size and complexity; creating a global and culturally diverse people strategy; differentiating your company in the marketplace; filling the pipeline from science, technology, engineering, and mathematics (STEM) disciplines; getting buy-in for total cost of ownership and life-cycle costing; and spanning boundaries across industries and value chains.

Managing Size and Complexity

Several people I interviewed described the sheer size and complexity of the company as simultaneously a strength and a challenge that needs to be addressed. A positive feature is that it allows for multiple checks and balances in BASF's decision-making processes. But, as with any large global organization, its size and matrix structure can slow down processes in a dynamic marketplace that doesn't wait for anyone. Ensuring that people can identify and access the right colleague(s) with whom to speak regarding a specific problem, product, or opportunity is an ongoing challenge. "We've gone to great lengths over the past few years to provide new tools for connecting and collaborating with colleagues throughout both the global organization and here in North America," said Rotenberg.[60] "Our internal social media collaboration tool connect. BASF is a prime example of this."

The company's Sustainability Knowledge Verbund (the "Verbund of knowledge around sustainability," that I quoted Wall as mentioning in Building a Culture for Sustainability) is a starting point for addressing this challenge. The Verbund consists of "networked nodes" of people within each business unit who will point employees in the right direction when they have questions. BASF is beginning the process of establishing such Verbunds at regional and business unit levels.

Knowledge sharing is essential to fully integrating sustainability throughout the large company. For example, when Wall leads BASF's participation in a sustainability consortium in the consumer goods industry, she looks for ways to reach out to the rest of the organization to ensure that of the 17,000 people in North America, and the113,000-plus people globally, those who have a need to know can access the information they need. This is a Herculean task, but one that BASF is addressing head-on.

Creating a Global and Culturally Diverse People Strategy

In our interview, Rossman described how a diverse team can initially be more challenging but in the long run produces better ideas and is more innovative: "A diverse regional team is harder to charter and to get going. But once it hits its stride, it really delivers a lot more than a homogeneous team. Once the team is unleashed to take their ideas and make them better, it gets more momentum, goes farther faster, and delivers better, longer-lasting results."[61]

Expounding further on the relationship between diversity, innovation, and collaboration, Rossman said, "It's harder to ascertain different styles and mold them into one high-performing team. But it's critical for innovation [since] the best innovation is collaborative." Rossman believes that the "collective IQ of the group goes up when you have that clash of cultures. Our ideas get better when you look through different lenses."[62]

Although the chemical industry has historically been one of the more conservative and male-dominated industries, it is now facing big demographic challenges as about 50 percent of its workforce becomes eligible for retirement in the next decade. "We'll need to reinvent ourselves. We'll need to be recruiting differently, and retaining differently," said Rossman.[63]

One significant way BASF is addressing these challenges is by encouraging and supporting a variety of employee affinity groups. "The groups are about helping people network. We don't establish these groups to keep people separate. We establish these groups to support inclusion. If we can create more feelings of comfort and inclusion, the quicker they can assimilate into the BASF culture," said Rossman.[64] The BASF-sponsored affinity groups include Women and Business, Asian Professionals, a Latin American group, Women Working in Construction, an African American group, and Alchemy, a group for the lesbian, gay, bisexual, and transgender (LGBT) community. All the sponsored groups have an executive sponsor with close ties to the group, said Rossman.

Differentiating Your Company in the Marketplace

Marketplace differentiation is a challenge and an opportunity for any business, and for BASF sustainability plays a larger and larger role in achieving that differentiation. BASF recognizes the growing need and desire for sustainability-enabling product innovations and has strategically targeted several sustainability-focused growth markets. "Our purpose statement, 'We create the chemistry for a sustainable future', says a lot about our company and our products," said Pagano.[65] "It says to our customers and our future customers that we have the expertise, the chemistry, and the commitment to help them meet their sustainability objectives."

Filling the Pipeline from STEM Disciplines

As I discussed in the Alcoa chapter in this book, many companies are having difficulty finding talent with technical skills in the STEM disciplines, and this is especially true in the United States. Several of these companies are creating partnerships with educational institutions to increase student interest, involvement, and performance in these subject areas.

Photo 4.2   Kids Lab student and the stretchy green goo she created. (© 2013 BASF. Used with permission.)

BASF, for instance, has created innovative school partnerships and programs such as Starting Young, which offers Kids Lab for elementary school children ages 6 through 12. Kids Lab is a global program designed to allow children to "experience the magic of chemistry through safe and engaging hands-on experiments that illustrate the positive effects of chemistry in our daily lives."[66] The program involved more than 8,000 children in North America in 2011.

Science Summer Academy—which in 2013 marked its third year—is offered through an ongoing partnership between BASF and Fairleigh Dickinson University (FDU), in Florham Park, New Jersey. With support from BASF, FDU hosts 20 high-potential high school students from schools throughout the United States for a two-week intensive science academy. Working in teams, the students conduct research and develop their own personal-care products using BASF materials. They learn about the chemistry used to create products, how to develop products, and how to market those products. The students receive transferable college credits from FDU and a certificate of achievement from BASF.[67]

BASF provided seed funding for the Institute for Enhancing the Teaching of Science and Math (IETSM) at FDU in 2009. IETSM's mission is to work with New Jersey STEM teachers, primarily in middle school, to enhance their science-and-math classroom-teaching skills. The teachers are taught STEM-related content, pedagogy, and research by FDU faculty.

BASF also partners with the American Chemistry Society (ACS) to identify and develop educational opportunities for minority talent. The company participates in the ACS Scholars Program, funding scholarships for these promising students.

Getting Buy-In for Total Cost of Ownership and Life-Cycle Costing

Even though BASF's innovations bring significant sustainability benefits to its customers, sometimes a new technology is more expensive than a traditional technology on a per-pound basis. BASF uses total cost accounting and life-cycle costing to make the case for such technologies. Sometimes, however, the markets and customers are simply not open to, don't understand, or haven't caught up with this new way of viewing costs, which poses a continuing challenge to BASF.[68]

Spanning Boundaries and Value Chains

A key to sustainability is working across boundaries, using multidisciplinary approaches to find solutions to complex problems. Collaboration and information sharing are essential—but hard to accomplish with a worldwide workforce of more than 100,000 people in numerous, relatively autonomous business areas. BASF's size and complexity make it difficult, but even more important, to seamlessly weave the various parts of the organization together so that everyone is not working in traditional silos under a hierarchical structure. Employing the concept of Verbund, BASF has created intricate networks in which sustainability experts and businesses interface across distances, functions, and levels. The Sustainability Knowledge Verbund (which I discussed earlier in this section in Managing Size and Complexity), for instance, is a key vehicle through which BASF is orchestrating and spawning boundary-spanning initiatives and behaviors.

The company has introduced several other innovative approaches that encourage cross-boundary collective efforts. I described two such approaches earlier in this chapter under Best Practices: the market/customer focus teams and the Simply Dare! empowerment program.

Importantly, BASF also looks outside the organization—and includes external stakeholders—as it explores and searches for innovations and breakthroughs in sustainability. "Any time you can get a collective effort to look at an entire value chain together, that's the way you make progress and that's the way of the future," said Wall during our interview.[69] And she participates in the Sustainability Consortium (www.sustainabilityconsortium.org), a group comprising diverse stakeholders from every part of the value chain who come together to tackle the issues confronting the industry from a sustainability perspective. I see this as an important trend toward friendly co-opetition in support of a more sustainable world.

Lessons Learned

Here I attempt to synthesize the wisdom of the many inspiring people I spoke with at BASF. Some of these lessons refer to endeavors and initiatives that, simply because of size restraints, I was not able to present earlier in the chapter. They represent a combination of perspectives that companies and individuals can take and actions they can perform when building a culture for sustainability. They are all interconnected and form a holistic view, but for coherence and simplicity I have organized them under 10 themes: leadership, alignment, change, communications, employee engagement, stakeholder engagement, corporate responsibility, product stewardship, marketing, and personal impact. My hope is that other companies will take from these what is useful and find ways to customize them to make them their own.

Leadership

- Garner senior executive support for your sustainability endeavors. Sustainability needs a strong visible commitment and a clear path from the highest level of the organization.
- Lead by example. Create practical, easily understandable examples to demonstrate what sustainability means for your company. Provide meaningful "proof points" that resonate with people inside and outside your company.

Alignment

- Provide the link to business success and business drivers. The ability to measure the business value of the things you are talking about is critical. Unless you can show the link to business value, you're relying on internal value systems, which are unique to each person.
- Align everything with sustainability, linking to it from the corporate purpose in the boardroom to the employees working in the mailroom. Embed sustainability deeply in the company's DNA.

Change

- Recognize that a culture for sustainability involves the entire system and that changing mind-sets is a long-term process. Don't forget that little things that are visible to employees, such as becoming more paperless, make an impression on employees and build their trust in your dedication to sustainability.
- Remember that innovation is a messy business. Accelerate adoption of leading edge, not bleeding edge, initiatives.

Communications

- Use technology to help your employees stay in touch, but realize it is easy to get overloaded. Technology is not a panacea, nor is it a substitute for human interaction.
- Connect with people face-to-face. This is the best way to reach people. "The best way to talk to people is to talk to people," said Rotenberg. To encourage more face-to-face communication, Rotenberg occasionally imposes "no e-mail Friday afternoons," because it is so easy to lose touch even with the people sitting right beside you.
- Respect and appreciate all your employees. Talk with them and, more importantly, listen to them, as they are the backbone of and greatest ambassadors for your company. Leaders can find many ways to talk with people directly, such as in town hall meetings and "lunch and learns." If everyone can't attend, sessions can be taped and subsequently shared for local site communications and shown during employees' lunch hours. Never forget that not all people in the company have computers; they also need to be included and listened to.

Employee Engagement

- Don't try to control sustainability, because you can't. Instead find ways to mobilize it by engaging your employees' hearts, minds, and hands. If you don't, you will not change the culture.
- Create friendly internal competition through reward and recognition programs and sustainability awards. BASF has a variety of such programs, including its Pioneer Awards, and promotes contests to encourage its people to take credit for their ideas.

Stakeholder Engagement

- Find creative ways to reach out to all your stakeholders. BASF's stakeholder group is quite varied, internally and externally, so the company employs several different kinds of strategies, tools, tactics, and objectives to reach them.

Corporate Responsibility

- Do the things the right way or you'll end up paying for it. Be responsible in the way you operate. Be responsible for your employees. Provide a good work environment. Transport your goods safely. Make and market products safely, and make sure they're used safely as well.
- Tell the truth, no matter what, and then that is all you have to remember. If you start doing things in a less-than-ethical manner, sooner or later it will catch up to you, and you'll lose your job and damage your company.
- Always place value on human life—whether the person is inside your fence line, outside your fence line, a contractor, an employee, or a member of the local community. Not only is it the right thing to do, but we all live in glass houses and society is always watching.
- Take care of legacy issues, where they exist, now (e.g., when you buy rights to a site that has legacy issues such as chemical spills, take care of them immediately).

Product Stewardship

- Make changes gradually in your product portfolio to include more products and solutions that are sustainable. Understand that it's a process; you can't switch it on/off like a light overnight. Apply a strategic filter and deselect products in your portfolio that don't meet your sustainable standards.
- Ask (and answer): Is there a healthier, safer way to produce this product? Can we use less energy, less water, make it more compostable, more recyclable?
- Raise minimum acceptable standards of what a great product or package is. One way to do this is by supporting smart regulations. Having the right regulatory environment raises the bar and creates barriers to entry for competitors who are less committed to sustainability. At the same time, it can promote innovation and healthy living (e.g., lead paint is no longer acceptable and has been completely replaced by low/zero volatile organic compounds [VOC]).

Marketing

- Link to what your customers and markets are doing to flag emerging opportunities within market segments. For example, BASF has identified and seized on new opportunities for ingredients in sustainable paint products used by small- to medium-size enterprises in the automotive industry.
- Create value for your customers through product differentiation. Having a differentiated product makes it harder for people to copy and more difficult for cheap imports to compete against.

Personal Impact

- Realize that learning to live sustainably does not require a sacrifice in your quality of life.
- Encourage employees to look from the outside in so they have an external driver in addition to one inside the organization. For example, look for partnerships with collectives or groups that are working on similar topics either within or outside your industry.
- Make sustainability personally compelling for people. Sustainability can generate excitement and energy and as such can motivate people in their day-to-day work.
- Help your employees think about how sustainability affects them personally and, given their specific responsibilities, what they can do to support sustainability in their job.

Frameworks, Tools, and Resources

BASF has produced a panoply of leading-edge frameworks, tools, and resources, many of which I have featured in this chapter. In addition, the company participates in numerous global organizations and uses external resources and proven off-the-shelf tools and methodologies. For ease of reference, they are listed here along with their websites.

External Participation

- Global Reporting Initiative (GRI; www.globalreporting.org). BASF has an A+ rating and is one of ten pilot companies spearheading new initiatives to see how far companies can go with transparency.
- The UN Global Compact (UNGC; www.ungc.org). Global CEO Kurt Bock sits on the UNGC board.
- Sustainability Consortium (www.sustainabilityconsortium.org).

- Dow Jones Sustainability Index (DJSI; www.sustainability-index .com).
- American Chemistry Society Scholars Program (www.acs.org).
- Responsible Care. A chemical-industry initiative to assure the safe and responsible use of chemicals (responsiblecare.americanchemistry .com).
- Green Sports Alliance (www.greensportsalliance.org).

BASF Tools and Frameworks

- EMS (Environmental Management System)
- SEE Balance (Social, Environmental, Economic)
- SET (Sustainability, Eco-Efficiency, Traceability)
- AgBalance
- Sustainability Check
- LCA (Life-Cycle Assessment)
- EEA (Eco-Efficiency Analysis)
- Total Cost of Ownership/Life-Cycle Costing
- Materiality Assessment
- Sustainability Knowledge Verbund

Conclusion

BASF is committed to creating the chemistry that will enable the company, its employees, its customers, and society at large, not only to survive but also to thrive in a sustainable future. To do so, the company continually examines megatrends that will shape the future for decades.

The company recognizes that humanity is already using one and a half times the earth's resources, and if this trend continues, we will be using the equivalent of three and a half worlds by 2050. This level of overconsumption is not sustainable.

In this context, everyone I spoke with at BASF recognizes that sustainability is the absolute key to BASF's future success. They recognize that by unleashing the talent of its people BASF can make a profound contribution to the sustainability of people, the company, and the preservation and regeneration of the world's natural resources for future generations. This requires that the company demonstrate its commitment to leading responsibly, steady management, and taking a long-term view.

Sustainability leader Charlene Wall summed it up this way: "As I look to the future, for people that are looking to get into this field, it's really exciting. As we see more and more activities within a business or within a function around sustainability, the field is rich and ripe for people who have a passion for sustainability. And those kinds of people will be the leaders for the future."[70]

CHAPTER 5

Bureau Veritas:
Leading by Example

We need to bring together the thinking with the feeling. If we force them, they won't do it. We need to bridge the gap between the brain and the heart. Move the emotion of the people to do things more automatically. We need to see the long-term benefits of doing small things that can contribute to the big things.

—Joshua Choong, 2012

What moved me most when I interviewed Bureau Veritas (BV) managers from around the world was their heartfelt commitment, in the face of almost unimaginable obstacles, to making a difference in the countries and communities in which BV operates. Malaysian-based Joshua Choong and Kah Yin Chan—whose teams have separately won environmental awards and who together were honored with the BV 2010 Biodiversity Award, the BV 2011 Education Award, and a BV 2012 Special Recognition Award—told me about numerous impressive actions BV employees at every level in Southeast Asia have performed over the past four years. In 2012 alone, the Special Recognition Award honored the Southeast Asia region, consisting of six countries and teams—Brunei, Indonesia, Malaysia, Singapore, Thailand, and Vietnam—for the following significant accomplishments: they helped rehabilitate the Pesanggrahan River in Indonesia, coordinated a massive collection of waste in Vietnam, organized and implemented a coral-conservation initiative in Thailand, cleaned natural sites with a local non-governmental organization (NGO) in Malaysia, implemented durable

Photo 5.1   Mother and son planting mangroves in Indonesia, World Environment Day, June 5, 2011. (© 2013 Bureau Veritas, Inc. Used with permission.)

green practices in Singapore, and participated in two programs recognized by local authorities in Brunei Darussalam. Motivated by a firmly held belief that their actions can positively improve the ecosystem and minimize environmental impact, BV managers, employees, and their families waded with their children on their backs through chest-deep water to replant the mangroves in Indonesia.

This chapter describes the work BV does on behalf of its clients and shows how it energizes its employees to lead by example, building a culture for sustainability both inside and outside its walls. It presents a variety of best practices that have been successful in unleashing the passion of BV's employees, transcending cultural differences, and going beyond legal requirements in countries in every region of the world. I summarize challenges BV continues to face and lessons it has learned as it seeks to embrace and embody sustainability in every way possible.

Taking Compliance to a Higher Level

BV is a world leader in testing, inspection, and certification (TIC) services, doing business in approximately 140 countries with 56 North

American offices. The company has eight global businesses providing a balanced portfolio of activities: the Marine business to make shipping safer through classification and inspection; the Industry business to assess equipment and processes from design to operation; the Inspection and In-Service Inspection and Verification (IVS) business for checking equipment and installations for safe, reliable operations; the Construction business for verifying building compliance with quality and safety requirements; the Certification business for helping clients improve performance; the Consumer Products business for making sure products meet standards and customer expectations; the Commodities business for inspection and testing in three segments—oil and petrochemicals, metals and minerals, and agriculture—and the Government Services and International Trade (GSIT) business for moving goods reliably between countries.

The environmental services BV provides include phase I environmental site assessments, subsurface investigations, soil and groundwater remediation, compliance and permitting assistance, underground storage tank closures and removals, and brownfield redevelopment.[1]

While BV serves its clients by providing verification and assurance services, it simultaneously contributes to their competitiveness in the marketplace. By going beyond compliance, BV not only supports its clients' "license to operate" but also helps elevate the standards for entire industries in which the companies operate. By providing added value, third-party verifications, and recommendations for improvement, BV inserts a level of ethics, impartiality, and integrity into the process that raises the bar for everyone.

Materiality, Assurances, and Verification

To help its clients monitor their environmental performance, BV performs audits for a wide range of certifications encompassing quality; environmental, health, and safety; security; corporate sustainability and social auditing; and integrated management.[2]

Verification

BV conducts third-party verification services for the Carbon Disclosure Project (CDP; www.cdproject.net) and is one of five partners for the CDP. BV provided me with examples of this process's use in such diverse industries as financial, snacks and beverages, foods, electronics, mining, and pharmaceuticals. Third-party verification is a systematic,

Quality
- ISO 9001:2000
- ISO/TS16949 (Automotive)
- AS9100 / AS9120 (Aerospace)
- TL 9000 (Telecommunications)

Environmental
- ISO 14001 (Environmental)
- Sustainable Forestry Initiative® (SFI)
- RC14001

Health & Safety
- OHSAS 18001 (Occupational Health and Safety Assessment Series)
- RCMS (Responsible Care Management System)

Security
- SRMS (Security Risk Management System)
- TAPA FSR (Freight Security Requirements)
- RCSC (Responsible Care® Security Code)

Corporate Sustainability / Social Auditing
- SA 8000 (Social Accounting)
- GRI (Global Reporting Initiative)
- AA1000

Integrated Management
- Enterprise Registration (Multiple sites under single certificate)
- Combined Management Systems (Multiple management systems)
- Supply Chain

Figure 5.1   © 2013 Bureau Veritas, Inc. Used with permission.

independent, and documented process, which in this case evaluates greenhouse gas (GHG) assertions by organizations. It is conducted according to agreed-upon verification criteria, such as those in the various subject-specific ISO standards and guidelines, for example, for carbon and GHGs, ISO 14064, ISO14067, PAS2050, and the GHG Protocol, whereby gaps are identified; and systems and underlying processes for the generation, collection, management, and reporting of performance data are verified.[3]

The verification process covers the following areas:

- Relevance. It ensures the GHG inventory appropriately reflects the GHG emissions of the company.
- Completeness. It accounts for and reports on all GHG sources within chosen inventory boundaries.
- Consistency. It uses consistent methodologies throughout the company to ensure meaningful comparison of emissions over time.
- Transparency. It uses transparent methods, assumptions, calculations, and estimates to address all relevant issues factually and coherently to provide a clear audit trail. It discloses any relevant assumptions

and makes appropriate references to the accounting and calculation methodologies and data sources used.

- Data accuracy. It makes sure that information is accurate and free from significant error.

John Stangline, senior consultant, BV North America, summarized the verification process when he said, "Information should achieve a degree of exactness and low margin of error necessary for readers to make decisions with a high degree of confidence."[4]

Assurance

Assurance is a wide-ranging term that captures an overall approach to providing confidence in information generated and reported by organizations relative to their sustainability position, progress, and performance. Assurance is delivered through a variety of compliance mechanisms, including formal audits, data and systems verification, and wider strategic engagements that can be subject or company specific. The assurance process applied to corporate sustainability reporting, for example, is designed to confirm that the "information reported is *right*, and that the *right* information is reported." The process should increase credibility with stakeholders, improve data reliability, enhance scores on sustainability indexes and rankings, provide practical recommendations for improvements, and identify strengths and weaknesses.[5]

The assurance process consists of five phases: scoping, planning, verification and assurance activities, finalizing and providing deliverables, and project review. It is used in virtually all industries to improve the quality and credibility of reporting.

Sustainable Supply-Chain Issues

BVs employees, customers, and other stakeholders must understand and find ways to address the many complex and systemic sustainability-related issues throughout their supply chains, often cutting across organizational, industry, regional, country, and other boundaries. The CDP, an international organization mentioned earlier that is focused on helping companies share environmental information, emphasizes the importance of obtaining information from supply chains. The Global Reporting Initiative (GRI; www.globalreporting.org) convened a Supply Chain Disclosure Working Group to develop recommendations for updated reporting guidelines. Clients who use precious metals in semiconductors and other products (e.g., cellphones, smartphones, tab-lets, and laptops) have become sensitized to the traceability of these met-als because of concerns regarding "conflict minerals" from certain areas of the world. These companies need to be able to understand their entire supply chain to ensure the minerals they are using are conflict-free, po-tentially a very costly and time-consuming process. This is just one of the many issues that companies face with respect to their supply chains. Reporting on supply chain issues and on how a company is addressing the issues of most importance to their company and industry is an in-creasing challenge.[6]

Defining Sustainability at BV

The people I interviewed at BV said that the company has essentially been "doing sustainable development"—which they view as "about 80 percent just common sense"—for more than 40 years. For BV, it is not a revolution but an evolution. "Take time to understand what has already been done and make it respectful of the past. Don't get rid of the past, and don't lose knowledge of past; it's important not to forget history. Then ask, Where do we want to be?" said Charlotte Breuil, BV's global health, safety, and environment (HSE) manager, auditor, and co-ordinator, located in Paris, France.[7]

Murray Sayce, BV's technical director, global assurance, explained that BV does not have its own definition of sustainability. Rather, it looks at how sustainability affects its 300,000 plus customers and cli-ents worldwide, ranging from large, global, and multinational corpora-tions (MNCs) to small- and medium-size (SME) companies. The key is understanding what sustainable development means for a specific client or company. Sustainability is interpreted differently depending on the unique challenges to and requirements of its customers.[8]

In its work, BV considers the three elements of the triple bottom line (people, planet, and profits) and, at the beginning of a relationship with a client, it seeks to discover what the client is already doing within each of these domains.

Leading by Example

BV is committed to leading by example and is adamant about having an internal culture for sustainability that is visible to its clients. "As we work for clients, we need to walk the talk," said Lisa Barnes, techni-cal director for sustainability services in BV's U.S. HSE group.[9] Barnes described how over the last decade sustainability has gradually evolved at BV. Originally it was focused solely on compliance, but as interest in the concept grew among executives and employees, its focus broadened. For example, initiatives have been implemented to reduce paper use, and some of the company's offices have gone to 100 percent electronic filing. In the past, BV often produced as many as 10 hard copies of a huge number of lengthy reports. The company has reduced paper use 6 percent from 2011 to 2012 and has goals for further reductions (the most recent goal is a 15 percent reduction). Now most reports are delivered in an electronic format such as PDF, and BV has found that clients typically prefer these over paper copies. When printing is required, the company prints double-sided and minimizes the use of color ink.

A key commitment for BV is reducing its own environmental footprint and improving its environmental performance by encouraging employees and business partners to do the same. The company applies to itself the same standards and criteria used by its clients, even though as a professional services organization, BV is not subject to the same level of risks, regulations, and observation.

Building a Culture for Sustainability

BV shapes its sustainability culture by keeping its employees informed and involved in what the company is doing and providing opportunities for employees to participate in myriad volunteer initiatives and on-site energy-, water-, and paper-conservation programs. Employee education builds awareness of such energy-conservation initiatives as turning off lights, computers, and printers when leaving offices or work areas, using double-sided print/copy options, and not adjusting thermostats. The emphasis is on communicating simple methods that employees can get involved in at the local level and that can easily be replicated in any company.

Energy conservation small steps include:

- Installing energy-efficient light fixtures or bulbs
- Limiting access to the control buttons of the heating and air-conditioning units
- Presetting thermostats with programmable after-hours and weekend energy-efficient settings to reduce cooling and heating costs
- Contracting vendors to service the air-conditioning and heating units on a regular basis to maximize cooling and heating efficiency and reduce electrical costs

- Installing motion-sensor light switches in work areas throughout the building offices, work areas, and restrooms
- Checking for proper insulation in ceilings and walls for buildings owned by BV
- Installing adjustable heating, ventilation, and air conditioning (HVAC) vents to prevent excess supply of cold/hot air to work areas throughout the offices

BV's water-conservation program includes:

- Installing new water-efficient toilets that flush only 1.6 gallons instead of the standard 3.5 gallons
- Promptly repairing leaking toilets and sinks
- Closing water valves under sinks a third of the way
- Equipping all faucets with aerators to reduce water usage
- Providing in-line filters to kitchen sinks and refrigerators, thus eliminating 5-gallon plastic bottles and water-delivery services

BV's paper-conservation program includes:

- Setting double-sided copy/print option as the default on all copiers and printers
- Recycling office paper waste
- Placing recycling bins near copiers
- Using smaller font on client deliverables
- Using and storing electronic files instead of paper files and folders
- Reusing scrap paper internally
- Avoiding printing e-mails

In sum, BV employees introduce site-specific initiatives to save paper and reduce printing, post stickers to remind people to conserve energy and turn off lights, send documents in electronic formats (PDF, CD, or DVD) to clients rather than paper whenever possible, and generally encourage each other to do their part. Employees are in some circumstances encouraged to work at home a few days a week to save gas, save money, and reduce their impact on the environment.

BV sees marked increases in employee engagement stemming from participation in sustainability initiatives. "Employees are excited to learn a new service and to be a part of something that matters, in the United States and the world. Employees are very engaged in what we're doing for our clients and how we can help them do better in this area. Most employees now want to work for responsible companies," said

Barnes. It is important that BV has an internal program and an external program, she said, because "people want to work for a company that cares about its employees, cares about the environment, and cares about the community." Barnes sees the employees as one of the most important stakeholders, along with the customers, investors, community members, and shareholders. "To have a good bottom line you need good employees. It all flows together," said Barnes.[10]

Safety: Not a Priority, an Absolute

The new BV CEO, Didier Michaud-Daniel, is so committed to safety that he has vowed to make it "not a priority, but an absolute."[11] To accomplish this, the company has introduced training programs, initiated topical campaigns, and communicates frequently about risks and how to prevent accidents. It has a training library and 11 e-learning modules in multiple languages regarding risks. It launches three to four global "Safety campaigns" a year to communicate key messages—with local discussions, questions, and feedback—about specific issues such as working safely at heights, reducing trips and falls, safe driving, and preventing accidents. It is rolling out safety talks and materials across the company in multiple languages.

These programs are being disseminated throughout the company via an internal HSE network that comprises 25 people around the world at the regional and country levels. BV's CEO sent all 52,000 managers an e-mail communicating the message: "You as managers must be involved in safety. If you're not already, get involved."

The company's approach is preventative: it encourages its people to report near misses and has developed leading indicators for safety, rather than merely measuring lagging indicators. As part of its goal to train 100 percent of its employees, it has introduced an HSE induction for 100 percent of its new employees.

On its website's TV channel, BV has posted a brief videotape entitled "Bureau Veritas Internal HSE" about its internal commitment to HSE. The video shows a significant decrease (30 percent) in energy consumption since 2008, mostly from lowered use of electricity.

Best Practices

I asked each of the managers I interviewed what they considered best practices in sustainability at BV and how these are achieved globally and in their part of the world. "We need to sustain momentum and motivation every day of our lives," said Kah Yin Chan, quality, health, safety, and environmental (QHSE) manager for Malaysia and Brunei. "Everyone has to realize what we are doing and how every individual impacts themselves, our environment, and our community as a whole." Chan explained that Malaysia developed green tips for what can be done at home and at work and described how her facility is working to raise awareness about reusing waste. Although Malaysia does not have mandatory recycling, local employees are committed to recycling—so much so that they are actively measuring and monitoring the amount of recycling they are doing. In this manner, the Malaysian management is working to "raise awareness not just one day but throughout our lives," said Chan.[12]

Joshua Choong, Southeast Asian technical, quality and risk, and health, safety, and environmental manager (TQR and HSE manager for SEA), said that "the environmental issue is only felt when it is on a big scale . . . but environment is a long-term, slow process."[13]

BV's overall environmental indicators comprise year-to-year comparisons of all energy, water, and paper consumption. As well as collecting this information, the company strongly encourages its entities to develop environmental-management systems in line with the ISO 14001 standard. Each new entity starting the certification process receives individual support from company teams and has access to documents based on the experience of entities that have previously been certified against the standard.

Choong told me that his team established a system using ISO 14001 to manage environmental impacts. The system enables them to continuously monitor key environmental metrics to ensure they are on the right track. They persuaded the CEO and employees in their facilities to proactively undertake sustainability-related activities on an ongoing basis.[14]

"We need to bring together the thinking with the feeling. If we force them, they won't do it. We need to bridge the gap between the brain and the heart. Move the emotion of the people to do things more automatically. We need to see the long-term benefits of doing small things that can contribute to the big things," said Choong.[15]

World Environment Day

BV participates actively in the United Nations–sponsored World Environment Day (WED) each year, and most all the people I interviewed at BV mentioned this as a best practice. WED was established by the UN General Assembly in 1972 to mark the opening of the Stockholm Conference on the Human Environment (www.unep.org/wed) and is commemorated yearly on June 5 as a way to stimulate worldwide awareness of the environment. WED gives "a human face" to environmental issues, as it empowers people to become active agents of sustainable and equitable development.[16]

BV began participating in the UN WED in 2009, and, at the time of this writing, has celebrated the day for four consecutive years. The initiative was launched at the company level to raise awareness and generate meaningful activities around the world. Actions have been launched and conducted in 65 BV entities, coordinated by local management, and supported by BV's regional sales and marketing teams.

Each year BV presents three awards, each on a different topic:

- Education. This award is for activities that educate people, families, children, or clients.
- Creativity. This award is for programs designed to generate creative and innovative ideas.
- This topic varies each year and is selected by the United Nations:
  - In 2012, the topic was "Green Economy: Does It Include You?"
  - In 2011, the topic was "Forests: Nature at Your Service."
  - In 2010, the topic was "Biodiversity."

In some cases, a special surprise award is given.

In its 2012 request for participation by BV locations, the company noted that "the green economy is crucial to reduce carbon emissions and pollution, enhance energy and resource efficiency, and prevent the loss of biodiversity and ecosystem services."[17]

Most of BV's WED activities have come from Asia, Latin America, and Africa. In particular, BV employees are very active in Southeast Asia (Vietnam, Malaysia, Singapore, Indonesia, Brunei, and Thailand). The Southeast Asia team encourages the employees, families, and clients to participate in the annual WED.

An internal BV jury decides who wins the awards each year, and the winning organization receives a wooden plaque engraved with its name. In 2010, BV's Malaysian team won the award for biodiversity. The competition was designed to address the following biodiversity challenge:

- Biodiversity is essential to maintain the ecosystems and hence for human well-being.
- A total of 17,291 species are known to be threatened with extinction, mainly because of human activities.[18]

The Malaysian team sought to reinforce eco-friendly and positive messages and behaviors. They organized a visit to the rain forest with the Malaysian Nature Society and picked up rubbish during the trip. BV employees organized a "go green, recycle for charity" event in front of BV's Kuala Lumpur office building in Malaysia to collect recyclable goods for donation via an environmental NGO (Pertubuhan Amal Seri Sinar). These activities were designed to raise awareness about Malaysia's biodiversity issues and to conduct collective actions beyond BV's borders, involving neighbors and other building tenants. Altogether, 800 kg of reusable goods and recyclables were collected.

In 2011, BV Indonesia won the 2011 Forests Award for its response to this challenge:

- Forests cover one-third of the earth's land mass, performing vital functions and services around the world which make our planet alive with possibilities.
- Global deforestation continues at an alarming rate: every year, 13 million hectares of forest are destroyed (size of Portugal).[19]

The BV Indonesian team proposed and implemented a project that involved acting locally on the depletion of mangroves by planting them in an area undergoing rehabilitation. In addition, the team visited mangroves to learn how the ecosystem works, created useful objects out of recycled material, and pledged to protect the environment. As a result, 105 mangrove trees were planted, and the team raised the awareness of BV Indonesia employees and their families, 50 of whom actively participated in the project. When I asked Choong why he and his team were so committed to this project, he explained that in Jakarta, Indonesia, the number of mangroves is diminishing, and, because Jakarta is located below sea level, "if nothing is done by society, one day the water level of the sea can overflow and flood all of Jakarta."[20]

That same year, 2011, the BV Malaysian team won the Education Award for their response to this challenge:

- Creating awareness, enhancing environmental friendly habits and life styles are the key to protecting the environment.
- Environmental issues are to be domesticated and people empowered.[21]

The team organized a tree-and-grass-planting program, involving visiting, tree planting, making pledges, and cleanup at the National Botanical Garden, Shah Alam. They organized a booth in front of BV's Kuala

Photo 5.2   Bureau Veritas employees and families collecting waste at a popular beach in Vietnam. (© 2013 Bureau Veritas, Inc. Used with permission.)

Lumpur office building collecting recyclable goods that they donated to an environmental NGO. The program helped develop awareness about waste management in the younger generation and promoted learning among BV's employees and their families about Malaysian forests and ecosystem issues.

In 2012, the BV Southeast Asia team won a Special Recognition Award in honor of the actions I describe in the opening paragraph of this chapter. For the fourth consecutive year, the entities in Southeast Asia were deemed by the jury to have performed "innovative and meaningful actions."[22] To honor them, the jury created this special award.

Community Involvement

Corporate social responsibility (CSR) at BV is led at the local level, where it carries out specific activities on behalf of the local communities in which the company operates. No one person is in charge of sustainable development, and, as noted before, there is no global policy. Although BV does not yet publicly report on formal policies or programs for community involvement, actions are communicated through the company's intranet portal. The company has a dedicated foundation; provides assistance, including financial support, to sustainability and CSR initiatives; and matches employees' charitable contributions. Although community initiatives are undertaken at a local level, they are consolidated regularly at the company level.

BV community involvement initiatives can be found in France, Haiti, the United States, Spain, Japan, and other locations. In France, the head office organized a Climate Care Day in partnership with the World Wildlife Federation. The team significantly reduced business travel by holding web and phone conferences, helping to finance the Arctic project aimed at preserving biodiversity in the Arctic. In Haiti, the company made a special effort to support recovery efforts after the devastating 2010 earthquake in which 200,000 lives were lost, 300,000 people were injured, and 1,000,000 were left homeless. In addition to financial contributions at the corporate and entity levels, spontaneous local initiatives were led by company employees to help the population of Haiti by partnering with NGOs already present in the country.

The BV U.S. corporate culture "strongly supports charitable efforts and the philosophy of 'giving back' to the local community."[23] As in the rest of the world, volunteer activities are initiated locally by each office, with considerable autonomy and variability in the nature of the projects. For example, employees may participate in a riverbank cleanup on a Saturday and donate their time to building houses for Habitat for Humanity on brownfield sites. A unique project initiated in Middle Torch Key, Florida, involved the restoration of Key Deer National Wildlife Refuge.[24]

In Japan, BV is a committed partner of the Cool Biz initiative to promote the responsible use of air conditioning to address global-warming issues. BV provides support to the Japan Committee "Vaccines for the World's Children" (JCV) to help eradicate polio in the Asian region (www.jcv-jp.org/english). BV employees collect bottle caps and recycle the caps for money that is then donated to JCV.

Challenges

BV faces many challenges in its quest to educate its clients, employees, and other stakeholders and accelerate their movement toward sustainability. Key challenges are highlighted here:

- *Working with different measurement systems and methods around the globe.* Globally, every country has its own methodology for measuring carbon, waste, water, paper, and energy. A tremendous amount of flexibility is necessary to customize these for use in each region and country in which BV operates. This challenge is addressed through encouraging and supporting global standards, such as ISO14001, while maximizing local autonomy in the implementation of the standards.

- *Overcoming preexisting stereotypes.* The company is sometimes challenged by preexisting stereotypes or attitudes toward clients from specific industries. One example is in the mining industry. Some people categorically reject the notion of mining, no matter how much the mining company is doing to minimize its impact on the environment. I learned that in one case, to address this challenge, the company invited an anti-mining activist into the client company for a month to observe all its operations. The activist was so impressed with what he saw that he subsequently became an employee at the mining company, where he now works to communicate with other anti-mining activists about how to reduce environmental impacts and safety hazards.

- *Fear of reaching out to stakeholders.* BV encourages its clients to engage with their stakeholders up front, but sometimes clients are afraid to ask difficult questions because of what they may hear. Over and over during my interviews, people at BV stressed the importance of communication, especially the willingness to listen to all stakeholders and recognize their concerns head-on rather than sweeping them under the rug. Openness and willingness to listen are key; companies should never pretend issues don't exist.

- *Bringing clients beyond compliance.* Because BV focuses on assurance, verification, and compliance, the challenge is how to bring clients and employees to a higher standard. Sometimes BV needs to take extra steps to show its clients the business value in going beyond compliance to address broader sustainability issues and concerns.

- *Changing employees' behavior.* Perhaps the biggest challenge for BV is the behavioral and cultural challenge of changing the culture in its own organization. Because BV is a worldwide leader in social responsibility and quality, health, and environment, people tend to think the company already is where it needs to be. They don't take time to ask, "Am I really that good?" And it can sometimes be difficult to encourage employees to become even better than they already are.

- *Making safety an absolute.* The problem is to create a safety culture in which employees are constantly alert and vigilant. It is especially critical for employees who may be working alone on a client site. Recently an employee on such a site in Japan had a serious accident, resulting in a broken bones and a head injury. The employee, a 60-year-old man, was standing on a ladder in a house. He was carrying documents in one hand when he removed his hard hat with the other, missed his step, and fell backwards from a height of two meters.

Lessons Learned

I asked each of the people I interviewed at BV to reflect on the lessons they've learned through their work within the company and with diverse clients around the world. Here are a few salient points gleaned from these reflections:

- Get to know a company's culture before trying to change it. Changing culture is not a "one size fits all" effort, and any change-management endeavor must start with an understanding of the company's unique culture. As Charlotte Breuil said, "If you can't get in through the door, get in through the window. Timing is everything."[25]
- Be patient; timing is everything. When working with people, it is important to view the change as an evolution—building on the knowledge of the past—and not a revolution.
- Practice what you preach. This is particularly critical in the professional services industry.
- Engage with all your stakeholders up front and listen. Address stakeholder concerns head-on and don't sweep issues under the rug.
- Ensure key performance indicators (KPIs) are in place.
- Be transparent and go public with your successes and your failures.
- Do more research up front and integrate sustainability services at an early stage.
- Don't just rely on numbers and analysis to engage employees. Rather, realize that employees already want to give back and contribute. It isn't necessary to provide financial incentives to persuade employees to participate in sustainability initiatives.
- Don't try to do everything at once.
- Focus on branding around sustainability to attract the kinds of employees you want; potential employees look at sustainability reports before deciding to come into a company. In fact, employees are the most important stakeholders of all and are the ones that read the reports the most.
- Report using GRI, but don't try to report on everything. Determine what is most important and material for the company, and then report on and focus on that. Companies that are most successful in reporting have identified a limited number of goals—such as paper and energy reduction—and communicate those broadly.
- Have a reporting system that includes clear documentation and consistent procedures. This is essential for companies that are thinking about reporting, or are already reporting, sustainability data to their

stakeholders. The data needs to be standardized and repeatable. Environmental-management systems help companies get ahead of the game with good documentation and procedures.

Frameworks, Resources, and Tools

BV uses several proprietary frameworks to support its clients' sustainability efforts. I discuss a few of these here.

BV Carbon

The BV Carbon tool was developed by BV internal experts to measure the company's CO_2 emissions and assess the efficacy of its environmental programs internally. The tool is made available on BV's intranet in three languages, along with a dedicated user guide and an e-learning module. BV Carbon measures the six main sources of carbon emissions on an ongoing basis: energy, water, paper, business travel, ozone-depleting substances (e.g., air conditioning), and waste. In 2011, BV expanded its use of the BV Carbon tool throughout the company, enabling identification of local action plans and environmental priorities to reduce its carbon footprint.

Vericert

Vericert measures the stage of maturity of a company's sustainability initiatives and how far it needs to go. The Vericert approach goes beyond certification; it identifies key processes and risks to which the company is exposed. It uses international guidelines or internal commitments and objectives as the measurement stick. Vericert services highlight the strengths and weaknesses in the company's management system that directly impact performance.

Veriperf

Veriperf is a web-based tool that gives clients access to third-party services from BV. The purpose is to assess and implement HSE best practices in multisite companies. Veriperf aims to measure a client's performance regarding how risks and opportunities are identified, measured, and managed in stages of maturity ranging from "having little in place" to "best practice." Best practice could include a fully implemented policy, clearly defined objectives and targets, processes that manage the risks and maximize opportunities, well-defined roles and responsibilities with adequate competence for the purpose, and systems for internal assurance and external reporting. The outputs from Veriperf measure the gap between the client's current state and best practice, enabling them to implement action plans for achieving improved control and performance over time. It is a tool that BV incorporates into the reporting and outputs of a typical audit or advisory approach when assessing its clients against set mandatory or voluntary compliance criteria.

Standards

BV uses a number of internationally recognized standards and frameworks internally and for its clients. Companies that implement quality-, health-, safety-, environmental-, and social-management (QHSES) systems to such standards as ISO14001, OHSAS18001, and ISO 9001 are considered, as Sayce told me, to be "ahead of the game, although this is now becoming more commonplace and therefore expected of the larger organizations with higher impacts and external investor and stakeholder interest."[26] He pointed out that consistency of data is essential for reporting and disclosure purposes. BV encourages companies to appropriately manage QHSES risks through the implementation of management systems that are externally certified to such standards for added rigor, recognition, and credibility. These systems help (1) to ensure companies have a systematic approach through clearly defined processes and documented procedures, (2) to address QHSES risks, (3) to continually review and revise the approach, and (4) to produce reliable performance data that can be used for external disclosure. Companies adopting these systems have an advantage over those that do not, in that there is a greater level of confidence in the information produced and less need to check internal systems. BV says it is more "than just a matter of having accurate data."[27]

BV's recommended standards for the management, continual improvement, reporting, and assurance of sustainability positions and performance are the following:

- Global Reporting Initiative (GRI; www.globalreporting.org)
- AA1000 series (including AA1000 Principles, Assurance Standard, and Stakeholder Engagement Standard) to ensure companies follow the principles of materiality, stakeholder inclusivity, and responsiveness in sustainability management and reporting (www.accountabil ity.org)

- ISO (www.iso.org) and related standards, such as
  ISO 14001, for environmental-management systems
  ISO 14065, the overarching standard for measuring GHG emissions
  ISO 14064 series (1–3) for the measurement, management, and verification of GHG emissions
  ISO26000, for social responsibility
  ISO50001, for energy-management systems
  ISO 9001, for quality systems
  SA8000, for social accountability (in the supply chain)
  OHSAS 18001, for safety and health management

In my interview, Sayce pointed out that this is not an all-inclusive list, and that other standards and frameworks are available as is sector specific guidance regarding sustainability best practices.

Summary and Conclusion

BV plays an essential role in compliance-related activities, helping companies reduce their environmental impacts, remove liabilities, and minimize risks. It encourages clients to go beyond compliance in myriad ways, some of which I've described in this chapter.

In working to create its own culture for sustainability, the company integrates simple strategies for reducing its environmental footprint into employee management and business activities. BV makes employees' health and safety at work and the minimization of the company's adverse environmental impact a prime duty and responsibility of the management and integrates it into business activities. Its energy-conservation program involves employees in water-, paper-, and energy-conservation initiatives in their offices and work areas.

BV is a model for global professional services companies seeking to go green and create a culture for sustainability. The inspiring stories of its employees around the world provide tangible demonstrations of what is possible when a company is highly committed and the employees, creative and motivated to craft and implement their own initiatives. I share these stories in the hope that they become role models that will lead to concrete actions in both the developing and developed world.

CHAPTER 6

Church & Dwight: Product Stewardship for Sustainable Prosperity

I believe in sound science. I don't believe in taking chances.
—Robert (Bob) Coleman, 2012

Arm & Hammer: A Heritage of Sustainability

Two brothers-in-law, Dr. Austin Dwight and John Church, started what became Church & Dwight in a small kitchen in 1846 with one product, baking soda, or sodium bicarbonate. Twenty-one years later, in 1867, Dr. Dwight's son James brought what became the iconic Arm & Hammer Vulcan symbol to his father's company. James had run a mustard-and-spice business under Vulcan Spice Mills, whose logo incorporated Vulcan, the god of fire in Greek mythology, who fashioned ornaments and arms for the gods. After the symbol—an arm with a hammer clutched in its hand—was placed on baking soda containers, people started asking for the product with the Vulcan on it and have been buying it ever since.

Today—167 years later—Church & Dwight Co., Inc.'s Arm & Hammer brand carries a reputation as one of the safest, most-trusted, high-quality, and sustainable consumer products brands in the United States.

In this chapter, I review the evolution of sustainability at Church & Dwight, present some of the company's best practices, and highlight key challenges the company faces and ways it is addressing them. I describe important lessons learned and provide recommended frameworks, tools, and resources.

A Heritage of Sustainability; a Successful Consumer Products Company

Over more than a century and a half, Church & Dwight has come far on its journey to sustainability, starting with its concern for the environment that has endured since the company's very early days. Over the past several years, it has begun to embrace the broader concept of sustainability and is dedicated to making the culture change that this concept represents.

The company was the first, and only, sponsor of the inaugural Earth Day, in 1970. Famously, the company's baking soda was used to clean the Statue of Liberty on that historic day. As far back as the 1880s, the company put trading card pictures of birds in every box of baking soda, with the inscription: "For the good of all, do not destroy the birds."

In my interview with Bob Coleman, senior manager, Office of Sustainable Development, I learned that Church & Dwight has been using 100 percent recycled board in its baking soda boxes for more than 100 years.[1]

Figures 6.1 & 6.2 "Useful Birds of America" trading card from a box of Arm & Hammer baking soda in the 1880s. (© 2013 Church & Dwight Co., Inc. Used with permission.)

In 1970, Church & Dwight introduced its phosphate-free laundry detergent. In 1972, it recommended that its customers put the yellow baking soda boxes in their refrigerators to keep them fresh and remove food odors. Over time, baking soda came "out of the box" and into myriad products, such as "super washing soda," which is a cleaner in its own right and a laundry detergent booster.

The company introduced liquid laundry detergent in 1988, but took another 10 years to come out with personal care products, after first entering the dental-care business with its Arm & Hammer toothpaste. Although Colgate and Procter & Gamble "owned the market," Church & Dwight thought if it could get only 1 to 2 percent market share, it would be satisfied.

The company challenged consumers to "try the product for a week or two" and promised them "you won't go back." It worked. Arm & Hammer dental products established themselves in the marketplace, and "one could say, gave us the confidence needed to continue innovating over the next 25 years," said Matthew Wasserman, director, global product and portfolio stewardship, Office of Sustainable Development.[2]

Today the Arm & Hammer dental products have a very loyal following and a market share of about 6 percent. This success gave Church & Dwight the confidence to step further into the intensely competitive and highly regulated personal care industry. It introduced its deodorant line in the 1990s, along with baking soda carpet deodorizers and more.

The company made its biggest leap in sustainability when it added the Essentials line, with a 98 percent reduction in colorant (i.e., almost dye-free). The line uses plant-based surfactants, and the company is insistent that it never sacrifices quality or performance.

Church & Dwight is now a consumer products company with a wide variety of brands. Eight of these—Arm & Hammer, Spinbrush, Oxi-Clean, Xtra, Trojan, First Response, Nair, and Orajel—represent approximately 80 percent of its consumer sales, and the company refers to these as power brands. In 2011, domestic household products made up approximately 47 percent of the company's total sales; domestic personal care products, 25 percent; and international consumer products, 19 percent.[3]

The company's Specialty Products Division (SPD)—approximately 9 percent of Church & Dwight's total sales in 2011—provides specialty inorganic chemicals, animal nutrition, and cleaners. SPD manufactures and sells various grades and granulations of sodium bicarbonate for a wide range of uses: baked goods, cosmetics, pharmaceuticals, kidney dialysis, fire extinguishers, and swimming pool products, among others.

Building a Culture for Sustainability

It's an Evolution Not a Revolution

Although Church & Dwight has a heritage of environmentally friendly practices dating back to its founding, in the last decade the company began to ask itself, What does sustainability mean to us? Does it mean our company will be on the cutting edge, using totally "green" ingredients in all our products? On the bleeding edge, being totally green and always acting to reduce our impact and preserve the natural environment?

As Church & Dwight was exploring these questions, it also began to explore sustainability's social and human aspects.

"Evolution on sustainability has been slow," said Coleman, "[which is] understandable since we're such a lean company, and we're very busy." A few years ago, Church & Dwight's Office of Sustainable Development presented a clearly articulated business case to senior management, got buy-in from the top, and designed a strategy to align with the business case. Once the business case and strategy were confirmed, the challenge in building its culture for sustainability became embedding it throughout the entire company, or "grabbing the attention of all the employees," as Coleman said. "If your employees are not on board, it's not going to take hold."[4]

Initially the company was unsuccessful in garnering alignment on its sustainability goals "up, down, and across the organization," he said, and as a result, it was unable to drive the required activities and develop the metrics for tracking and achieving its goals.

Michael Buczynski, program manager—stewardship, Office of Sustainable Development, described the evolution as a "gradual building of awareness and sense of responsibility, communicating throughout the organization as well as with our customers. Sustainability is a journey, and for us, this is the journey we have embarked on: Build employee involvement and awareness to the community."[5]

What Does a Culture for Sustainability Look Like?

Church & Dwight views corporate social responsibility (CSR) as the umbrella under which sustainability is nested. CSR represents the master plan for the company: the social aspects, code of conduct, integrity, ethics, environmental and product stewardship, and business sustainability.[6]

The company demonstrates a culture for sustainability in its end-to-end thinking, including life-cycle considerations that treat economic, environmental, and social challenges as one—by clearly and strongly communicating its vision and its plans to implement the vision, and by providing specific ways that all employees, managers, and executives can contribute. Best practices include tying sustainability business drivers (e.g., saving energy and water, minimizing waste, and improving carbon footprint) to employee performance management. Among its diverse employee engagement initiatives are a volunteer cross-functional sustainability committee to drive communication and awareness; a variety of educational activities such as "lunch and learns" and fairs; departmental competitions for carpooling and paper and energy saving; and a newsletter that reports metrics and employee efforts.

It's in the Mind-Set

When I asked what a culture for sustainability looks like at Church & Dwight, Coleman said, "A culture of sustainability is in the mind-set."[7] This involves thinking and acting sustainably in employees' everyday behavior and practices. "There's a responsibility to do the right thing. We're never going to put someone at risk to save money," said Buczynski.[8] It starts with understanding—knowing what sustainability is all about. He explained, if employees "have the mind-set of doing what's right for the environment and the business, the rest takes care of itself." A great example of this in action is the steep growth in the company's Employee Giving Fund (EGF), which is described in detail in the Best Practices section of this chapter. Coleman believes that if you do right for the environment, society will benefit. And if you do right for your business, society will also benefit.

Respecting and Learning from Failure

A key aspect of the culture for sustainability at Church & Dwight is how it deals with failure. Coleman said, "The beauty of this company is you don't get blamed for failure. . . . You know things don't always make it. You try your best, and you move on." He described how the company examined a product introduction failure and learned from it. A key question the company asked itself is, "Are we going to be a leader at any cost or a company that does the responsible thing and takes what comes? We won't lead at any cost. We'll lead where it makes sense and meets our business objectives. We know that we always have something else coming up the pipeline."[9]

Reporting the Bad with the Good

Church & Dwight is concerned about reporting what is relevant to its business and reporting accurately. As Coleman told me during our interview, "We won't report incomplete data. We report bad with the good. It's not going to stop us from reporting. We even had a postmortem on the Essentials line to say here's what we think happened. It's not going to stop us from being innovative. I'm still hoping the cleaner in the Essentials line that was discontinued will come back. It was a truly innovative product."[10]

An example of the company's transparency is its voluntary ingredient disclosure, which can be found on its website (www.churchdwight.com) under Brands and Products. Here customers and other stakeholders can do an ingredient search for any of the company's products.

Best Practices

Church & Dwight is committed to fully engaging its more than 4,000 employees worldwide in a variety of activities, simultaneously providing education, building team camaraderie, and having fun. Some of the key activities designed to encourage employee involvement at all levels and across the company are described here, including an annual Earth Day celebration (which I had the opportunity to participate in), a friendly competition called Pay the Piggy, myriad small steps employees can take both at home and on the job to make a difference, and a highly successful EGF to support local community charities. In addition, best practices for strategically embedding sustainability in the company's business practices are its Business Impact Matrix and Material Safety Data Sheet program (MSDS).

Celebrating Earth Day

Since 2008, a key employee touchpoint is Church & Dwight's annual celebration of Employee Earth Day held at the company's Princeton, New Jersey, headquarters. Coleman and one of the company's sustainability volunteer committees (SVC)—a cross-functional committee that includes people from marketing, transportation, logistics, HR, IT, R&D—design and coordinate the one-day event. Outside the corporate headquarters, a volunteer team sets up tables with interactive activities, exciting demonstrations, and giveaways, such as tree seedlings and T-shirts, which show employees the wide variety of ways they can personally get involved in promoting more sustainable practices, inside or outside the company. Various programs from local and regional colleges and universities showcase their educational and outreach programs.

Figure 6.3   Church & Dwight's invitation to the company's 2010 Earth Day celebration. (© 2013 Church & Dwight Co., Inc. Used with permission.)

Coleman followed up on the first event with an employee survey, and learned that employees loved it. In fact, the first such sustainability Earth Day event was so successful that 103 people volunteered to participate in future events. To keep it manageable, Coleman established a volunteer committee composed of 8 to 12 people to coordinate the activities of the committee and told them they could stay on as long as they like. I asked Coleman about the participants and learned that although there is a great deal of diversity among them, they are primarily middle management in their thirties through fifties. They join "because they have a passion for it. Ideas just start flowing in meetings, so much so you sometimes have to rein them back to stay focused on what we're trying to do," said Coleman.[11]

When I asked about the payback to the company for investing in such events (the approximate cost of the event itself is $1,500 to $3,000), Coleman said that the true payback is the increased employee awareness and commitment to sustainability. As the volunteer committee coordinates the agenda for the entire year, its members speak to employees, and their passion is contagious. Said Coleman, "Some who stop and

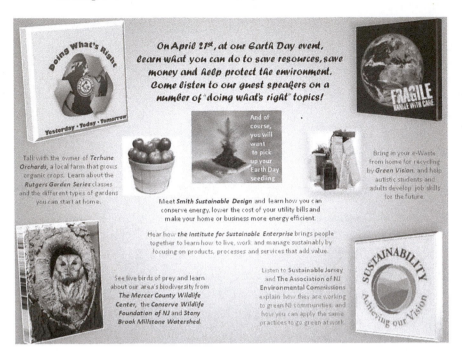

On April 21st, at our Earth Day event, learn what you can do to save resources, save money and help protect the environment. Come listen to our guest speakers on a number of "doing what's right" topics!

And of course, you will want to pick up your Earth Day seedling

Talk with the owner of *Terhune Orchards*, a local farm that grows organic crops. Learn about the *Rutgers Garden Series* classes and the different types of gardens you can start at home.

Bring in your e-Waste from home for recycling by *Green Vision*, and help autistic students and adults develop job skills for the future.

Meet *Smith Sustainable Design* and learn how you can conserve energy, lower the cost of your utility bills and make your home or business more energy efficient.

Hear how *the Institute for Sustainable Enterprise* brings people together to learn how to live, work and manage sustainably by focusing on products, processes and services that add value.

See live birds of prey and learn about our area's biodiversity from *The Mercer County Wildlife Center*, the *Conserve Wildlife Foundation of NJ* and *Stony Brook Millstone Watershed*.

Listen to Sustainable Jersey and The Association of NJ Environmental Commissions explain how they are working to green NJ communities, and how you can apply the same practices to go green at work.

Figure 6.4   Church & Dwight's Exhibitors at the company's 2010 Earth Day celebration. (© 2013 Church & Dwight Co., Inc. Used with permission.)

listen have a true interest in how they can be greener."[12] Some employees ask what they can do at home and at work to save the environment and how their department can contribute.

The volunteers and employees discuss how they can reduce waste through recycling and cut down on energy use in their departments. They speak to people face-to-face in their own departments and encourage cross-functional communication by visiting adjacent or other departments with which they interact. Coleman said that people are much more willing to respond when the communications are person-to-person and focused on what they can actually do to make a tangible difference.

Pay the Piggy: Igniting Friendly Competition

Church & Dwight has for several years conducted a friendly competition known as Pay the Piggy. When someone leaves her office without turning out the lights, she receives a note on her desk requiring her to "pay the piggy" $1. The money goes into a fund for the local groups participating in the competition, and, at the end of the year, the groups use the money to hold a celebration. Ironically, in this case raising money is a bad thing (i.e., it represents a lack of energy efficiency), so the department that raises the least money is the winner. The program is a practical way of raising employee awareness and having some fun.

The company's local Olympics, held every fall, is another employee engagement activity designed to build pride in the company in a social setting. Local teams compete against each other in a variety of events. Coleman has found that people are very competitive and will "go all out" to try to win recognition for their departments or teams.[13]

In this way and others, Church & Dwight creates friendly competitions by turning employee activities into contests. The employees competed to see who could save the most money by turning off lights and using natural light, and saved $20,000. They competed to see who could save the most money on printing, and saved $7,000 by using double-sided pages. The key, according to Coleman, is to publish the metrics to show how much total money was saved for the company through these competitions.

Over time, the little things begin to add up. A program started in the corporate office spreads into "green teams," or SVCs, in plants. At the time of the interviews, there were a total of three SVCs, in the United Kingdom, the United States, and Canada.

Employee Giving Fund and Volunteerism

The leaders and managers I spoke with at Church & Dwight said that Human Resources has a "tremendous employee focus" that fuels employee engagement. An employee activity committee oversees the company's efforts on employee contributions to local charities through the EGF and provides opportunities for employees to volunteer their time and energy. The company sees this as a way to provide a huge social benefit and involve employees at the same time.

Until almost a decade ago, the company had one major fundraising program every year, a United Way internal campaign that raised between $50,000 and $75,000 a year. At a town hall meeting, the employees made it clear that they would like to be able to donate to charities of their choice, the leaders reviewed Church & Dwight's charitable policies, and EGF was born.

The company holds quarterly town hall meetings at which, for one and a half hours, all the business leaders, HR, and the legal departments discuss the business. Transparency is evident in these meetings as the leaders describe both what the company is doing right and where improvements need to be made. They not only inform the employees about the state of the company, they also "take the pulse of the organization like a thermometer" by giving the employees their ears. They take what the people say seriously, consider their suggestions, and respond to them.

When employees said they wanted to give to charities with which they have personal connections, the company's CEO Jim Craigie decided to give back to organizations that impact the company and are within the communities where the employees live and work. The company created a 501(c)(3) nonprofit organization, EGF, to accept financial donations for employees' chosen charities. Employees give tax-deductible contributions to the EGF earmarked for their charities, and the company matches the employee contributions dollar for dollar.

The EGF represents a major social aspect of sustainability at Church & Dwight and is a significant part of the company's commitment to CSR. Established in 2005, this program has grown each year, rising to almost $1 million in 2012. The fund has distributed more than $3.6 million to charitable causes and has awarded more than 690 grants, 149 of them in 2011 alone.[14]

Under the EGF, funds have been raised for a wide variety of social and community charitable purposes, including hunger relief, disadvantaged youth, homelessness, health, domestic violence, the environment (e.g., local watersheds and wildlife), save the animals, animal rescue, and education.

The leaders I spoke with told many touching stories of how these funds have been used. The company donated $500,000 to Feeding America, and another $500,000 was divided among nine local food banks to feed struggling individuals and families in New Jersey. Other funds went to providing direct emergency relief, medical services, and emotional counseling. Church & Dwight collected and donated over 1,000 items of food, toys, backpacks, and pet supplies to numerous local organizations. On a global basis, it contributed $20,000 to the American Red Cross to help the people of Japan following the 2011 earthquake and tsunami.

Volunteer Opportunities

The company provides up to four employee volunteer opportunities per year, each of which involves between 10 and 20 people. This enables about 50 to 80 employees, out of 800 in Church & Dwight's corporate and R&D headquarters in Princeton, to participate for half a day each year in these programs. In the summer, the company runs a Homefront Kids Camp in which employees can volunteer to help homeless and disadvantaged youths. Employees raced in a Relay for Life to raise money for cancer research and walked a Heart Walk for the American Heart Association. They donated money and products, and volunteered their time, to local schools, fire departments, children's hospice, sports clubs, United Way, local Special Olympics, and other local community charitable organizations.[15]

Partnerships with NGOs

Church & Dwight has established several collaborative and long-standing public private partnerships with nonprofit environmental organizations, among the most long-standing and successful are its relationship with World Wildlife Fund (WWF) and the Nature Conservancy.

Photo 6.1   A member of Church & Dwight's Inaugural C&D Stream Cleanup Team removes trash from the shores of Carnegie Lake in support of the Stony Brook Millstone Watershed Association. (© 2013 Church & Dwight Co., Inc. Used with permission.)

Management System Supporting Programs

Responsible Care

The U.S. chemical industry's Responsible Care is a voluntary program that helps members improve environmental, health, and safety performance beyond levels required by U.S. environmental and safety regulations and standards. The program was established in 1988 by the American Chemistry Council (ACC). As a member of the ACC, Church & Dwight, through its SPD in the Chemicals Group, is committed to implementing the principles of Responsible Care and its Responsible Care Management System (RCMS). It does so by tracking and publicly reporting performance based on economic, environmental, health and safety, societal, and product-related metrics. The company's environmental safety organization (ESO) provides ongoing training and guidance to assist in plant maintenance of RCMS, provides the required internal system audits, and continues to support the various RCMS programs within the company.[16]

Each year, the company has a third party conduct a Responsible Care Audit as a part of the Consumer Specialty Products Association (www .cspa.org).

In 2011, the audit identified five strengths in the company's sustainability program, including continued concern with sustainability, publication of sustainability reports, issuance of its quarterly Business Impact Matrix, and continued improvement to its MSDS program, which I discuss later in this chapter.

Product Care

The company considers its membership in Product Care, a division of the CSPA, to be a demonstration of its commitment to product safety and environmental protection. The CSPA is a trade association representing approximately 240 companies that manufacture and sell hundreds of well-known consumer products. Its purpose is to create cleaner and healthier environments for household and institutional customers. As a member of Product Care, Church & Dwight pledged to develop management principles across seven product life-cycle areas ranging from design to anticipated disposal needs.

Business Impact Matrix

The Business Impact Matrix is an internally produced spreadsheet, updated quarterly, that focuses on specific issues the company considers challenges. It provides current information about activities regarding these challenges, a priority scheme, relevant trade associations, and internal contacts. It also covers recommendations for how the company can work more effectively with regulators to ensure it is in compliance. The Business Impact Matrix is considered a best practice at the company because it provides a highly effective way of communicating about sustainability and other strategically important issues to upper management, and is heavily relied on by the legal department.

Product Stewardship

At Church & Dwight, sustainable development and product stewardship go hand in hand. Both are about creating a balance between the economic, environmental, and social aspects of its business. The goal of each is to provide principles of management practice, leadership, and training by which the company can provide safe and effective products for its household consumers and commercial, institutional, and industrial customers. The company is dedicated to operating responsibly in the design, development, and manufacture of its products, and advancing human health, environmental quality, social well-being, and economic growth.[17]

Michael Buczynski leads the product stewardship function in Church & Dwight's Office of Sustainable Development. He described the company's commitment to product stewardship in an internal document in these words: "We are committed to the enhancement of human health and quality of life through the safe-and-effective formulation, production, and sale of products and ingredients that provide desirable benefits for household, commercial, and institutional customers and consumers. These activities include our careful risk assessment of ingredients and products, labeling for safe use, poison control services, and customer inquiry."[18]

Material Safety Data Sheet Ingredient Disclosure

Paul Sieracusa, executive vice president, research and development and executive champion for sustainability and product safety, coined the phrase, now prominently on the wall in the corporate headquarters' building entry, "Products for Healthier and More Sustainable Living." This section describes some of the practices at Church & Dwight that translate this vision into reality.

Buczynski explained how product stewardship is managed at the company by taking the general requirement to use a MSDS to a higher level—full-ingredient disclosure.[19] Broadly used and legally required, an MSDS is a key aspect of product stewardship and occupational safety and health. It was designed to provide workers with procedures for working safely with and handling chemical substances. It is widely used for cataloging information wherever chemicals are used. Formats may vary within and across nations depending on national requirements.

Full-Ingredient Disclosure

The company goes above and beyond the requirements to provide specific product-safety information and full-ingredient disclosure, making the MSDS easily searchable and readily available to its end-use consumers on its website (www.churchdwight.com/brands-and-products/msds-ingredient-search.aspx).

The company's product and safety overview stands up for the consumer's basic right to know what is in the products they are using and how safe they are. The overview states that the company "recognizes that it is important for consumers to know the contents of the products they use in their homes." It guarantees that the company's products "have been thoroughly evaluated and are used safely and effectively by millions of people every day." Here Church & Dwight is upholding its long-standing commitment to the environment. The following quote, also from the overview, gives us a sense of why the company considers its use of MSDS a best practice: "We are proud of the reputation and trust that our products have earned with consumers. We are committed to building upon our legacy of providing consumers with products that are better for their families and their homes, with a focus on improving the sustainability of those products."[20]

Animal-Testing Policy

The company's animal-testing policy, which is available in the product-safety overview, demonstrates its dedication to ensuring and protecting animal welfare: "We use only materials already known to be safe. It is our policy not to test on animals, and we also request that suppliers not test any materials or products on animals, unless required by law or regulation." The policy goes on to explain the company's fundamental values and approach for implementing this: "We take a detailed and deliberate approach to evaluating our ingredients and products for potential toxic effects from expected sources of exposure. If there is a question about a particular potential toxic effect related to an ingredient, we would look for a substitute ingredient, or conduct testing using a validated alternative (i.e., nonanimal) test method such as *in vitro* and clinical safety studies."[21]

Reducing Waste, Energy, and Water

Church & Dwight monitors the annual energy use, water use, wastes, and greenhouse gas (GHG) emissions of its operations and implements control and reduction strategies to address any increases resulting from the continued success and growth of the company. Even with significant growth in sales and revenue, the company has reduced utility costs by controlling or reducing energy and water use.

Its manufacturing sites focus on waste management and have implemented a number of waste-reduction programs. The company's Lean Six Sigma and cost-savings programs have been instrumental in achieving process efficiencies, reducing energy consumption, and decreasing waste. As a result of these efforts, Church & Dwight's total energy use fell by 9 percent in 2011 (compared with its 2010 use) and has fallen 24 percent overall since 2008. The company considers this "a remarkable accomplishment" given the growth of the businesses and the increase in manufacturing operations over the same period.

Even though some of its products and operations are quite water intensive, its water use has decreased 5 percent per year on average since 2008 as a result of product concentration, water reuse, and process improvements. Overall water use fell more than 11 percent from 2008 through 2011, and new water-management and water-reduction strategies are under way to maintain this downward trend in 2012 and beyond.

With regard to waste management, the company is minimizing the amount going to landfill. Its Leadership in Energy and Environmental Design (LEED)-Silver facility in York, Pennsylvania, became a zero-landfill operation in 2011 with all process waste being treated, recycled, or used for energy recovery. These efforts have resulted in an overall 11.4 percent reduction in GHG emissions since 2008, an average 3.8 percent reduction per year.

Challenges, Trade-Offs, and Conundrums

Church & Dwight recognizes the environmental impacts associated with its operations and products and makes a conscious effort to reduce those impacts. According to the company's 2011 sustainability report, Church & Dwight understands there is "always room for improvement given the challenges [it] faces due to continuing company growth," but nevertheless is "committed to keeping the trend lines moving in a downward direction."[22]

I asked each person I spoke with about the challenges the company is confronting. Here I provide a brief explanation of seven such challenges and how the company is addressing them: (1) integrating sustainability into a successful business; (2) being sustainable versus touting it; (3) consumer perceptions that green costs more, and finding a workable trade-off; (4) tree hugging, cutting edge, or bleeding-edge? (5) altruism versus meeting market expectations; (6) meeting customers and consumers where they are; and (7) determining whether natural ingredients are always better.

Integrating Sustainability into a Successful Business

Coleman described, from a change-management perspective, the struggle he has trying to integrate sustainability into a very successful business: "When you're successful, people don't want to change. I look at our heritage of environmental sustainability and I feel it slots nicely. However, sustainability today as a triple-bottom-line concept is a culture change from a purely environmental sustainability approach. We have a heritage of environmental sustainability or responsibility, but we're not so successful we don't need to change anything. Our ability to effectively integrate sustainability thinking and practices into our business can be a contributing factor in helping to sustain our future success."[23]

Coleman said that, largely because of the strength of its brands, the company had a banner year even at the height of the recession, in 2009. Because of its value brands, he said, it is "hard to get people to understand we need to change. I have to communicate that I'm not trying to change our business model. I'm trying to enhance it. And there's no reason we can't integrate sustainability into our business to enhance it to drive success."[24]

Being Sustainable versus Touting It

Since 1846, Church & Dwight—as we saw earlier—has demonstrated its commitment to "being the change it wants to bring about in the world," as Mahatma Gandhi famously said. But at the same time, the company has never touted its commitment to "green" or sustainability.

The challenge for the company now is to authentically gain traction for how far it has come on its journey to sustainability. It struggles with being heard by customers in an increasingly cluttered and competitive marketplace in which companies are making more and more claims about being green and sustainable every day. In my own work with corporations, I've noticed that it is especially difficult to make such claims in a marketplace characterized by the "seven sins of greenwashing."[25]

Meeting Customers and Consumers Where They Are

Church & Dwight makes it a practice to talk with its customers, such as Wal-Mart, and to consumers so it can understand their needs and meet them where they are. The company has identified different consumer segments and targets its product portfolio to meet their needs. The smallest segment of the green market, according to Wasserman, is the "tree huggers who absolutely want to make sure everything they buy is organic, as local as possible, and coming from sustainable places." Wasserman believes that in 2012 this segment represents "less than 10 percent of consumers, a very small percentage who are buying strictly on that." A much larger percent of consumers would buy green, or sustainable, products, he said, "if the cost is the same and the product performed no worse (or at least as well)."[26]

With its Arm & Hammer Essentials line, which displays the Environmental Protection Agency's (EPA) coveted Design for the Environment (DFE) logo, the company gained many insights about consumer behavior. The first Essentials product was a detergent four times more concentrated than most, or a "super concentrate." The company offered consumers an empty 32-ounce squirt bottle with a small bottle of concentrate. Consumers were to fill the empty bottle with water and a small amount of the concentrate. If the line were successful, it would have "incredible advantages" from a sustainability perspective: because the company would not have to ship as much water, it would take many trucks off the road, reducing its impact, saving transportation costs, and reducing GHG emissions. In addition, the product would take less shelf space wherever it was sold. Megastores such as Wal-Mart embraced it; it was consistent with their commitment to environmental sustainability and saved them money.

Despite all these advantages, Church & Dwight's first foray into the completely green market was a failure. The product was introduced in 2008. Months passed. A year passed. People were not buying it. The company ran promotions, but it still wasn't selling. The consumers didn't get the concept and would not buy an empty bottle. There were stories of people telling the salesperson at the register, "They forgot to fill this!"

Even though Wal-Mart loved the product and struggled to market it, it was gone after a year to year and a half (see more about the Essentials line, including the products that still exist [mentioned in the Tree Hugging, Cutting Edge, or Bleeding Edge? section]). In retrospect, Wasserman said, "consumers were confused. Had we had a little more time, maybe we could have sold the first bottle full and then sold concentrates after that." The company pulled the product off the shelf, he said, because "the numbers didn't work."[27] Although the company really thought "it had a winner," said Coleman, it learned an important lesson from this failure: "You have to educate the consumer."[28]

Consumer Perceptions that Green Costs More; Finding a Workable Trade-Off

A major challenge for companies going green is consumers' apparent—or at least initial—unwillingness to pay more for green or sustainable products. The people I interviewed at Church & Dwight believe that, for the most part, it does cost more to make green products, particularly to make ones that perform at the same level as more traditional, less-green products. And those green products that cost the company less, or at least the same as, traditional products, often will not work as well.

The question is, Is there a workable trade-off? "To be completely green, that is, to not use any ingredient that is on anyone's 'do not use' list, anywhere in the world, to meet consumers' performance standards, and have it not cost more you can't make it work," said Wasserman. The company does, however, seek to use only those ingredients that are generally regarded as safe (GRAS), and it takes into account not just their direct impact on consumers but also their potential impact on the environment. Wasserman is adamant that "there are lots of things we can do and do that are safe for people and safe for the environment."[29]

Tree Hugging, Cutting Edge, or Bleeding Edge?

Because the company never compromises on performance, I was told, it won't produce the greenest brand possible if it believes it won't perform to its consumers' expectations and satisfaction. The company, said

Buczynski, is committed to providing safe, well-performing products that its consumers can use responsibly. It continues to listen to consumers, as we discussed earlier, meet them where they are, and determine when educating them will be effective and advantageous.[30] Church & Dwight does "not want to be on the bleeding edge, to force society to go in a certain way. We're not big enough to do that," said Wasserman, "but as one of the smaller companies, we can be influential."[31]

Despite the market failure of its first Essentials item, the company has continued to develop and market other products in the Essentials line to meet consumer needs and demand for environmentally friendly laundry and personal care products. They have less chemical load, are made with plant-based surfactants, and are almost completely dye-free. Today the Essentials line has three major products: laundry detergent; fabric softener, made with vegetable-based softener; and an underarm deodorant, which stops odor but won't stop wetness (antiperspirants use aluminum salt to prevent wetness). The Essentials' tag line is, "Harnessing the power of nature."

Altruism versus Meeting Market Expectations: "Rallied and Actively Prepared"

Church & Dwight sees a continuum between being purely altruistic, at one extreme, and strictly paying attention to economics, at the other. As a publicly held company (CHD on the New York Stock Exchange [NYSE]), it is committed to taking care of its shareholders, but at the same time, it is committed to finding an appropriate balance with the three elements of the triple bottom line (social, environmental, and economic).

To be true to its sustainable values and meet market and consumer expectations, the company changed its strategy in 2010 to one of "being actively prepared." This means "keeping our thumb on the pulse of consumers (and all stakeholders) at all times," said Wasserman. "We look at all that information and do our best at 'guessing' what [will] happen over the next two or three years, and prepare now for the next three years." He gave me this example to illustrate his point:

> If our competitors seem to be rushing to move everything from synthetic chemicals to plant-based chemicals, then let's start looking at our supply chain and figuring out if that's possible. If we think there are a number of bills currently being floated at the state

or federal levels, let's engage in the debate, be part of those conversations. Then we can use that information to prepare ourselves for the next three years.[32]

The mantra at Church & Dwight is, "Rallied and actively prepared."

The Natural Question: Are Natural Ingredients Always Better?

As the company seeks to meet consumer's demand for "natural" ingredients, Buczynski explained, "we can create chemicals that are better than what nature created." He drew a clear distinction between natural and chemical when it comes to the product's performance: "Performance is the beauty of chemistry. Through the beauty of chemistry, we can create a natural degreaser that nature never intended." The "natural" question, he said, then becomes, "Did nature intend to create for industrial uses we now have?" He believes in the company's tagline: "Better living through chemistry."[33]

Lessons Learned

Here is a synopsis of Church & Dwight's lessons learned on its journey to sustainability:

- Find out what's important to your executive suite and make sure it resonates; make it relevant.
- Do the right thing. Have a conscious attitude toward products from conception (R&D) through commercialization.
- Use sound science to figure out the best ingredients to put into your products. Don't take chances.
- Be transparent: Report the bad with the good. Report what's relevant to your business and what you can be accurate about.
- Find ways to work positively with regulators.
- Educate the consumer to help her get past the confusion in the marketplace.
- At any moment, the actual isn't as important as the goal. It is the goal that gets everyone moving in the right direction.
- Build and leverage your network.
- Identify and address hot spots in the world. Discover what's important to the world and how to address those needs.
- There's no one silver bullet.

Frameworks, Tools, and Resources

Research and Development 4DRD Platform

To support its corporate sustainability and product stewardship objectives, Church & Dwight uses a 4DRD platform—discover, develop, deliver, and delight—for the development of its product packaging and formulations. The four Ds stand for these four phases:

- Discover innovative new products and concepts.
- Develop them.
- Deliver them to customers.
- Delight the consumer.

At a minimum, the 4DRD standards are centered on regulatory compliance. But they go beyond that, taking into account consumer inputs and insights when developing new products and creating existing product modifications. This helps ensure that the products are safe and effective for its consumers, customers, and the environment. According to the company's 2011 sustainability report, "We manage project activities from concept to launch to assure the quality, safety and performance of every product we launch, and as a means of addressing and reducing the environmental impact of our product portfolio in an effort to make our products more sustainable."[34]

The Sustainability Consortium

Church & Dwight is a Tier 1 (i.e., founding) member of the Sustainability Consortium (www.sustainabilityconsortium.org), which it describes as "an independent organization of diverse global participants who work collaboratively to build a scientific foundation for driving innovation and improving consumer product sustainability." To facilitate communication of sustainability-related product information based on the entire product life cycle, the Sustainability Consortium is developing the Sustainability Measurement & Reporting System (SMRS). This standardized framework helps companies design better products, manage sustainability in their supply chain, and articulate product sustainability to consumers.[35]

Johnson & Johnson Sustainability Best Practices Tool

Church & Dwight uses a tool developed and shared by Johnson & Johnson to quantify, track, and reduce energy, water, and waste in its plants' manufacturing facilities. Wasserman described the tool as "very robust" because, he said, it asks all the right questions.[36]

In the introduction to its Sustainable Energy Best Practices tool, Johnson & Johnson said, "Improving energy performance of buildings reduces operating costs, reduces environmental footprint, and enhances occupant comfort."[37] The tool is on a user-friendly Excel spreadsheet and comprises a series of checklists regarding management practices and continuous improvement; energy purchasing and monitoring; air handling (HVAC); motors and pumps; boiler systems; chiller systems; electrical and on-site generation; lighting; compressed air; and manufacturing and other load reductions.[38]

The Sustainable Energy Best Practices checklist provides guidelines for creating and implementing a sustainable energy-management program that can be implemented at the component, process, system, and organizational levels. The best practices are designed to help energy and plant managers cost-effectively reduce energy consumption while meeting regulatory requirements and maintaining product quality.[39]

Standards

Church & Dwight uses a number of internationally recognized standards and frameworks, and participants in several trade associations. Some of these are listed here:

- Responsible Care/Product Care (www.cspa.org)
- Global Reporting Initiative (GRI; www.globalreporting.org)
- Green Chemistry Principles (www.epa.gov/sciencematters/june2011/principles.htm)
- American Chemical Institute (ACI; www.portal.acs.org)
- American Cleaning Institute (ACI; www.cleaninginstitute.org)
- National Sanitary Foundation Trade Association (www.nsf.org)

Conclusion

As Church & Dwight looks to the horizon across its global operations, it will continue to support environmental, safety, sustainable development, and product stewardship programs to enable the design and manufacture of products for healthier and more sustainable living. The key areas of strategic focus include:

- Energy-, water-, and waste-reduction efforts at its plants
- Environmental and safety support for plant startups

- Maintenance and continual improvement of all sustainability, environmental, safety, and training policies and programs
- Expansion of Lean Six Sigma projects
- Efforts to go beyond regulatory compliance to deliver products that meet its customer and consumer needs
- Product life-cycle considerations and carbon footprint improvement in its product-development efforts
- Participation in the Sustainability Consortium[40]

I was particularly impressed with the authenticity and keen insights provided by Bob Coleman in the company's fifth annual sustainability report. In his "Program Perspective,"[41] Coleman described the company's accomplishments and hurdles along with future efforts needed to sustain the company's move to sustainability.

The report stated clearly that "integrating sustainability into our business operations was not an easy task. The increased complexity of our present day company, as well as the complex concept of sustainability in general, required that we first get our feet wet and go after more attainable objectives."[42]

As we have seen in this chapter, an environmentally friendly heritage does not guarantee a sustainable company in the twenty-first century. Both Coleman and Buczynski talked about the gradual nature of the company's evolution to sustainability in all its complexity, which encompasses more than a commitment to the environment. In fact, as I have seen in companies across the world, it almost always requires a cultural change—perhaps even a transformation.

Through its Office of Sustainable Development, the company actively monitors a broad spectrum of sustainability indicators in order to stay current regarding changes and best practices "as the sustainability paradigm continues to evolve," said Coleman.[43]

CHAPTER 7

Ingersoll Rand: Integrating Sustainability into the Heartbeat of the Company

If you can make sustainability another business lever, you'll be much more successful in changing culture and changing the behavior.

—E. Jefferson (Jeff) Hynds, 2012

Addressing Global Challenges

For 140 years, Ingersoll Rand has been about solving big problems, making a transformational impact on a global scale with its products and services. Its invention of the jackhammer transformed city landscapes and—together with the invention of the rock drill—the mining industry. The company's air conditioners bring comfort to the world. Its chillers and refrigeration products enable food and pharmaceuticals to stay fresh, making more foods available to more people and saving lives. Solving big problems "is part of who our company is and what we've delivered," said W. Scott Tew, executive director, Center for Energy Efficiency and Sustainability (CEES) at Ingersoll Rand.[1]

The company continues its legacy into the twenty-first century by creating sustainable products and services. Today, Ingersoll Rand is committed to addressing formidable global challenges such as climate change and energy efficiency—seeing the former as "a global threat to future social, environmental and business performance"[2] and the latter as key to a less-energy-intensive way to support growth in the United States and in developing markets. Regarding these challenges, Ingersoll

Rand suggests that "with the instability of energy costs and global challenge of climate change, energy efficiency provides the opportunity to invest available capital in growth, to innovate and create new jobs."[3]

One broad-reaching way Ingersoll Rand both addresses climate change and increases energy efficiency is by creating more-efficient and more-intelligent buildings. In the United States, residential and commercial buildings account for 41 percent of energy consumption and 40 percent of total greenhouse gas (GHG) emissions. Ingersoll Rand is working with policy makers and customers on the future of energy efficiency in buildings, taking an approach that embraces improved energy-efficiency standards, reduced energy intensity, incentives, and more.[4]

To ensure the sustainability of the earth and its people, Tew identified global megatrends that must be addressed:

- Resource scarcity (4 billion people are affected by water scarcity)
- Ecological decline (80 percent of fish stocks are over, or fully, exploited)
- Disparate prosperity (1.3 billion people have no access to energy)[5]

Ingersoll Rand pays close attention to these when developing its products and services, always with an eye toward minimizing their environmental impact. The company is mindful of other global megatrends as well, including the following:

- Globalization (international trade and foreign investments have tripled from 1992 to 2011)
- The rapid acceleration of digital connectivity
- The need to feed and provide energy to a growing population that is exhibiting patterns of increasing consumption
- Rapid urbanization, in particular in areas with emerging economies such as China and India[6]

Building a Culture for Sustainability

Today Ingersoll Rand, a diversified industrial company with more than 46,000 employees in more than 100 countries, is a world leader in commercial, residential, and industrial markets. It provides products that enhance air quality and comfort in homes and buildings; transport and protect food and perishables; secure homes and commercial properties; and increase industrial productivity and efficiency. The $14 billion global company is a family of brands—Club Car, Ingersoll Rand, Schlage, Thermo King, and Trane. Ingersoll Rand's stated purpose is to "advance the quality of life by creating and sustaining safe, comfortable and efficient environments,"[7] and it embraces the triple-bottom-line definition of sustainability, which it views as a mind-set, not just another initiative.

Recently Ingersoll Rand formed the CEES with the goal of integrating sustainability into all business functions in the company. And it has launched a behavior-based sustainability program to integrate sustainability into the heartbeat of the company by educating and engaging all its employees. Ingersoll Rand positions sustainability as a competency-strengthening opportunity and builds it into its talent programs as a focus area for leadership development.

What Does a Culture for Sustainability Look Like?

To address the big challenges, Ingersoll Rand realizes it needs to fully integrate sustainability into the way it does business and ensure that it is manifested in how everyone in the company approaches the work that they do every day. Ingersoll Rand not only looks at how the company instills a sustainability mind-set internally, but also seeks to determine how it can help its customers become more sustainable, understand how its products and services impact its customers, and figure out how it can help its customers create value with minimal negative environmental impact.

How to Get There

Here I present the key approaches the company uses to move forward on its journey to sustainability, based on the interviews I conducted in 2012 with a cross-section of leaders, managers, and individual contributors at Ingersoll Rand and the CEES, several 2011 and 2012 Ingersoll Rand presentations, and secondary research I conducted in 2013. These approaches encompass strategic, organizational, and structural actions that help Ingersoll Rand drive sustainability internally with its employees and externally with its customers, suppliers, shareholders, partners, and other key stakeholders.

Taking a Strengths-Based Approach and Developing New Capabilities

Taking a strengths-based approach, the company identified its core competencies, asking the question, What are we great at? At the same time, it identified five strategic capabilities it had to develop further to enable it to address the global challenges presented earlier:

- Grasping opportunities—teaching its people how to discover and seize opportunities and how to teach others to do the same
- Using cradle-to-cradle design principles such as life-cycle assessment (LCA)
- Expanding its resourcing and manufacturing strengths and competencies so that they encompass product use and end-of-life phases
- Identifying market opportunities by developing a better understanding of unmet customer needs
- Developing partnerships with key stakeholders to cocreate customer solutions

Building Partnerships to Facilitate Progress

The company recognized it needed to develop collaborative partnerships with key stakeholders to cocreate solutions to the major challenges facing the world. "The future is networks of companies, because problems are becoming so large and complex," said Chris Tessier, director, communications, CEES.[8]

During the past decade or more, the company has developed, cultivated, and benefited from a wide range of strategic partnerships in four categories:

- *Industry associations.* These include the Alliance for Responsible Atmospheric Policy (ARAP; www.alliancepolicy.org), EDF Climate Corps (www.edfclimatecorps.org), GEO Exchange (www.geoexchange .org), and the National Association of EHS Management (NAEM; www.naem.org).
- *Governmental groups' frameworks.* These include the Montreal Protocol on Substances that Deplete the Ozone Layer in association with the United Nations Environment Programme Ozone Secretariat (www .ozone.unep.org/new_site/en/montreal_protocol.php) and the United Nations Framework Convention on Climate Change (UNFCCC; www .unfccc.int/2860.php).
- *Nongovernmental organizations (NGOs).* These include the Alliance to Save Energy (ASE; www.ase.org), the Business Council for Sustainable Development (BCSE; www.bcse.org), the U.S. Business Council for Sustainable Development (USBCSD; www.usbcsd.org), and

the World Business Council for Sustainable Development (WBCSD; www.wbcsd.org).
- *University-affiliated organizations.* These include Duke University's Center for Energy Development and the Global Environment (www .fuqua.duke.edu/edge), and Fairleigh Dickinson University's Institute for Sustainable Enterprise (www.fdu.edu/ise).

A complete list of CEES partners can be found on its website (www .cees.ingersollrand.com/pages/partners.aspx).

Recognizing the Inextricable Link between Sustainability and Premier Performance

"A sustainable company, when you look at the data, is a premier-performing company," said Senior Vice President, Innovation, and Chief Technology Officer Paul Camuti, articulating the link Ingersoll Rand sees between sustainability and premier performance. "We think sustainability is a business driver just like any other business driver. It helps us reduce our costs, increase our revenue, enhance our brand, increase our profit. We're doing sustainability because it makes good business sense," he said, "not because it's some good philanthropic idea to get points with the government."[9]

To drive Ingersoll Rand to premier performance, the company developed three enterprise-wide strategic imperatives related to sustainability:

- *Operational excellence,* with a dedication to implementing lean thinking (i.e., minimizing waste) and sustainability throughout the company's value stream
- *Growth through innovation,* with a particular emphasis on emerging markets and services
- *Creation of a progressive, diverse, and inclusive culture*

Tying Sustainability to the Company's Brand, Promise, Vision, and Purpose

Sustainability is embedded in Ingersoll Rand's vision—"a world of sustainable progress and enduring results"—and in its purpose, which I presented earlier in Building a Culture for Sustainability.[10] And, speaking with Ingersoll Rand's leaders, I discovered that sustainability is the company's raison d'être. Camuti said, "That's what we do; it's woven into our promise to the customer. This does two things. It provides a linkage from our vision to what we're actually doing. And it ensures that we are holding ourselves accountable to the customer [for] delivering on that vision."[11]

Creating a Rallying Point and a Focus Area for Alignment

An essential step in the journey to sustainability at Ingersoll Rand was developing a rallying point and aligning all activities and decision making with it. Camuti said, "You can't underestimate the amount of time [you need to take] at the beginning to be thoughtful in developing your plan and [in considering] how it will evolve over years." Establishing the CEES was one important step, but "the key thing for embedding [sustainability] in the culture is alignment." "You can't declare victory too early," Camuti said. If you do, he warned, "people delegate their thinking to the group. Embedding it means we're making it align with everything we're doing, not a separate set of activities for our employees to do or a separate thing we're discussing with our customers or our supply chain. Our thinking is that this [culture for sustainability] will evolve from awareness and focus to a distributed way of thinking about things."[12]

The company's sustainability commitment gained momentum when CEES established the Sustainability Strategy Council/Steering Committee, composed of senior leaders from multiple businesses and functions. The council sets priorities and provides advice concerning key sustainability initiatives. It meets on a quarterly basis to discuss strategic opportunities related to sustainability and then integrates them into Ingersoll Rand's overall business strategy.

Translating Sustainability into Customer Value

Ingersoll Rand translates sustainability into customer value in a variety of ways, with sustainable design principles and total life-cycle management, the responsible use of natural resources—including energy, water, air—and, as we will see throughout this chapter, its people. The company is committed to complying with, and exceeding, industry standards and certifications.

Camuti used the example of one of its premier products—chillers—to show me how these commitments are translated into tangible actions. Ingersoll Rand's chillers are used in heating, ventilation, and air-conditioning systems (HVAC) in large buildings and industrial processes. Sustainable design principles allow the greatest possible waste reduction in manufacturing, and the chillers consume the least amount of energy. The company considers the entire life cycle, and there is a clear path to recyclability. "We want to be able to service the product in a really efficient way through remote connectivity. In this way, we encourage everyone to think about the value stream starting with our suppliers and extending to our customers," said Camuti.[13]

Camuti explained how Ingersoll Rand's sustainable mind-set is embraced and embedded throughout the value chain:

> We would be pressuring our suppliers to do the same [things we require of ourselves]. If we're going to supply the most efficient chillers, we would need motors that are the most efficient, e.g., finding efficient motor suppliers and passing along that efficiency gain. Thinking about the value stream over the life cycle leads you to a different way of approaching the business than someone who is not thinking about it from a sustainability perspective.[14]

Setting a Small Number of Strategic Priorities

Ingersoll Rand identified numerous possible strategic priorities by conferring with internal stakeholders, customers, and global thought leaders. First, the company held a workshop with key internal stakeholders. Second, company representatives called on customers in an attempt to better understand their unmet needs. With global thought leaders, they looked at the global megatrends to discover markets that might unfold in the future as a result of these. The company also held regional input and listening sessions around the world.

Company leaders systematically worked through all the inputs gathered from these meetings and distilled the 100 things they *could do* into the 5 things they *would do*. Thus, hundreds of suggestions became the five strategic capabilities and the three enterprise-wide strategic imperatives I identified earlier in this chapter.

Best Practices

Here I describe how Ingersoll Rand is embedding sustainability in the heartbeat of the company through its employee- and customer-centered initiatives. With the visible support of enterprise leadership, the company is trying to engage all its employees in self-organizing green teams under a common framework. The intent is to encourage Ingersoll Rand employees to think about and devise sustainable solutions for customers that take advantage of the company's core strengths and the capabilities it is in the process of building.

Capturing Employees' Hearts and Minds through Employee-Centered Initiatives

Ingersoll Rand is committed to making sustainability a widely held value that becomes a central part of how its employees live and work every day; it is going beyond compliance, or simply "following the rules." Gretchen Digby, director, global education and engagement, CEES, explained that Ingersoll Rand wants to help its employees find ways to integrate sustainability and "apply it to everything we do." She called this behavior-based sustainability. It is similar to "behavior-based safety," in which safety becomes a value that is fundamental to how you live and everything you do.[15]

Ingersoll Rand has created numerous programs to excite employees about sustainability and provides myriad tools and programs to encourage them to take action. In her white paper "Step Up to Sustainability," Ingersoll Rand Sustainability Specialist Katie Pogue notes that "employee networks are the driving force creating a culture change for sustainability [at Ingersoll Rand]," and highlights two of the programs that I discuss later in this chapter: "Together, Green Teams and One STEP Forward program participants create a worldwide network of sustainability champions at Ingersoll Rand who are enabled to bring sustainable values into the workplace and spark a culture change."[16]

Green Teams

Ingersoll Rand's green teams are volunteer grass-roots groups of employees who improve their facility's environmental performance, encourage and educate their colleagues about triple-bottom-line sustainability (people, planet, and profit), and work with and in their local community on triple-bottom-line issues. Although green teams have been active at Ingersoll Rand for more than a decade, in 2011 the company formed a global network of such teams—which is, significantly, sponsored by the senior vice president of integrated supply chain and global operations and vice president of global services—and an intranet portal to coordinate them. Since then, green teams have become a driving force for culture change, greater sustainability, and environmental action at the company. They are both an outlet for employees' passion and a means of increasing employees' enthusiasm and dedication; Ingersoll Rand considers these teams "one of our most successful engagement programs."[17] As an added bonus for employees, participation in the teams is considered a form of accelerated development.

Through kaizen events—group activities designed to continually improve all functions and involve all employees—the green teams identify areas of improvement in the company. In addition, the green teams' results in certain areas are measurable, and, through a robust set of processes, the company tracks their impact on key performance indicators (KPIs) such as energy consumption and reduction, water consumption, and waste-to-landfill reduction (see the sidebar Measured Impact of Green Teams in 2012). It also tracks the number of people participating in green team–led activities. This data is reported within the company's environment, health, and safety (EHS) performance system.

As well as producing the noteworthy results listed in the sidebar, these teams, as I mentioned earlier, are also leading to higher levels of employee engagement and satisfaction. In its 2012 internal survey of employee satisfaction, Ingersoll Rand found that company sites with green teams scored significantly higher than sites without such teams; people on green teams are less likely to look for a job outside the company (indicating a higher retention and lower turnover rate); and people on green teams are more likely to refer a friend to the company for potential employment. Green teams are considered one of the company's big sustainability success stories.

The number of green teams at Ingersoll Rand doubled from 25 in 2010 to 52 in 2011 and again to 110 in 2012. As of July 2013, there are 133 such teams and their number is still growing.[18] Although the goal is

---

MEASURED IMPACT OF GREEN TEAMS IN 2012

- 2,470,000 pounds of reduced waste to landfill
- 5,650 metric tons CO_2 emissions reduced
- 37 billion British thermal units (BTUs) energy conserved
- $770,000 in annual savings associated with Green Team projects
- Almost 7,000 employees actively engaged in more than 450 sustainability projects, Green Team activities or events

Source: © 2012 Ingersoll Rand, "Delivering Results 2012," 15.

eventually to have a green team at every one of the company's sites, as is
the case with its safety committees, the company has not made this mandatory. Instead of forcing green team participation on people, the company helps the teams expand organically by communicating the benefits
of their activities. In 2013, Ingersoll Rand set the following goals: registered green teams in 100 percent of its manufacturing locations and at
least 17 percent of total employees involved in green team activities.[19]

Green Team Certification

In 2012, the company switched its focus from increasing the number of
teams to increasing the effectiveness of its current teams. Toward this end,
Ingersoll Rand developed a certification program that evaluates, measures, and strengthens the teams by providing resources, processes, and
recognition. It formally recognizes teams' work on projects at company
sites and in the local communities where they are making a difference.

Green teams are eligible to apply for one of five levels of certification,
each representing a higher level of maturity: (1) beginning, (2) evaluating
(Certified), (3) improving (Silver), (4) succeeding (Gold), and (5) leading (Platinum).

To qualify for certification, regardless of its stage of maturity, a team
must address all three triple-bottom-line aspects of sustainability: environment, with specific projects planned, in process, and completed;
economic, including metrics and reporting; and social, including people
and community.

The Silver certification is given to teams that

- implement environmental projects in key areas such as waste, water,
  and energy;
- broadly communicate measurable successes;
- track project results using standardized metrics such as kWh and gallons; and
- participate in sustainability-related activities outside the workplace—
  at home or in the community.

The Gold certification is given to teams

- whose actions have resulted in significant performance improvements;
- that have been locally recognized for their facility's environmental excellence and whose actions have been incorporated into their business
  operating plans;

- that regularly track and communicate their project results to local employees and the Green Team Advisory Council;
- whose results are translated into operational cost savings and productivity gains;
- with strong levels of participation, supported by frequent employee-engagement activities; and
- that actively coordinate volunteer activities within the local community.

In 2012, a Special Award for Exceptional Performance was given to a team in Dublin, Ireland, "in recognition of its consistent commitment to implementing green activities."[20] The Dublin team was also acknowledged for its year-over-year improvements and its consistency in seeking out new opportunities.

The company recognizes a sampling of certified teams in a brochure on the CEES website, which provides profiles of Gold-certified green teams around the world (www.cees.ingersollrand.com/Pages/sustainability_successes.aspx).

The Green Team Advisory Council

The volunteer Green Team Advisory Council, representing every function and sector in the company, meets quarterly to find ways to further support the burgeoning green teams. This council maintains governance by continuously reviewing and modifying the framework if needed, annually reviewing all certification applications, and reviewing and advising on sustainability project fund requests.

Sustainability Champions Drive Change

The company relies heavily on sustainability champions to inspire employees and motivate them to change their mind-sets and behaviors. Ingersoll Rand considers them key resources and advocates for change and action within their respective functions and work sites.

Nominated by their managers, the sustainability champions represent employees at all levels, business units, and departments of the company. I found it noteworthy that many of them come from Ingersoll Rand's sales and service organization. In some cases, the regional or district general manager is the sustainability champion and the leader of the team delivering the training. Digby said that it is "quite powerful when someone at that level takes the time" to run local sustainability training.[21]

The Sustainability Workshop

A unique sustainability workshop is a central component of Ingersoll Rand's employee sustainability education; it was designed to build awareness, change behaviors, and drive results. When describing the workshop and its effectiveness, Digby stressed that what is presented "doesn't come across as merely statistics or buzzwords" and you must "engage the heart first."[22] The workshop helps sustainability champions make a personal connection to sustainability principles and encourages them to apply what they have learned to their work and their lives. According to Ingersoll Rand, they "commit to building a culture where every employee understands why sustainability matters and how they can apply sustainability practices in their offices, homes, and communities."[23]

All sustainability champions participate in this highly interactive, experiential, one-day workshop. By the end of 2012, the company had held 14 of these workshops and trained 335 sustainability champions.[24]

The workshop includes the following topical areas:

- What is sustainability?
- What is personal sustainability?
- Why should this matter to me?
- What does sustainability mean at Ingersoll Rand?
- How can I lead a work-related sustainability project?
- How can I effectively engage coworkers?
- What are the next steps?[25]

During the workshop, participants do a facility walk-around to identify opportunities for improvement. For example, a finance person might notice a lighting opportunity. Although he had never thought about it before because it's not in his functional area and he had not been engaged or knowledgeable enough to care, it has now moved onto his radar screen. Digby described the types of issues people notice and convert into actions: "We went into one plant with so much low-hanging fruit and little simple things, like motion sensors, turning off lights in offices, everything from removing a lightbulb in a vending machine that's not needed to see the M&M's to a complete redesign of a department to how the maintenance guy sees ways to save on compressed air."[26]

After the workshop, the participants' identified projects are registered and tracked. As a visible and continual reminder of what she discovered and committed to in the workshop, each participant writes out her personal commitment on a big red card that she posts over her desk.

Two Ways to Build a Lunch Box

A creative exercise in which people build two lunch boxes helps to reinforce four *P*s: people, planet, profit, and progress. Subgroups of participants within the workshop are asked to first design a lunch box focusing only on profit; they are encouraged to make the lunchbox as unsustainable as possible. Then they do the reverse, focusing on sustainability and the four *P*s; now they are encouraged to be as creative and "outrageous" as possible.

Deborah Kalish, program manager, CEES, and a sustainability champion herself with expertise in LCA, told me she has seen people come up with fabulous ideas while doing this exercise. "People get enthusiastic and become evangelists; it's a great way to increase engagement," she said.[27]

Cross-Cultural Differences

Ingersoll Rand has conducted the sustainability workshop around the world, and, in the process, has discovered the primacy of cross-cultural differences in the successful global implementation of the program. In my interviews at Ingersoll Rand, it became clear to me how important it is to recognize these differences, to be sensitive to them, and to evaluate the various aspects of the program from a cultural perspective when preparing to bring it to a new culture. In the Czech Republic, for example, the people already have sustainability mind-sets, but "they were never given the platform to voice them," said Digby. In formerly Communist countries, she said, you can't give out the red cards, because the people, still influenced by their nation's Communist heritage, will think that if they don't do what's on the card, they will be punished. Digby added that "it is critical to keep the volunteer nature of the program so that champions continue to feel empowered—not forced—to take action."[28]

Because Europe "has been doing these sorts of things better and longer, the Europeans in general have a higher level of consciousness around energy and waste than [people] in the U.S.," said Digby, and this must be taken into account when readying the workshop for use in European countries.[29]

One STEP Forward-Personalizing Sustainability

Ingersoll Rand recently launched One STEP Forward, a program designed by CEES, to increase employees' awareness about global challenges and shift their mind-sets and behaviors at work and at home. With the program, the company "aims to personalize sustainability for

Photo 7.1   Employees at a One STEP Forward event. (© 2012 Ingersoll Rand. Used with permission.)

every employee and begin a movement that starts within the walls of our company, but quickly moves beyond, and has lasting impact in homes and communities."[30] It hopes to do this by making employees comfortable about taking initiative and by ensuring them that their managers and the company are behind them when they do this.

Digby explained that the idea for One STEP Forward came to her after she heard a sustainability champion comment, "If each of us just takes one step forward, we have a collective impact that is almost immeasurable."[31] It occurred to her that a program based on this concept would encourage Ingersoll Rand employees to "step up to sustainability." And in synch with the sustainability champion's comment, Ingersoll Rand introduced the program to employees with this inspirational message: "It only takes one pebble to start a ripple, one falling domino to begin a cascade of action, and one person to inspire others."[32]

When developing the program, the company invested a significant amount of time trying to understand employees' perspectives. Using consultants involved in creating Wal-Mart's "My Sustainability Plan," Ingersoll Rand conducted benchmark research in two companies: Duke Energy and Nissan. It learned that although many employees are eager to take individual action, they either don't know how to or don't feel comfortable doing this at work, primarily because they don't know the extent to which they will be supported.[33]

ONE STEP FORWARD

At Ingersoll Rand every employee owns sustainability. One STEP Forward introduces STEPs (sustainable, transformative, encourages others, and personal), or actions, that employees can take to personalize sustainability. These STEPs are defined as

Sustainable: Contributes to a better world
Transformative: Supports you in living your values
Encourages Others: Inspires colleagues, friends, and family
Personal: Connects to something personally meaningful

These easy, effective actions are collaborative, have a positive and measurable impact, can save costs, and influence others in their department/site/community to take action. Examples of STEPs include:

- Only printing documents when necessary, and printing double-sided
- Reducing waste-to-landfill by adding recycling bins in plant and office workspaces
- Working with a team to plant trees or flowers at a company facility
- Using personal mugs instead of disposable cups for hot beverages
- Reducing waste-to-landfill at home by utilizing recycling and composting

Source: © 2012 Ingersoll Rand, One STEP Forward Public Announcement.

Values: From Home to Workplace

Looking at Ingersoll Rand's employee-centered programs holistically, I became convinced that more than anything else, sustainability is a value at the company. After this value is embraced, it gradually becomes a way of living and working. This process starts with a shift in mind-set: people become conscious of sustainability. Then that mind-set influences the way they see the world: they begin to view everything they do through a sustainability lens. Kalish believes values start with the family and home first: "If you talk about what's important to people in their personal life first, it becomes part of their daily life."[34]

Life-Cycle Thinking

Kalish, who is an expert in LCA processes, gave me an example of the sustainability mind-set at work within the company.[35] Shortly after participating in a sustainability workshop, she worked with one of the manufacturing teams to conduct a screening-level LCA on steel doors. Kalish and the manufacturing team realized that the company was using a great deal of water to prevent some of the steel doors from corroding and thought, Why don't we use a different steel that doesn't require water to remove anticorroding oils?

She created a "value stream map" and conducted a "hot spot analysis." Value stream mapping is an approach used in lean manufacturing to design and analyze the flow of materials and information necessary to bring a product or service to a consumer. In the business world, hot spot analysis is a screening-level LCA and a cost-effective way to gain a high-level view of a product's environmental footprint. It helps identify the points from which the biggest environmental impacts originate, giving the company information it can use to maximize reductions in the product's environmental footprint.

Kalish and team discovered that replacing the steel with a different steel not requiring special oils would reduce costs, be better for the environment, and help to attenuate impending water-scarcity crises. Kalish told me that although it clearly is just "common sense," she wouldn't have been sensitive to it had she not taken the sustainability workshop. "It's all about the culture," said Kalish.[36]

Creating and Sustaining Customer Value

Ingersoll Rand's overriding commitment to customer value has led to several best practices that I found both unique and potentially transferable to other industries and organizations. In this section, I will explore some of these: Ingersoll Rand's methodologies for segmenting its market, building its green portfolio, and employing disruptive and open innovation. With these foundational building blocks in place, the company's application of "outcome-driven innovation" (ODI) to sustainability challenges represents a profoundly important contribution to the future of sustainability.

During our interview, Tew cited the work of Clayton Christensen several times. This intrigued me, and I wanted to learn more.[37] So I perused Christensen's work that I might better understand it and the value it could bring to addressing sustainability megatrends. I read his three best-selling books—*The Innovator's Dilemma* (2011; first edition published in 1997 by Harvard Business School Press), *The Innovator's Solution,*[38] and *The Innovator's DNA*[39]—and, in this section and the chapter's conclusion, I introduce some of my insights into his work. I extrapolate and extend these insights in chapter 11 of this book.

Segmenting the Marketplace

Tew described how the company successfully applies market research techniques based on Christensen's work to segment the underlying needs of its customers. "In the past we focused on the product features. We turned that around to redefine the products in terms of how the customer understands it," said Tew.[40]

Through my research I learned the essential distinction between classical market segmentation and the disruptive innovation approach Christensen and Raynor presented in *The Innovator's Solution.*[41] Typically marketers segment the marketplace by type of product, price, and the demographics and psychographics of those individuals or companies that represent their customers. Unfortunately, these categorizations all too often lead to failure in the marketplace; three-quarters of all new product-development efforts are commercially unsuccessful. Why?

Christensen suggests that the answer is that these companies do not take into account the way customers actually use and experience the products in their lives. His disruptive innovation approach is based on the notion that customers "hire" products to do specific "jobs" and provides a new way to think about and conduct market segmentation. "Knowing what job a product gets hired to do (and knowing what jobs are out there that aren't getting done very well) can give innovators a much clearer road map for improving their products to beat the *true* competition from the customer's perspective—in every dimension of the job," said Christensen and Raynor.[42]

Ingersoll Rand used this approach to identify three distinct types of farmers who were using its products. Rather than asking them what types of features they'd like to have in a product, the company asked them what problems they needed the new product to solve, or to put it another way, what job they needed the product to do. Through this process, it identified farmers' problems that it could translate into a specific set of needs. "The company was able to apply its segmentation scheme to create a concise series of only seven or eight key questions for sales people to ask its customers. Once identified, the needs of each farmer segment would be better served," said Tew.[43]

Creating a Green Portfolio through Open Innovation

The process of redefining problems based on the customer's need instead of product features—a process Ingersoll Rand calls open innovation—was applied by Ingersoll Rand in the creation of its green-product portfolio. The company was "very successful in identifying and developing new technologies that would simultaneously help its customers and its business," said Tew.[44]

Ingersoll Rand's touchscreen controls for its compressors is one innovation that was created using open innovation. In a process based on Christensen's ideas described earlier, "customers look at the 'job' of controlling equipment," said Tew.[45] He suggested that one problem customers might have with traditional equipment (i.e., equipment that uses a regular keyboard rather than a touchscreen) is "dirt collects under the keys." Now that Ingersoll Rand knew this was a problem, it could figure out a solution and, in the process, develop a product that customers would want. "By getting people to redefine what they want from a technology from the perspective of customer need, instead of the features of a particular product," the company was able to introduce a very successful product that met the needs of its customers, according to Tew.[46]

Photo 7.2   Examples from Ingersoll Rand's green portfolio. (© 2012 Ingersoll Rand. Used with permission.)

The open innovation approach enabled Ingersoll Rand to conduct research around key sustainability challenges and explore new opportunities to ameliorate them. For example, Tew said, the company is now using
open innovation to "find technologies that can help us reduce GHGs."[47]

Outcome-Driven Innovation

Tew explained how the company embraced ODI, a theory and practice
Anthony Ulwick introduced. Ingersoll Rand used ODI to significantly
extend the open innovation process and apply it specifically to sustainability challenges. Because I think that ODI, especially the way Ingersoll
Rand uses it in developing its green portfolio, is a significant breakthrough, I will summarize the ODI process here.

ODI is a strategy and an innovation process based on Ulwick's needs-
first approach, in which "companies first learn what the customer's
needs are, then discover which needs are unmet, and then devise a concept that addresses those unmet needs."[48] "It links a company's value
creation activities to customer-defined metrics. . . . With an 86 percent
success rate," said Ulwick, "ODI helps companies make product and
marketing decisions that ensure the growth of core markets and the successful entry into adjacent and new markets."[49]

Ulwick developed the ODI methodology over 19 years of research. It
is founded on the following eight "discoveries," which take a holistic
and end-to-end view of the innovation process:

(1) When it comes to innovation, the job, not the product, must be
    the unit of analysis.
(2) A job map provides the structure needed to ensure all customer
    needs are captured.
(3) When the job is the unit of analysis, needs take the form of
    customer-defined metrics.
(4) ODI's "jobs-to-be-done" principles apply equally well to design
    innovation.
(5) The opportunity algorithm makes it possible to prioritize unmet
    needs.
(6) Opportunities (unmet needs) dictate which growth strategy to
    pursue.
(7) Scattershot brainstorming doesn't work; sequenced and focused
    idea generation does.
(8) Concepts can be evaluated with precision against customer-defined
    metrics.[50]

Applying ODI to Sustainability Challenges at Ingersoll Rand

Ingersoll Rand realized it could apply ODI methodology and concepts to sustainability challenges. It identified 22 key customer needs related to sustainability, each of which it translated into potential green-product characteristics. The needs included decreasing GHG emissions, managing and minimizing the product's use of potable water, reducing environmental hazards in products, and managing energy.

After defining these needs and determining 22 product characteristics that fulfilled them, the company created a survey for customers asking them how important these characteristics are to them and how satisfied they are currently with their ability to meet these needs. For example, regarding minimizing GHG emissions, how important is that to you, and how satisfied are you now? The company analyzed the answers, using a quantitative algorithm to identify opportunities for product innovations that are important to customers but not currently well satisfied.

Ingersoll Rand combined this analysis with a competitive analysis of how well its products and services stacked up against its competition for each of the 22 product attributes. Using an algorithm it developed, Ingersoll Rand determined which of the 22 product characteristics represented the best opportunities to meet customers' needs in a way that the customer is willing to pay for. "The sum total of the 22 characteristics is how customers view green products," said Tew.[51]

The idea is to discover and address unmet needs in the sustainability space—such as better management of energy, water, and waste, and avoidance of environmental hazards—that can also lead to the identification of specific opportunities for the company. Some of these opportunities are best met through its entrepreneurial and consulting practices, said Tew.

At the time of the interviews, Ingersoll Rand had not yet fully rolled out the results of this work to its product-development teams and was working with a third party to develop a software tool to automate and pilot the process.

"Customers have a huge desire to solve some of these issues, like GHG and managing water," said Tew. "We know there's a market there. Can we produce a solution that customers will be willing to pay for? Are customers willing to pay 5 to 7 percent more if they can get the total green job done?"[52]

Sustainability Examples from Ingersoll Rand's Green Portfolio

Here I highlight a few examples of Ingersoll Rand's green-product portfolio, with particular focus on the job the products are doing from a sustainability perspective. It is important to reiterate that the company's mission and vision are fundamentally related to advancing sustainability.

Ingersoll Rand's Green Portfolio, according to its 2012 Sustainability Supplement, "is the top echelon of those solutions representing a best in class environmental design and maintains top quartile performance relative to competitors."[53] Each of the products in the company's green portfolio delivers one or more of these environmental benefits:

- Energy efficiency, GHG emissions or criteria pollutant emissions during use
- Use of recycled input material or minimized waste at the end of its useful life
- Resource efficiency across the product life cycle or the inclusion of renewable materials[54]

Based on its ODI study described in the previous section, the company continues to evolve its product-development process, incorporating sustainability as a core piece of the framework. In 2012, the company formally launched the Ingersoll Rand Product-Development Process (PDP), which is designed to ensure that the company assesses risk, sustainability, and intellectual property throughout the entire product-development cycle.[55]

Trane Intelligent Services

As an example of meeting customer needs, Ingersoll Rand developed an offering called Trane Intelligent Services. These services give its customers remote connectivity to their buildings, so they can adjust the performance of buildings daily, hourly, or even by the minute. "This intelligence allows continuous data collection, rigorous analysis, and specific recommendations for building optimization and efficiency."[56] This obviates the need for Ingersoll Rand to send out engineers in trucks to make these adjustments, thus reducing GHG emissions and lowering Ingersoll Rand's costs. The equipment providing the remote connectivity is in the building itself and is connected to the customer via the Internet.

High-Performance Buildings

Tew explained the concept "high-performance buildings" and the company's unique value proposition in this space. While green buildings represent a measurement or snapshot of a building's environmental potential, he said, high-performance buildings take into account all the operations and services related to how that building actually operates, and the design of the building. "It's at a higher level and adds a greater degree of sophistication. We find that while buildings may be designed green, they don't always perform at that level," said Tew.[57]

By accounting for the actual performance of the building in terms of its sustainability, security, and other factors valued by the customer, the approach to creating high-performance buildings "considers the whole building. . . . Sustainable design principles guide new construction, while operational protocols and maintenance best practices ensure that buildings perform optimally over time. No matter what their age, high performance buildings use energy and water resources efficiently, while creating a positive occupant experience."[58]

Large-Chiller Business

Ingersoll Rand's Trane China controls and contracting team addressed sustainability needs when it built a prepackaged-chiller plant for a new baby-care manufacturing facility in southern China. The chiller is 20 percent more energy efficient than "more conventional solutions" and saves up to 40 percent on installation costs. It integrates "proven chiller technology, efficient systems design, and advanced controls to produce and distribute chilled water in the most energy efficient and cost effective way," said Ingersoll Rand in its 2012 Sustainability Supplement.[59]

Hybrid Diesel Electric Refrigeration

To keep perishable food fresh longer, the company introduced the Thermo King UT series of refrigeration trucks. These hybrid diesel–electric refrigeration cargo-transport trucks respond to two significant customer needs: the need to safely transport high-volume specialty cargo such as fresh foods and perishables and the need for operational (and operator) efficiency. These trucks, according to Ingersoll Rand, "allow optimum load management while maximizing fleet profitability."[60]

The new refrigeration unit reduces emissions and waste by running on electricity when parked and while driving, eliminating the need for an independent engine in the refrigeration unit. The unit is 10 percent more fuel efficient than traditional diesel-powered transport refrigeration systems and is lighter and quieter. At the same time special in-cab features—including a display with symbols understood by operators around the world—increase operator efficiency.

This new technology is helping Ingersoll Rand's customer Dean Foods—the largest dairy processor in the United States and owner of one of the largest refrigerated direct-store delivery-and-distribution networks in the food and beverage industry—reduce its carbon footprint while increasing operational efficiency and cost savings.

Club Cars

A division of Ingersoll Rand that makes golf carts and utility vehicles, Club Car is the world's largest manufacturer of small-wheel, zero-emission electric vehicles and is on the forefront of environmentally responsible zero-emission vehicle (ZEV) technologies. "Club Car electric vehicles offer a cleaner, quieter alternative to gas without sacrificing performance," according to Club Car's website (www.clubcar.com).

Camuti used one of Club Car's initiatives as an example of the benefits of ODI. He said that using the ODI process the company successfully persuaded many of the vendors that supply the components for the Club Cars to use reusable containers and packaging.

Camuti characterized the results of ODI at Ingersoll Rand: "It's not one big, macro thing. It's literally a thousand individual things going on throughout the company. And most [of these results] are locally driven."[61]

Challenges

Ingersoll Rand is in the business of helping people and organizations become more sustainable. The company has set a high bar for itself regarding the megatrends it has identified and the global challenges associated with them. It is committed to addressing these challenges head on in the most effective and efficient ways possible. As we have seen, the company is methodical, customer-centric, and holistic, determined to engage all its stakeholders both inside and outside the company in the journey to sustainability.

Here I discuss four sustainability challenges the company is facing and how it is addressing them. The first challenge is embedding sustainability holistically throughout its organization, culture, and brand. The second challenge is consistently producing solutions that customers are willing to pay for so that its sustainable products and services, and the company as a whole, remain financially viable. The third challenge is finding ways to create a customer pull instead of a technology or vendor push. The fourth challenge is managing through influence without authority, and it pertains specifically to CEES.

Embedding Sustainability Holistically in the Culture and the Brand

Several people I interviewed spoke about the need, as Camuti put it, "to constantly remind people how everything we're doing relates to sustainability."[62] This is particularly noteworthy because, as we have seen, Ingersoll Rand has in so many ways already embedded sustainability throughout the company and offers so many reminders to its employees that they will be supported when acting sustainably and taking on new sustainability initiatives.

The goal of the company is to incorporate sustainability so seamlessly, holistically, and transparently that employees no longer see themselves "as doing specific acts around sustainability anymore; they're just doing their jobs," said Camuti.[63] And that job, as seen by the company, is all about its employees helping its customers become more sustainable themselves. "As we move to making it part of our standard routine, [our employees] would be thinking about how this impacts our customers," said Camuti.[64]

As sustainability becomes deeply embedded in every aspect of the company, however, it creates a conundrum: The company could run the risk of losing the focus, perspective, and differentiation that sustainability brings to it both internally and externally. So the challenge is how to find the right balance between a concentrated and singular focus on sustainability and ensuring that employees, customers, and other stakeholders appreciate Ingersoll Rand's unique value proposition in the sustainability marketplace.

Producing a Solution that Customers Willingly Pay For

Ingersoll Rand has been in the business of solving big problems for 140 years and intends to stay in business forever so it can keep doing just that. This requires, however, that the company keep its sustainability products and services financially viable. E. Jefferson (Jeff) Hynds, director, innovation, said simply, "We're a business and here to make money."[65]

Hynds explained that "if [a product or service] costs more, there are not a lot of people who are willing to have the sustainable solution. If it costs the same, people will choose the green solution." So the company's job is to help its customers identify those products and services that are worth paying for. "Nobody will buy a product just because it's green. The product has to do the functional job it was designed to do first. When you turn the hand wheel on your car, if the car didn't turn the way it's supposed to turn, no one cares that it's a hybrid. When it's done, you are allowed the opportunity to differentiate your product against your competitors on sustainability-related issues," said Hynds.[66]

To meet this challenge, Ingersoll Rand built a clever and systematic methodology based on ODI (which I discussed earlier in Applying ODI to Sustainability Challenges at Ingersoll Rand) to help discover and address unmet customer needs. The company's approach to ODI enables it to work backward to uncover and then address customers' needs (e.g., those regarding water, waste, and energy).

Customer Pull versus Technology or Vendor Push

Camuti told me there is an ongoing debate among marketers about whether it's better to use customer pull when introducing new products and services to the marketplace or technology or vendor push. "We're pretty pragmatic about that"; he said, "in terms of innovation, we'll take both."[67]

We have already seen how Ingersoll Rand's approach to ODI incorporates *both* a customer pull (by uncovering customers' unmet needs) and a technology or vendor push (by creating products and services that address these needs). "What we've done here around mission and vision of the company around enduring progress on safe, comfortable, and efficient environment actually frames up our employees' thinking about potential solutions for customers that would address a sustainable value proposition for our customers," said Camuti.[68]

Managing through Influence without Authority

CEES is in the difficult position of having influence but not having authority. "We have to figure out something that someone else in the organization is willing to work on. We can't mandate it, but can only use our influence skills and persuasion," said Hynds.[69]

Camuti said that CEES's role has been gradually changing, enabling it to become a highly effective catalyst for change rather than an organization that constantly pushes people to shift their mind-sets and behavior to get things done: "The CEES mission has evolved over time . . . going from being a push and providing rails under which we're trying to get the organization to think about sustainability to really capturing the thinking that's going around and evolving what goes on."[70]

Lessons Learned

I invited each of the people I interviewed to reflect on his or her experiences and lessons learned from Ingersoll Rand's ongoing journey to sustainability. Here are some of the key takeaways from their responses, not all of which refer to topics I covered in this chapter.

- Engage the heart first.
- Think about your company's legacy and build on it, tying it to sustainability.
- Focus on building a high-performance organization and you will create a sustainable one.
- Remember that it's not "one big, macro thing, but a thousand individual things going on." And while small things send the signal that it's working, "you can't declare victory too early."[71]
- Align sustainability with and embed it in everything you're doing; it's not a separate set of activities.
- Communicate the value of sustainability in business terms to shift people's thinking. Remember the epigraph to this chapter: "If you can make sustainability another business lever, you'll be much more successful in changing culture and changing the behavior."[72]
- Take a top-down and bottom-up approach. Translate sustainable behavior into business practices. Make middle management accountable for business objectives.
- In branding, don't make sustainability campaign-specific. Rather, have it woven and incorporated holistically into your culture and your brand.
- Stopping doing certain things to change behaviors and culture is as important as starting to do certain things.
- Build wide networks because problems are becoming so large and complex. The future is networks of companies and organizations working together to address seemingly intractable problems.
- Lead by example. Exemplary behaviors of executives can show employees the way.
- Piggyback on other programs that are successful rather than competing with them. For example, offer slides to others for their presentations.

- Pay attention to global issues when rolling out programs. Respect cultural differences. Find a local champion and engage the international team to review your training materials so you can modify for different countries. Where possible, include live on-site translations.

Frameworks, Tools, and Resources

Ingersoll Rand employs numerous existing frameworks and global standards on sustainability. These include the following:

- Extensive LCAs that include a full cradle-to-cradle LCA study with Environmental Product Declarations (EPDs) are integrated into the company's design process. Three ISO standards used by the company are associated with LCAs: ISO 14025, 14070, 14080.
- The Carbon Disclosure Project (www.cdproject.net).
- GaBi (www.gabi-software.com/databases).
- SimaPro (www.pre-sustainability.com/simapro-lca-software).

Ingersoll Rand's internally developed frameworks and tools include the following:

- High-performance buildings (see High-Performance Buildings section under Best Practices).
- Ingersoll Rand PDP is a rigorous, standardized enterprise-wide process that helps the company accelerate customer-based innovation while enhancing productivity and efficiency. Through the PDP, the company ensures that sustainability is built into each stage of a product's development from ideation to end of life. Embedding sustainability as a component of PDP ensures the product meets customer's sustainability needs while reducing the product's overall environmental footprint. The tools used as part of this process may include risk assessment of materials provided by the supply chain, formal or customized LCAs, and others.
- Vitality Index for Innovation. This index represents the percentage of revenue generated from products and services introduced within the last three years. The goal is 25 percent.
- Integrated reporting. The company uses an integrated approach to annual financial and sustainability reporting.
- To create their own report in a PDF format, visitors may go to the company's website (www.ingersollrand.com) and select the elements

that most interest them from the 350 pages of support documents accompanying the yearly sustainability supplement.

Conclusion

Ingersoll Rand is a major player in the global sustainability movement. It offers myriad best practices and leads the way in several key areas. Here I cite four critical Ingersoll Rand contributions to the journey to sustainability that I observed during my interviews and discovered in my research.

The first and most outstanding contribution for me is the creative and systematic manner in which the company integrates ODI with the megatrends relating to sustainability. The company's relentless focus on providing customer value, especially in the context of societal and global sustainability challenges, serves as a model for other businesses.

Second, the company's holistic approach, and determination to effect enterprise-wide change in all functions and aspects, helps it stand out from the fray. I was particularly impressed with the many creative ways CEES is involving and energizing its global workforce in support of sustainability initiatives.

Third, the company's commitment to life-cycle thinking and implementation is critical to an authentic cradle-to-cradle view of products and ultimately to reducing its total environmental footprint and impact.

Last but certainly not the least important, the company's focus on the human side of sustainability, including its dedication to capturing employees' hearts and minds, is as pragmatic as it is inspiring.

During our interview, Joe Wolfsberger, former vice president, EHS, at Ingersoll Rand, described in 2012 the journey to sustainability as a journey through three doors: The first door is *awareness*—driven by sheer force of will. The second door is *process*—standardizing the work through training, green teams, and numerous other process improvements.[73] The third door is *culture*—building a culture of ownership for each person's behaviors and also for those of the people next to them.

As we find ways to move individually and collectively through these three doors, the world may shift a little on its axis and become more sustainable for us all.

CHAPTER 8

Pfizer: Growing Leaders through the Global Health Fellows Program

I've always had an interest in public health and hoped to gain a deeper understanding of the barriers to care and the opportunities to improve health-care delivery abroad.

—Michael Benigno, 2012

Pfizer is one of the largest and most diversified companies in the global health-care industry with over 100,000 employees worldwide. Its purpose is to "innovate to bring therapies to patients that significantly improve their lives."[1] Pfizer recognizes that engaged employees are key to its success and strives to make the company a great place to work by creating a culture of opportunity, accountability, and inclusion.

One of Pfizer's flagship Corporate Responsibility programs is the Global Health Fellows (GHF) program, an international corporate volunteer program that I feature in this chapter. The purpose of the program is to leverage the skills of Pfizer's employees to strengthen access to, quality of, and efficiency in health-care delivery across the globe while also enhancing the skills and experiences of the employees. In partnership with leading international health nongovernmental organizations (NGOs), Pfizer places employees in three-to-six-month assignments, each of which is designed to address a global health issue and improve care for underserved populations. Colleagues work hand-in-hand with community-based partners to help improve health-care systems while gaining new perspectives on global health challenges and on how the public and private sector can work together to address them.

The program has won tremendous recognition from human resources, business, and public relations media, such as *HRNews, PRNews,* and *Fortune,* and organizations such as the Society for Human Resource Management (SHRM). Among the honors it has received are the 2007 Global HRNews Corporate Citizenship Award, the 2008 PRNews Award, 2011 HVO's Golden Apple Award, and 2013 PRNews Award honorable mention in the Employee Volunteer Program category.

The program helps to develop the next generation of Pfizer leaders through hands-on exposure to global health challenges and patient populations in emerging markets. During assignments, Fellows use their professional medical and business expertise to promote greater access to health services while also honing their skills and improving their effectiveness in a range of areas, including communication and other competencies necessary for strong leadership.

Since 2003 when the program began, more than 300 Pfizer employees have served as Global Health Fellows working with more than 40 partner organizations in more than 40 countries. The assignments help strengthen the health systems in these countries by training health

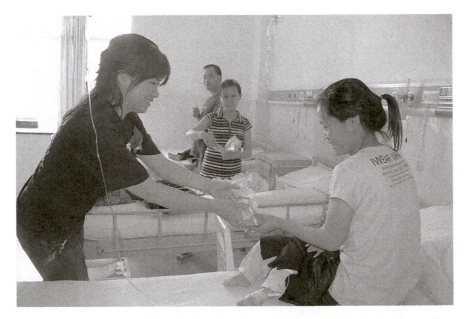

Photo 8.1 2012 Pfizer Global Health Fellow Connie Lieu working in a free children's clinic in rural China conducted by Project HOPE in partnership with a team of doctors and specialists from Shanghai Children's Medical Center. (© 2012 Oonagh Puglisi. Used with permission.)

workers, improving service delivery, and enhancing management of medicines, vaccines, and technology.

This chapter provides the how's and why's of the GHF program so it can be used as a model for other companies. After establishing the context from a global health perspective and exploring the program in depth, I present a case study of Michael Benigno, a 2012 Global Health Fellow, through his own eyes. I describe Benigno's experience working in Africa on a three-month assignment with the NGO IntraHealth International. The purpose of his assignment was twofold: to produce a guide for conducting cost-effectiveness analyses (CEA) for two interventions: the first was designed to prevent mother-to-child transmission of HIV-AIDS through the provision of mother support groups; and the second was to increase use of prenatal care through community support mechanisms. After offering this in-depth look at one Global Health Fellowship, I present the program from the view of one of Pfizer's NGO partners. Throughout, I highlight the ways in which the GHF program affects the participants, the partner NGO, Pfizer, and most important, the people in the local community whose lives are transformed—and potentially even saved—as a result of this program.

A Shift in Pfizer's Philanthropy

The GHF program (www.pfizer.com/ghf) started in 2003 as a way of addressing Pfizer's concerns regarding the HIV-AIDS crisis and the need to share Pfizer's employees' expertise through skill-based volunteerism. This represented a radical departure from the common approach to philanthropy and originated with Pfizer's then-CEO Hank McKinnell's visionary idea to fundamentally rethink the company's concept of philanthropy, which was largely focused on giving products and money.

Pfizer developed a framework through which the company would donate its people to select NGOs for specific periods of time to help them address global health challenges, such as HIV-AIDS. Because the new focus was on the people end of the business, Human Resources (HR) was brought on board to help design the process end to end.

Managing and Aligning Partnerships

Oonagh Puglisi, part of the Corporate Responsibility team at Pfizer, currently manages the design, development, and execution of the GHF program and works with many business functions across Pfizer, including HR, corporate communications, and security on its implementation. In addition to the GHF program, the Corporate Responsibility team is responsible for annual reporting, corporate social responsibility (CSR) re-porting, reputation polling, social investment, and taking a philanthropic approach to all assets. They direct financial, product, and HR to help align these assets with the company's core focus. They help ensure that Pfizer's social investments are aligned with the company priorities, so they simultaneously affect both the company's business and social objectives.

The Corporate Responsibility team works in partnership with a variety of NGOs, the U.S. Agency for International Development (USAID), associations, and health networks, many of which are also partners in the GHF program. The team conducts trend analyses to ensure there's a clear fit with the core needs of the nonprofits they serve. These collaborations not only involve partnering in the design and execution of the program itself, but also provide great opportunities for thought leadership in international health and extensive in-depth information exchange across the for-profit and nonprofit sectors. Pfizer selects partner organizations through an RFP ("request for proposal") process for a two-year partnership cycle.

Global Health Fellows Program Evolution

The GHF program has evolved in several distinct ways over the past five years (2008–2012). What began, in 2003, as an open-ended program in which the NGO partners chose the locations for the fellowship field assignments, has become a program that is keenly aligned with Pfizer's core expertise, overall strategy, business goals, and targeted emerging markets. Now Pfizer selects those countries and areas that are most aligned with key emerging markets, where there is a strong need for support, and where Pfizer can make a tangible impact. In addition, it has broadened its scope from assisting on single-issue projects to strengthening the overall health system in the countries in which it is working. Toward this end, it helps build the capacity of its NGO partners to scale up their programs so they can expand and deepen their impact. Examples include addressing supply chain issues and supporting health prevention programs (non-communicable diseases, oncology), and business-development functions.[2]

GHF had grown at one point to include 40 different NGO partners, but, as Pfizer refined the program, it narrowed this to 12 NGOs in 2011. Reducing the number of partners enabled GHF to develop deeper, long-term projects that would have a much larger impact. Choosing a smaller group of GHF partner organizations with two-year projects was a strategic planning exercise. Partners are chosen on the basis of a number of criteria. In addition, they must show the social and business

Photo 8.2   2009 Pfizer Global Health Fellow Arshia Ghani (far left) participates in a maternal health training session for expectant mothers in Saihara,
a village in rural Uttar Pradesh, India. Part of the Millennium Development
Goals, such antenatal care educates women with the hope of reducing maternal
and infant mortality. (© 2012 Oonagh Puglisi. Used with permission.)

impact their two-year project would have to their organization. Working with NGOs in an iterative manner, the Pfizer internal team reviews
and evaluates proposals through the lens of the company's core expertise and strategy.

Based on this strategic planning exercise, the program developed a
new strategic direction for the GHF, clustered around three core issues.
It then identified specific goals, metrics, and results to measure the return on investment (ROI) for each issue in tangible, quantifiable terms.
The three core issues are as follows:

- Supply chain issues
- Health-prevention programs related to Pfizer's core product lines
  (e.g., noncommunicable diseases)
- Health-systems strengthening

Regarding strengthening health systems, GHF began to include business development and entrepreneurial fellowships in which Fellows work to help NGOs build finance systems, accounting systems, and communications and marketing systems; craft sales and distribution strategies; and boost HR and organizational development.

In 2012, GHF committed to each of the 12 NGOs it had selected for a two-year period, offering 23 total fellowships. Three of those fellowships are focused exclusively on supply chain issues, and all are strategically located in Africa. The countries covered by the 23 Fellows are China, India, Tanzania, Kenya, Ethiopia, Uganda, and Rwanda.

Five Fellows are examining supply chains to identify gaps and needed training, quality-control problems, and other issues that affect access to health care. For example, one Fellow is examining Kenya's health ministry with respect to supply chain gaps that may require additional resources, training, or expertise. Others further down the supply chain are supporting quality control with pharmacists or a particular clinic setting.

In addition, as GHF has grown, a robust communications network has evolved comprising Fellows, alumni, NGO partners, and others. I will discuss the alumni component of this in the Michael Benigno case study.

Global Health Fellows Program Overview

The GHF program has several essential components:

- Pfizer, through a competitive process, selects NGO partner organizations to host fellowships over a two-year period.
- Pfizer and partners collaborate to develop fellowship plans and identify key intended results.
- Pfizer employees apply and interview with partner organizations. Pfizer covers salary, benefits, and costs of hosting the Fellows.
- Fellows report their key deliverables and progress back to Pfizer managers, and these are integrated into their annual performance reviews.

Benefits to Pfizer and Beyond

GHF provides several benefits to the company and to the world, most notably delivering a strong ROI and playing a role in developing leaders for the future.

Managing and Measuring Return on Investment

The GHF program ROI is measured in terms of both its business and social value. Specifically, each of the following three goals is measured by the following associated metrics:

- Goal: Develop and maintain trust and respect among critical international health stakeholders and communities.
  - Metric/Result: In 2011, 100 percent of GHF partners report fellowships assisted in accelerating sustainable change in health-care-delivery efforts.
- Goal: Build inside knowledge base on health-care delivery in key markets that could inform business-localization strategies.
  - Metric/Result: In 2011, 84 percent of GHF Pfizer managers believed the fellowships significantly enhanced employees' understanding of the global marketplace.
- Goal: Increase employee engagement and motivation to continue a path of excellence at Pfizer and in the health field.
  - Metric/Result: In 2011, 94 percent of Fellows agree that after their GHF experience, they are more motivated to perform at a higher level in their Pfizer job.
  - Metric/Result: In 2011, 94 percent of Fellows agree that this program is important in developing professional skills.

Leadership-Development Value

The GHF program represents a significant investment on the part of the company in leadership development; from the participants' perspective, the value is equally significant. For the company, the Fellows become ambassadors for Pfizer in locations around the globe. For the employee, GHF provides a developmental opportunity to gain field experience and grow professionally. It gives the Fellow a global perspective on the scope and scale of what Pfizer does, which she can then use to map out her next career moves within the company. It helps the Fellow approach her job with a new and expanded lens. The experience becomes an essential part of her development plan.

Global Health Fellows Program Process

The program is open to all Pfizer full-time employees. To apply, a Pfizer employee must have been with the company or any of its affiliates for at least three years and have received a meets expectations performance rating for each of the three previous years. An important requirement is that the candidate's manager support the application and sign off on it, being fully aware that the Fellow will be away for three to six months.

Application Process

The three-step (internal, Fellow alumni, and NGO partner reviews) online application process is very competitive. Candidates apply a year in advance of the fellowship. First the application goes through an internal review (Is the form complete? Does the applicant have manager support?). Program managers work with HR to ensure they are getting top candidates. In 2011, 100 out of 85,000 to 90,000 employees applied. But the company is not looking for large numbers; it is looking for the highest-quality employees. Normally there are about three applicants for every one position available, and the program is budgeted to fund and work with up to 25 Fellows per cohort per year.

After the internal review, the application goes through a review by GHF program alumni. Three or four alumni rate the application based on three key criteria:

- Motivation (Why does the candidate want to apply?)
- Goals (What does the candidate want to get out of participation and bring back to the company?)
- Skill set (What skills does the candidate have that qualifies her to work with an NGO?)

Most Fellows speak English. Some areas require that they also speak another language. For example, Fellows going to China should be fluent in Mandarin. For fellowships in India, it is helpful if the applicant speaks Hindu.

The alumni and internal reviews net the most suitable applicants, who are then presented to the NGO partners. Each NGO is given a choice of two or three candidates, whom they interview in a process much like a normal job interview. They look to see how the candidates fit into their organizational culture. The NGO partner has the final say, selecting the Fellow from the candidate pool of two or three.

Managers Need to Adapt and Support

The viability of a particular candidate's fellowship depends on his manager's support. This support starts with a conversation early in the application process, and if the candidate is selected, a plan must be put in place well in advance of the fellowship.

The way in which the manager organizes and offloads the Fellow's work during his absence is very important, and it requires building in the time to plan it carefully. How will the manager handle the person's absence for three months? How will he divide up and assign the Fellow's work to others during this period? How can the reassignment of the work provide opportunities for others to learn and grow? There is no one prescription because each scenario is unique. Managers are encouraged to find ways in which the team left behind can be incorporated into the experience and gain from the new work. How can they create situations in which everyone is a winner, and at the same time help ensure the absent Fellow's projects are completed?

Who Are the Fellows?

Overall, the program attracts candidates from middle management—usually at director and senior director levels—although Fellows have ranged from administrative personnel to vice presidents. The average age is mid-30s, and the average applicant has been at Pfizer seven years. Some Fellows have not previously been in the field or traveled a lot. Many Fellows have families. Some are single, married with grown children, and with and without any children. The Fellows are encouraged to go to the field locations on their own, without their families. They have no trips home during their fellowship. Ultimately life-stage timing is a key factor, as the fellowship has to take place at the right time in the Fellow's personal and professional life.

Preparing for the GHF Program

Once the Fellow is accepted into the GHF program, the company goes to great lengths to prepare him for the experience, beginning with an extensive orientation process comprising five distance-learning modules. These five modules give the Fellows information about (1) health and security, (2) their responsibilities as Fellows, (3) information technology, (4) cultural adaptation and sensitivity to time (especially encouraging them to be patient), and (5) communications. The last module covers internal communications, communicating in the field, and media. Each Fellow is provided a media contact for use if approached by media outlets in the field. In addition to the online modules, there are eight live web-based calls to review such topics as pro bono consulting, international development, business reviews of host countries, and review of protocols and policies relevant to the Fellow's assignment.

In addition, Pfizer's Alumni Business Network, through the Round Support committee, assigns each current Fellow an alumni "buddy" or two with whom he can share his thoughts and feelings before, during, and after the program.

In-Country Process

Pfizer works with the NGO to select the Fellow's accommodations and pays all program-related costs, so there is no additional cost to the NGO. The Fellows receive full salary and complete benefits (as if they were performing their regular jobs in their offices).

Each Fellow has an in-country manager, who is an employee of the NGO partner. The Fellow works with the NGO to map out the work and develop her list of deliverables and intended achievements.

This information is shared with the Fellow's manager at Pfizer, as is the feedback the Fellow receives from the NGO during and after her assignment. It is included in the Fellow's Pfizer performance review. Her work in-country is considered part of her professional talent development and is a percentage of her Pfizer performance management objectives for the year, with the percentage depending on the length of assignment. For example, a six-month assignment is 50 percent of the Fellow's Pfizer objectives. After returning from the assignment, the fellowship often provides great opportunities for the Fellow to take on additional responsibilities on her work team by, say, leading training sessions, doing public speaking, or leading the team.

Reentry

Although the experience is very inspiring for the Fellows, they often find it difficult to go back to their everyday desk jobs. By several accounts, the biggest surprise is the reverse culture shock, which is a huge challenge.[3] Fellow alumni are uniquely positioned to help returning Fellows cope with the reverse culture shock of reentry and advise them regarding using their in-country experiences to inform their work at Pfizer and continuing nonprofit work.

GHF program Manager Oonagh Puglisi was herself a Fellow. At Infectious Diseases Institute (IDI) in Kampala, Uganda, in 2009 she strengthened communication among IDI staff, patients, and partner clinics that supported overall IDI strategy. She "got a hands-on and birds-eye view of the work her NGO was doing," she said, which gave her a new approach to her Pfizer work responsibilities, increased vigor, and a desire to continue volunteering on her own. "Many Fellows return home after fellowship feeling that they have learned so much more from their colleagues and host country culture than they thought possible. They want to do more, so they keep volunteering and supporting their NGO team," she added.[4] Many continue to volunteer with NGOs long after they have returned from fellowship.

Although it's a challenge to talk about their experiences, Fellows want to, and Pfizer provides specific opportunities for this, giving returning Fellows a platform to reach business leaders. Back at Pfizer, Fellows first present to their own teams. Then they often become part of a speaker series through which they can talk about a topic such as their supply chain work or their work with their NGO partner.

Alumni Continue the Work

Over the past 10 years, since GHF's inception, the alumni have remained active. As we've seen, they participate in the selection of Fellows, help prepare them for their experiences in the field, and mentor them through all stages of fellowship, including their return to home country.

In 2011, the alumni decided to establish a formal platform and networking group through the GHF Alumni Business Network, which now has five standing committees that support the vision of the network as a recognized "think tank" group within Pfizer designed to share GHF insights and innovations through meaningful collaboration across the business.

Alumni, in coordination with the GHF program team, have spent the last year building this network's foundation, vision, and mission. Their projects include annual education and recruitment; publication of *Connected,* their quarterly newsletter; the leadership speaker series mentioned above; and the naming of site champions at various Pfizer locations. The champions become primary contacts for the GHF program at these sites; they are responsible for leading local events and answering questions from colleagues. They are working on increasing the visibility of the GHF program. The alumni incorporate these network activities into their Pfizer development plans to ensure their managers are supportive of this mentoring and development opportunity and to gain approval for the time needed to focus on these activities.

Results

Although GHF alumni retention is about the same as in the rest of the company, the program is seen as a retention advantage for Pfizer's best and brightest. "People come back inspired, motivated, and engaged; they are more proud to work at Pfizer than ever," said Puglisi.[5]

Puglisi emphasized that even while on assignment, Fellows are enhancing their value to Pfizer in many ways, including expanding their talents and gathering useful information. "[Working] five days a week," putting in extra time on the weekends, "taking on a lot, loving what they do, the Fellows bring back observations and give market and business intelligence that is valuable to Pfizer," she said.[6]

The Alumni Business Network uses this local information to organize and connect with Pfizer's business. For example, an alumnus visiting from Germany presented a highly valuable briefing document about what Pfizer employees need to know when they go to India, which was used by a vice president working in India.

Case Study: Global Health Fellow Michael Benigno

The Context: Preventing Mother-to-Child Transmission of HIV-AIDS

According to Mothers2Mothers and Pfizer, without any intervention, about 40 percent of children born to HIV-infected mothers will contract HIV. This equates to more than 400,000 new HIV infections worldwide each year. Interventions, such as those that Pfizer and its NGO partners support, can potentially reduce this to 5 percent.[7]

Benigno Decides to Apply to GHF

Michael Benigno had been with Pfizer seven years when he applied to the GHF program. He decided to apply because he wanted to use his research skills to improve access to health-care services for women and children in the developing world.

As a statistician and analyst, Benigno believes math can be used to solve very large complicated problems. His job entails using sophisticated statistical techniques to determine where medicines are being taken, what kinds of patients are taking them, and what kinds of doctors are prescribing them. He enjoys this, but wanted to work for a time on a hands-on project with actual human beings rather than on projects in which people are merely statistics.

Benigno's boss, Kirsten Axelsen, was a Global Health Fellow in 2006. Over the years she discussed the GHF program with Benigno and whetted his appetite. In 2011, he decided to apply. The application process was a lengthy one, and he spent many hours writing several essays about the impact he thought he could make through the GHF program. In particular, he explored and sought ways to apply his mathematical modeling and statistical skills to help relieve people's suffering and improve peoples' health outcomes in developing countries.

Perfect Fit

Benigno's current position as a director in Pfizer's Worldwide Policy division and his previous work in the company's management science and global market analytics group—together with his graduate studies at Columbia University—made him the perfect fit for a policy analytics position at IntraHealth International (www.IntraHealth.org). IntraHealth is a 30-year-old NGO that addresses global health challenges primarily in the developing world. It develops and implements innovative methodologies and programs for providing basic health care, strengthening service delivery, accessing resources, and conducting interventions for HIV-AIDS and other infectious diseases.

He wrote his master's thesis on how psychosocial stressors affect low-income women and children, in particular how certain psychosocial environments inhibit proper pre- and postnatal care.

In Ethiopia

Three months after discovering he had been accepted into the program, Benigno was deployed to Addis Ababa, the capital of Ethiopia, located on a plateau where it was temperate weather all year round. He lived in a 12-to-13-room guest house near his office. The NGO took care of making his living arrangements. The guest house was a bed and breakfast, located above an art gallery that displayed the work of local artists. He ate crepes and tea for breakfast. He walked to work. The people spoke the ancient "Amharic" language, but many people in the capital also spoke English because they learned it in schools. The area was very safe for Westerners and foreigners.

Program Goals

IntraHealth was very clear about what it needed: to determine the cost-effectiveness of its set of interventions for the prevention of mother-to-child transmission (PMTCT) of HIV-AIDS. In order to raise the funds

Photo 8.3   Michael Benigno (far right) with local IntraHealth staff at the Addis Health Center, Addis Ababa, Ethiopia. (© 2012 Oonagh Puglisi. Used with permission.)

necessary to continue this program, IntraHealth had to demonstrate that such programs make a difference.

IntraHealth had data on the PMTCT program going back several years. Determining its cost-effectiveness required performing sophisticated statistical analyses on epidemiologic and financial data and compiling demographic information gathered through interviews and visits to health centers.

"Pharma companies are very data rich," Benigno told me when I met him, "but need to turn that data into information."[8] His assignment provided him an opportunity to do just that.

The Assignment

As noted earlier, Michael's assignment was to create new methods and produce a guide for conducting CEA for two interventions: the first was designed to prevent mother-to-child transmission of HIV through support groups for the mothers and mothers-to-be; the second, to increase use of prenatal care and PMTCT services by creating a demand for them in the community at large.

The NGO held support groups for HIV-positive women at the local community's health center every week. When they first joined the groups, the women had very little knowledge about HIV. Fear permeated their culture, and the stigma attached to women who were HIV positive was so intense that women were afraid to seek treatment. So it was important for IntraHealth not only to identify HIV-positive women and get them on drug therapy, but also to (with the help of the World Health Organization [WHO]) educate them about their condition and address the psychosocial issues in their culture.

The key to the success of this latter part of the program was empowerment: dissipating participants' fear and showing them that they could live a full life with HIV-AIDS. This was accomplished partly by having the groups run by women who had gone through the program themselves. The examples of these leaders' success and strength showed participants that their lives need not end because their husbands had left them or they had been thrown out of their homes—situations in which such women found themselves too often in this region. It was risky to be open about an HIV-positive status.

The support groups also provided a safe place to transmit life-saving knowledge. Benigno told me that most of the participants didn't know that they could nurse safely or that if their children took *one* dose of *one* drug prophylactically, it would protect them from the virus. (The drugs used were all generic and Pfizer had no incentive or role in promoting any products.)

Benigno analyzed data from almost 1,300 HIV-positive women in Ethiopia, a subset of whom had participated in these support groups. To meet his goal, Benigno had to convince funders of the value of IntraHealth's work. This required standardized metrics that could easily be understood by a variety of audiences. In his search for such metrics, he discovered techniques that had been developed years before by the World Bank but had fallen out of use. He introduced the staff to new measures and ideas for assessing cost-effectiveness. He presented his results to the NGO, crafted a training regimen for use by the Ethiopian staff, and produced a guide for conducting CEA of IntraHealth's PMTCT programs.

Armed with this regimen and guide, the local staff can now conduct these analyses themselves.

Michael Makes a Difference

How much is a life worth? Through his analyses, Michael and the IntraHealth team showed that the rate of HIV infection was lower in the children of women who had gone through the PMCMT support group intervention and that the program was very cost-effective.

Communicating the findings to an international audience of public health professionals required speaking the standardized language of development economics. Programs are often evaluated on their ability to prevent a patient's living a single year with a disease. In technical terms, the goal of the program was to minimize the number of "disability adjusted life years," or DALYs, caused by HIV infection. This number is weighed against the financial cost of running the program, including staff time and logistics. Benigno determined that the cost of preventing a year lived with HIV through the use of the mother support groups was a mere $130—significantly below the threshold for cost-effective interventions in Ethiopia established by the World Bank and WHO (almost $1,000 per DALY averted). To the delight of IntraHealth, the PMTCT support program was extremely cost-effective.

The results of the study were presented in Africa at the December 2011 International Conference on AIDS and STIs (ICASA; www .icasa2011addis.org). Creating a presentable piece of external research had not been in the original scope of Benigno's work, and having the results accepted at an international conference was a welcome surprise for everyone. The NGO could now show that the cost-effectiveness of the program had been vetted by outside researchers.[9]

Benigno attributes much of the success of his GHF project to Patricia McLaughlin, at the time IntraHealth's country representative/ CPMTCT project director, a dynamic woman from Chicago who worked in Africa for 30 years. He described her as "assertive, capable, and effective, negotiating red tape and cultural difference to acquire the crucial data" that made his study possible.[10]

Benefits to Pfizer and Stakeholders

The GHF program helps build a culture for sustainability through employee engagement and leadership development. During my interview with Michael Benigno, it became clear that the program enhanced Benigno's leadership and management skills, making him a more effective leader. His participation in GHF rekindled his passion for serving people through the delivery of health-care services, which resulted in his becoming a more connected and engaged employee. "Through the GHF program," he said, "I was able to work on issues that affect people's access to health care, allowing me to keep a pulse on these issues. The challenge of making a difference in the health-care field is very fulfilling and motivating for me."[11]

Moreover, Benigno met GHF objectives that I have not yet mentioned. One of these is to "sharpen your skills"—both soft skills, such as communication, and technical skills, such as those he used in the statistical analysis work.

Benigno reported, for example, that he became a better and more culturally sensitive communicator. When he arrived in Ethiopia, he found it necessary to disabuse people of the notion that his being there had anything to do with the way they performed their jobs or with any deficiency on their part. Benigno quickly learned how to be very diplomatic and sensitive to the nuances of the culture.

Regarding technical skills, Michael learned new methods for conducting CEA that were applicable in an international setting. He aggregated these, developing a way of measuring ROI and quantifying benefits based on measurements and methods that could be understood globally.

Perspectives from the NGO: IntraHealth International

The WHO has identified a number of countries—including many in Africa—with critical shortages of health workers and access to health care. In this context, IntraHealth International, the NGO that hosted Michael's fellowship, is committed to empowering health workers to better serve communities in need around the world by improving health worker performance, strengthening health systems, harnessing technology, and leveraging partnerships to ensure that people have equitable access to high-quality health-care services. According to assistant director of Program Development, Karen Stegman, IntraHealth strengthens health workers and the systems that support them across the globe.[12] Headquartered in the United States, IntraHealth works in 30 countries with a staff of more than 600.

IntraHealth is a capacity-building organization that partners with local stakeholders, such as health-care providers and managers, trainers, and pre-service institutions. It has project offices staffed by local or regional employees and works within local government strategies and existing public health systems. Its approach is holistic; it takes into consideration the entire health-care system within a country, working to strengthen it and ensure that "local entities are well-positioned to sustain and build on the work without us," said Stegman.[13]

During our interview, Stegman spoke enthusiastically about Intra-Health's partnership with Pfizer and described myriad ways in which it is mutually rewarding.[14] Over the past seven years, the program has evolved shared goals and a shared understanding of what each organization has to offer.

Several factors contribute to its success. One is the accessibility of Pfizer's staff, said Stegman: "They seek out open communication and set clear expectations up front." Second, she noted a marked "emphasis on taking the program to the next level of rigor and focusing on results and sustainability." "The Pfizer team are true professionals who are really appreciated," she said.[15]

IntraHealth has had eight Global Health Fellows so far, including Michael Benigno. Although Stegman doesn't get to be with them in-country, she receives inspiration from the Fellows themselves. When Benigno returned from his fellowship, he gave a presentation at Intra-Health headquarters in Chapel Hill, North Carolina, that Stegman said "was highly impactful for everyone."[16]

During our interview Stegman said the key is picking the right person for the assignment—aligning the candidate's skills with the needs of the NGO—and that Pfizer does a very good job of selecting candidates for IntraHealth to choose among. IntraHealth appreciates that Pfizer offers two or three choices and gives the NGO the opportunity to conduct its own interviews, thus ensuring the right match. IntraHealth develops job descriptions that are in line with the key skill sets Pfizer's Fellows have to offer.

Attitude and mind-set is important, Stegman said, especially open-mindedness and respect: "You don't want the attitude of 'I know better' and 'I'm going to teach them' what they don't know . . . as this won't work." It is vital that the candidates demonstrate appreciation for the people they are working with and seek to learn from their counterparts. It is also critical, said Stegman, that "the local stakeholders are well-versed in the opportunities and challenges they are facing and are seeking collaboration and new approaches. The important thing for the Fellow is the ability to transfer their specific capacity or area of expertise to the local stakeholders."[17]

In sum, from the perspective of the NGO, in order to have a successful and sustainable partnership it is important to

- Be clear about the needs and expectations up front
- See yourself in the role of a facilitator rather than a doer

- Find a way to build metrics (they are extremely important; the challenge is they can also be expensive and tough to implement)

Global Health Fellows Program Challenges

GHF is meaningful and beneficial to the Fellows, the NGOs, Pfizer, and society at large, but like all growing programs, it faces a variety of challenges. I summarize the key challenges here:

- Right match: Ensuring the right match between a candidate's skills and mind-set, and the needs and goals of the NGO requires significant work up front. In particular, the Fellows need to be prepared to work independently and take initiative.
- Time frame: There is an inherent tension between a private sector company, its cycles and schedules, and urgent needs in the real world.
- Duration of the fellowship: Currently the fellowship lasts three to six months. Although Pfizer managers prefer the shorter, three-month duration, the NGOs would rather have the Fellow for six months to a year. A limited time in the field puts more pressure on the Fellow to hit the ground running and on the NGO to make sure the project assignment is achievable within the designated time frame.
- Availability of time and resources: To accomplish the goals of the Fellow's project, Pfizer managers, the candidate, and the NGO country staff need to invest the necessary time and other staff resources to ensure its success.
- Transition to the Fellow's assignment and back to Pfizer: The transition back seems particularly difficult for many Fellows, and as discussed earlier, can result in reverse culture shock.

Lessons Learned

For companies thinking about introducing a program modeled after, or similar to, the Pfizer GHF program, I summarize here some of the key lessons learned.

Establish the Value

- Focus on business value and make sure the program is closely aligned with your business. Make it more than a nice philanthropic thing to do. Position it as a business growth opportunity.

- Especially for pharmaceuticals, concentrate on building reputational capital in countries where the work takes place. Help the local people understand why the Fellow is in their country and appreciate the significant investment the company is making. Clearly communicate that the company is not there for drug research or development, but strictly for reputation enhancement and professional development.
- Give employees on the ground experience in emerging and growing markets, especially East Africa, India, and China. This international experience is invaluable for high-potential talent working in a global marketplace.
- Provide uniquely valuable learning experiences for the Fellows that strengthen their professional, technical, and communication skills. Give the Fellows an opportunity to apply their skills and contribute in tangible and important ways.

Manage the Partnership

- From the company's perspective, the process of selecting the right NGO partner is extremely important. Make sure to select partners who are able to effectively manage and host the Fellow. A strong partner equals a strong fellowship.

Garner Support Top-Down and Bottom-Up

- Executive and CEO visible—and behind-the-scenes—support is critical to launching such a program. Grassroots collegial support for the program and the Fellow is equally critical to ensuring successful implementation.

Conclusion

The Pfizer GHF program can become a model for other companies as they strive to build a culture for sustainability. It simultaneously enhances employee engagement, develops the emerging leaders' technical and soft skills, and helps demonstrate the company's enduring commitment to CSR.

CHAPTER 9

Sanofi: Putting the Patient First

Our whole focus is patient-centric. This is core to who we are and integrates CSR into everything we do.

—John Spinnato, 2012

What has inspired me most as I've come to know Sanofi and its people over the last 10 years is their extraordinary level of caring and humanity, manifested in the company's overriding commitment "to improve the health of all seven billion people on the planet."[1] Whether this translates into helping people in Africa with neglected tropical diseases (NTDs) such as sleeping sickness or Buruli ulcers; vaccinating 2 million children under age five who still die each year from preventable diseases; addressing the needs of the 63 million people with diabetes in India; training 15,000 midwives in 15 countries to reduce maternal mortality; developing and delivering orphan drugs for patients living with such rare diseases as Mayze; or tackling the proliferation of diseases resulting from climate change, Sanofi applies its vast expertise in chronic diseases to a wealth of situations around the world, helps others learn from its experience, and in general, is part of the solution. With humility, the company recognizes that it cannot accomplish such formidable goals by itself and recruits full participation of a vast array of stakeholders. Sanofi explicitly and intentionally develops strategic partnerships with international institutions, nongovernmental organizations (NGOs), health professionals, and patient organizations across the globe. The company understands that its substantial and ambitious commitments require an engaged, inspired, and talented workforce that is continually developed and reinvigorated. At the center of its universe is the patient, its true raison d'être.

Today, Sanofi is a global health-care leader with more than 110,000 employees in 100 countries throughout the world. It embodies the triple bottom line in 12 key corporate social responsibility (CSR) priorities, which are organized in four "pillars": Patient, People, Ethics, and Planet. The company's internal and external communications breathe life into a multitude of CSR initiatives for its employees, who become ambassadors for the company's many best practices, notably those providing wider access to medicines and sustaining a healthy planet for patients.

This chapter explores some of the diverse, innovative programs, strategies, and platforms through which Sanofi supports CSR and sustainability: Partners in Patient Health (a dedicated area of corporate affairs), wellness programs, local and national volunteerism and community outreach, diversity and inclusion strategies and platforms that include employee resource groups (ERGs), and supplier diversity and sustainability initiatives. I describe how Sanofi defines and creates a culture for sustainability and present best practices, including its approaches to workforce and leadership development, along with the challenges it faces and ways it is stepping up to those challenges. Based on interviews with a cross-section of leaders, managers, and employees from a variety of functions, I synthesize numerous lessons learned. I discuss a number of the key partnerships that Sanofi participates in, and frameworks and tools that Sanofi uses, so others who are not as far along can learn from them and incorporate similar approaches into their own journeys to sustainability.

Building a Culture for Sustainability

What Does a Culture for Sustainability Look Like?

For John Spinnato, vice president, North America Corporate Social Responsibility and president, Sanofi Foundation for North America, "The key to a culture for sustainability is full participation, to make everyone feel they are part of something greater and bigger and to have an impact on patient's lives, whether it be in a small way or a greater way." In an ideal state, Spinnato said, "for every major decision, and a lot of minor decisions, people need to stop and ask, 'What is the impact to the organization within our key pillars'?"[2] Spinnato told me that although the financial bottom line has always driven every corporation's decisions, Sanofi wants to develop a culture in which people stop and look at the impact on the environment and the impact on our social structure before making decisions. Aside from this being the right thing to do, he

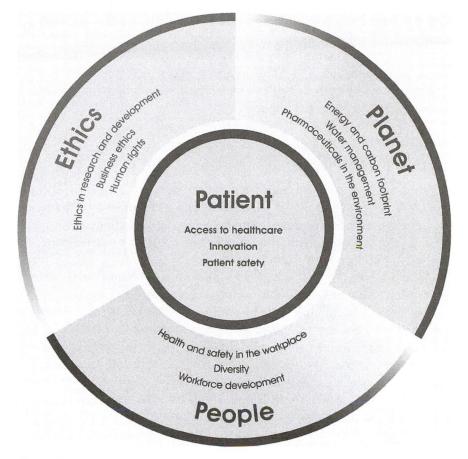

Figure 9.1   Sanofi's Four CSR Pillars and 12 Priorities. (© 2012 Flag. Used with permission.)

explained, if those decisions are not examined holistically, they could have tremendous negative ramifications for the image and reputation of the company. Looking forward, Sanofi seeks to ensure that every time a decision is made, the people making the decision "reflexively understand what CSR means and whether that decision has an impact on society at large and an impact on the environment, as well as on the bottom line."

Leadership and Vision

Several people I spoke with said that it was leadership and vision that drove this change. Although the patient has always been Sanofi's focus, the company's priorities shifted even more in that direction as its product portfolio declined. And it was "the patent cliff that caused everyone to stop and reflect on what are we going to do differently," said Peter

Loupos, senior director, advocacy, Partners in Patient Health.[3] The actual and impending loss of patents caused the leaders at Sanofi to ask and answer the question, Why does Sanofi really exist? Once the answer came clearly into focus"—"The company exists to serve the patient"— Sanofi began to reorient itself so that everything is done with the goal of improving the lives of the patient.

How to Get There

A Passion to Help People

So now undergirding all Sanofi's commitments is "a passion to help people." Patient centrality is manifested in a holistic view that encompasses the prevention of disease and an emphasis on wellness. "Research and development scientists truly want to find a cure for diseases, and not just push pills into the system," said Loupos.[4]

As a diversified health-care-solutions company, Sanofi strives every day to find innovative solutions to intractable problems, putting people at the center. For example, to address the exponential rise in the number of people living with diabetes in India, Sanofi introduced AllStar, an affordable and reusable insulin pen. Sanofi further demonstrated its commitment to staying close to the patient by manufacturing AllStar locally, in India, becoming the first global manufacturing company to manufacture such a device locally. In Israel, Sanofi introduced a novel solution by inserting Quick Response (QR) codes on some of its insulin products. These codes can be scanned using a smartphone to measure the patient's glucose levels. Customers can also scan the QR code to watch a video presentation on how to inject insulin.

Evolving from Environmentalism to Social Consciousness to Innovation

Sustainability at Sanofi began with a strong commitment to the environment, which was embodied in efforts such as those to properly manage the company's chemical waste and to reduce its power and energy, CO_2 and greenhouse gas (GHG) emissions, and water usage. Over time, the company started looking at the social aspects of sustainability, "helping mankind to live better healthier lives and reduce the cost of health care. We wanted to be a good local and global citizen and started donating vaccines in developing countries," said Loupos.[5]

The people I interviewed told me that the company never saw sustainability as a trade-off or a barrier because leaders at Sanofi quickly became aware of the ways in which sustainability could help the company be more efficient and thus actually save it money. Finding new drugs, treatments, and cures could drive up revenue and profitability. And as more revenue and profits become available, a virtuous cycle is created, allowing for greater R&D investments to create more innovative solutions.

Over the years, the culture evolved to be more socially conscious. When Sanofi was put on the Dow Jones Sustainability Index for the first time, the company did not view it as a CSR initiative. But over time, environmental sustainability and socially beneficial initiatives came together at Sanofi under the umbrella of CSR.

Providing Access to Medicines and Reducing Health-Care Costs

In his "Senior Management Interview" in Sanofi's 2012 Corporate Responsibility Report, CEO Christopher A. Viehbacher explains that the company "decided to focus on areas where we can make a real difference and have the most impact."[6] Chief among these is access to quality health care, given that approximately one-third of the world's population—more than 2 billion people—currently has no access to even the most essential care of this sort. Viehbacher attributes this to the following fundamental problems: "the lack of infrastructure, medical professionals to diagnose and treat, education and awareness of diseases, supply chain, transport/storage and of course, funding."[7] Later in the same report, the company states that "Sanofi believes that enabling individuals to assert their right to health means facilitating access to quality medicines and vaccines to benefit as many patients as possible, whether they live in developing, emerging or developed countries."[8]

The company views the role of the pharmaceutical industry largely as capacity building, which can be manifested in such efforts as long-term development aid programs, increasing awareness through education and campaigns, and providing the necessary training for health-care professionals. When limited by costs, companies can be still be directly involved by:

- Developing solutions that are better suited to patients' needs
- Adapting the company's commercial offerings to economic conditions
- Supporting the production of generic versions of its own products, including by manufacturing them
- Contributing to innovative strategies and programs that improve health outcomes beyond access to medicines, such as access to prevention, diagnosis and follow-up, especially when it comes to chronic diseases (e.g., cancer, diabetes, mental illnesses)[9]

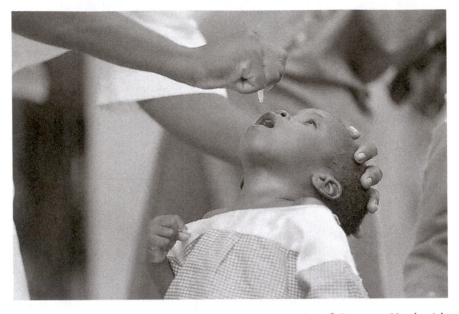

Photo 9.1   Polio vaccination in Africa. (© 2012 Sanofi Pasteur. Used with permission.)

Because Sanofi has the resources, experience, expertise, size, and geographical presence, it can and does go beyond merely donating medicines in an attempt to help address the underlying problems Viehbacher pinpointed earlier. For example, the company created a dedicated Access to Medicines Department to work with partners to analyze needs and then work together to find solutions. This department provides health care for "the neediest patients in resource-poor countries," including medicines for "malaria, tuberculosis, NTDs (sleeping sickness, leishmaniasis, Chagas disease, Buruli ulcer), epilepsy and mental disorders."[10] It takes a holistic approach that combines tiered pricing to make medicines affordable to everyone with information and education programs for all links in the health-care chain and research and development with a future focus.

Sanofi recognizes that current levels of health-care spending are not sustainable. It believes that through innovation pharmaceuticals can help reduce health-care costs, for example, by eliminating unnecessary hospital stays.

Fostering a Culture of Innovation

Sanofi's commitment to innovation is fueled by its recognition of demographic trends, the need for health-care reform, and an ever-increasing demand for new treatments for the world's growing and aging population. At the same time, a culture of innovation can help the company become more sustainable as continuous improvement of its manufacturing processes help it become more efficient and cost-effective internally. Its "open innovation" strategy, centered around business decentralization, enables its research and development organization to be more effective by "maximizing synergies and convergence around a hub model, leveraging economies of scale, and improving [its] R&D cost structure."[11]

Connecting with Employees in Every Function

The key to creating a culture for sustainability is reaching people in every function by explaining its connection to what they do every day. Whether in finance, internal security, information technology, research and development, manufacturing, human resources, or supply chain and procurement, a direct line can be drawn between the work employees do and sustainability. Each employee at Sanofi needs to have a clear line of sight and understanding of how her work affects the company's ultimate beneficiary—the patient.

Best Practices

Many of the best practices at Sanofi are inspired by two important questions: Where do we start? and What will benefit society the most? Furthermore, "it's not just about giving money, it's about building a partnership," said Sabrina Spitaletta, associate vice president, corporate social responsibility and social investments. "If we don't have a strong relationship and understanding of each other's strengths and areas for development, how would we know what to propose? . . . It needs the dialogue, so the thinking can evolve. There are all these different variables . . . if we keep doing it the same way, we're never going to get a better outcome."[12]

Partners in Patient Health

Three themes have emerged that exemplify Sanofi's commitment to making systemic improvements in patient health care. The first theme is encouraging patients to be actively engaged in their own health. The second theme is working closely with patients to safeguard their healthcare interests and defend their rights in times of significant change. The third theme is bringing all stakeholders together to collaboratively and synergistically drive innovative solutions to challenging health problems.

A great example of the latter took place in March 2012 when Sanofi brought multiple groups of executives together. For the first time, Sanofi and each organization had a chance to hear what each other was doing. The organizations included Faster Cures (a Milken Institute center), the Michael J. Fox Foundation, Multiple Myeloma Research Foundation, the Coalition against Major Diseases (CAMD; a part of C-Path, the Critical Path Institute), the Life Raft Group, and the Chordoma Foundation (discussed in The Story of Josh). Loupos described the event as an "incredibly enlightening experience" for both Sanofi employees and the other participants. New collaborative research opportunities organically emerged. The participants described this one-day event as "enlightening" and truly "inspirational," said Loupos, who quoted participants as saying, "I was reenergized" and "I will look at my job differently."[13]

The Story of Josh

I was particularly inspired by the story of a young man named Josh Sommer who took his health into his own hands by forming the Chordoma Foundation. When Sommer was 18, he was diagnosed with a rare cancerous skull-base tumor called a chordoma (this tumor can grow anywhere along the spine, starting at the base of the skull, where Josh's was). To help himself and others suffering from this rare tumor, Sommer simultaneously became a patient, an expert, and a scientist, studying chordoma at Duke University for two years. He created the foundation and originally worked with two federally funded research scientists. Sommer shared his cell lines with the researchers, and because of this, they were able to learn more about the disease than ever before. Sommer had the cell lines but didn't know how to get them tested, and the scientists had the mechanisms for testing them and using them to understand this genetic condition.

The foundation and the research it sponsors continue to explore these mysterious tumors, developing treatments, providing patients with principles for making decisions regarding their treatments, and more. Research into the genetic mutations present in these tumors—with the hope of pinpointing those that cause chordoma—continues. "All it took was getting everyone in the same room," said Loupos.[14]

Local Volunteerism and Community Outreach

Giving back to local communities and volunteerism is a priority in Sanofi's North American social investments initiatives.[15] Sanofi provides volunteerism opportunities for all employees and continues to expand these as the company evolves. Currently they involve all sites in North America and encompass all the company's businesses and functions. The global company, for example, has established Sanofi Volunteer week as an annual event in multiple regions of the world and extended it to an entire "season," October through December.

Ellyn Schindler, director, home state public affairs–Pennsylvania, Sanofi Pasteur U.S., proudly described a community fund-raiser she runs annually in Pennsylvania's Pocono Mountains through her Pennsylvania Sanofi facility (community.sanofipasteur.us), which conducts research and development and manufactures influenza, tetanus, and diphtheria vaccines.[16] The complex of Sanofi Pasteur locations in northeast Pennsylvania form the only comprehensive site in the United States for the Pasteur business in Sanofi.

The company pays all the event costs for the Pocono Mountains Community Fundraiser so that all the money raised through ticket sales and donations goes to the local charities. A steering committee reviews submissions from charities in or serving Monroe County and selects the winning charity, each of which receives between $25,000 and $55,000 on average.

In 2011, the awards went to Big Brothers, Big Sisters, and the Girl Scouts. The event at which they were announced was run, as it is every year, like an "Academy Awards of the Poconos," said Schindler.[17] Under a big tent, the head of the local chamber of commerce acts as master of ceremonies and presents an oversized check to the charity. Sanofi makes a donation to the winning recipients in addition to the amount collected directly through the fund-raising efforts. In 2011, the fund-raiser raised more than $1,455,000 for nonprofits in Monroe County and attracted more than 2,000 employees and several hundred contractors.

Schindler was enthusiastic about how much fun the event is for everyone. Executives get out on the dance floor, there is a lobster bake, and everyone mixes with everyone else. "The nonprofits receiving the money are overjoyed. . . . Everyone from the company has pride because they are really helping out the local community," she said.[18]

In addition to this extravaganza, Sanofi Pasteur holds local drives and volunteer events involving hundreds of employees throughout the year, every year—2012 was the seventeenth year it has conducted such drives—to build sustainable and close relationships with the community in which the employees live and work. It organizes an employee drive for Head Start children and their families. Around Thanksgiving, it brings food, gently used clothing, and snow boots to families and fills holiday wish lists.

Schindler summed up the impact of community volunteer efforts on the employees:

> If you could see the room filled to the brim with all sorts of gift-wrapped packages . . . People take such pride in the fact that they work here. It's great for employee morale. Anytime you have a group of employees who are coming together to work together and help others in need at the same time, gives you a sense of pride, creates a bond with you and your colleagues. It's a really special way of bringing everyone together.[19]

Schindler insisted that this pride translates into results for the company as well: "Employees appreciate how the company goes above and beyond in all these areas. [It] makes them want to go above and beyond in the life-saving work they do every day. We have employees who have worked here for 40-plus years. They have such a passion for the company's vision to be a good corporate citizen."[20]

Wellness Programs: Health in Action

Among its 12 CSR priorities, Sanofi focuses on three key priorities in the People pillar: health and safety, diversity, and workforce development. Regarding the first People priority—health and safety—Sanofi's Employee Wellness and Prevention strategic platform promotes a healthy lifestyle among employees. It provides resources and education that emphasize healthy nutrition, regular physical activity, and prevention management.

"You can't expect people to engage in their health if the culture doesn't support it," said Nuala Culleton, director, internal prevention and wellness, at Sanofi's corporate headquarters in Bridgewater, New Jersey.[21] In this newly created position, Culleton develops and implements a variety of initiatives to bring the entire organization to a new level of prevention and wellness based on lifestyle changes. She sees this as a three-to-seven-year process of behavior change, which must be embedded in and supported by the culture. Sanofi reported that, according to the World Economic Forum, such programs "can help prevent up to 40 percent of cardiovascular diseases, cancer, lung disorders, and other chronic diseases."[22]

Culleton started the process by creating a wellness committee, which developed a branded Health in Action prevention-and-wellness platform. Sanofi uses RedBrick Health in Minnesota (www.redbrickhealth.com)

Photo 9.2   The fitness center at Sanofi's headquarters in Paris, France. (© 2012 Daniel Rousselot/Interlinks Image. Used with permission.)

to provide its employee health-and-wellness programs and services. These include a free, completely confidential, online interactive health assessment and screening to help individuals understand their current health status. Once they complete the assessment, they receive a personalized "HealthMap" with a list of recommendations to improve their health. In addition, participants in the RedBrick programs gain points that can be redeemed for merchandise. They receive points each for completing the health assessment and screening and additional points for participating in healthy activities on a continuing basis.[23]

The follow-up programs include personalized support through phone coaching and online interactive resources. In RedBrick's phone-based condition-management programs, health coaches work "one-on-one with individuals who have been diagnosed with a condition or a disease or who have been identified as at risk to develop a condition." The coaches "provide outreach, education and support services to promote adherence to treatment guidelines, prevent exacerbations and optimize functional status."[24] The programs typically last between 6 and 12 months and cover such conditions and issues as asthma, blood pressure management, cholesterol management, chronic obstructive pulmonary disease (COPD), diabetes, heart disease, and heart failure.

RedBrick's phone-based lifestyle-management program coaches provide education and support services to enable employees to take charge of their own health. For example, the coaches help clients recover from injuries resulting in low-back pain, prevent further injuries, and avoid back pain by setting goals, developing muscle endurance, reviewing occupational workstation ergonomics, and teaching proper body mechanics and posture. Other phone-based lifestyle programs focus on the following:

- Healthy food choices that will improve an individual's nutrition
- Lifestyle changes that will support an individual's physical activity goals
- Stress management through learning about stress triggers and strategies for dealing with them
- Tobacco cessation
- Weight management
- Healthy pregnancy

Again, the programs typically last between 6 and 12 months, depending on the specifics of the individual's goals and current physical condition.

RedBrick's online health-and-wellness programs are self-directed so individuals can pace themselves as they make improvements in their well-being and health. These programs focus on chronic pain management, diabetes, healthy back, insomnia, living with a chronic condition, nutrition, stress management, tobacco cessation, weight management, and physical activity. A physical activity tracker called Boost allows individuals to measure the effects of every kind of activity they engage in.

Sanofi is committed to creating a culture throughout the company that incentivizes healthy lifestyles. Healthier Trails offers points for a 12-week program in which employees walk up to 600 miles. In many locations, the company provides walking trails, a fitness center, an on-site pharmacy and clinic, and other amenities to encourage employees to improve their health. Managers are encouraged to fully participate and lead by example. The company's benefits cover 90 percent of employees' in-network health-care costs. Flu shots, colonoscopies, and annual physicals are covered at 100 percent.

Sanofi's on-site diabetic coaching program is open to employees, adult dependents, and retirees. The program provides regular face-to-face visits with a certified diabetic coach, on-site physician visits, nutrition counseling, and incentives.

CSR Ambassador Program

The CSR Ambassador Program is a broad-based grass-roots approach, developed by Spitaletta, to excite employees about the value of CSR and engage them in CSR initiatives across the company. She partnered with Human Resources (HR) to make this available to employees and to present professional-development opportunities from a different perspective. Employees may be from any function; they must have a passion for the community, for learning more, and for sharing with their colleagues. The program is completely voluntary, and participant ambassadors work with their managers to make time for this role.

Each CSR ambassador attends monthly calls or webinars to learn from various CSR professionals throughout the company. When they are comfortable with the information, they share it with their teams and begin educating and enrolling employees in, for example, CSR, volunteerism, and health-and-wellness programs. The ambassador's role is one of education and awareness: first learn about it, and then share about it. If they need more technical background, they come to the CSR department to learn more. When I asked Spitaletta why she thought this would work, she explained that an informed "peer-to-peer approach is a powerful way to spread a message and to inform employees."

As of summer 2013, the company had 70 CSR ambassadors from a variety of functions and levels. The program continues to expand.

Diversity and Inclusion

As a global health-care company, operating in a world that is "characterized by broad diversity, which is reflected in the highly diverse needs of patients and consumers," Sanofi "embraces diversity as an opportunity."[25] Its importance to the company is shown by its placement as the second priority in the People pillar in the company's 12 CSR priorities. The company works proactively to promote diversity throughout its businesses, patients, suppliers, and employees.

Because the phrase has different connotations to different cultures, Sanofi customizes its approach to diversity and inclusion to the various countries and localities in which it operates, while maintaining a global policy of embracing diversity in its broadest sense. In 2012, Sanofi locations across the world participated in International Women's Day. Also that year in France, where Sanofi's world headquarters is based, the HR employees took diversity and nondiscrimination e-training, including training about people with disabilities. In the United States, all employees participate in a Diversity and Inclusion Awareness e-learning program. A separate, targeted training is required of managers. In 2011 affiliates in 18 countries arranged to offer diversity training for more than 2,189 Sanofi employees.[26]

Diversity plays a major role in providing the close focus Sanofi's people need to tackle complex problems. An example is in the company's fight against the increasing prevalence of diabetes in specific racial and ethnic groups. Lara Jones, head of U.S. Diversity and Inclusion, told me that the numbers of Hispanics and Blacks, or African Americans, with diabetes are growing. Changing the trajectory of these numbers and ameliorating the disease's effects on patients demands an understanding of these groups' cultures and languages.

Jones told me that the company strongly believes that diversity in the workforce creates more innovation and is better for business and that Sanofi is highly committed to acting on these beliefs to change people's mind-sets. "If we don't think about our people processes from a diversity and inclusion mind-set, including recruiting, talent development, succession planning, and performance management, and view those processes through a diversity lens, we're missing something," said Jones.[27] She pointed out that gender differences are especially important, given that women are much more likely to be caretakers and 80 percent of health-care decisions are made by women.

When it comes to diversity of thought, Jones emphasized the concept of inclusion, whether it is for people with disabilities, veterans, or others who may be too often forgotten. To promote diversity and inclusion throughout its employee base, Sanofi supports a "mosaic" of ERGs: Women Inspiring Sanofi Excellence (WISE); ADVANCE (Alliance for Diversification, Inclusion, and Engagement), which focuses its efforts in support of African American, Latin American, Asian American, and LGBT (lesbian, gay, bisexual, and transgender) employees; ParentsConnect for working parents who want to address work–family issues, and VETS, which supports veterans transitioning out of active duty and engages Sanofi members of the military and those who are passionate about veterans causes. The groups focus on community and business issues and their members' personal and professional development. For example, groups explore how different communities respond to health issues affecting them. They can then provide insights into marketing approaches that bridge formal marketing practices and tap into employees participating in the ERGs.

Jones told me that the WISE group was so successful that it won the Healthcare Businesswomen's Association (HBA) ACE Award in 2010. The ACE award is presented each year to one company's women's leadership program and stands for *Advancement, Commitment,* and *Engagement* of women in the health-care industry (www.hbanet.org). In October 2011, Sanofi sponsored the Women's Forum Global Meeting, in Deauville, France (www.womens-forum.com/meetings/detail/global-meeting-2011) where its WISE Mentoring Program was featured as a best practice. Jones told me the WISE session at the Forum was very well attended, and generated considerable excitement among the attendees.[28]

When I met with Jones, Sanofi was in the process of forming a diversity and inclusion council, co-chaired by the senior vice president for the company's Global Services Division, who is also the executive champion and sponsor. The council will comprise representatives from across the business, and ERGs will report to it. Jones considered this a major step forward in embedding the diversity and inclusion strategy throughout the business.

Supplier Diversity and Sustainability

Through its supplier diversity initiatives, Sanofi brings its diversity perspective to a critical set of its stakeholders. Specifically, the company is committed to opening up opportunities for small businesses and minority-, woman-, veteran- and service-disabled veteran–owned businesses. Sanofi believes that this initiative can play a central role in developing and nurturing relationships in the communities it serves, thus being mutually profitable and beneficial.

Head of Supplier Diversity and Sustainability Kathleen Castore described the value to the business of its supplier diversity initiatives: "[They] promote innovation and an entrepreneurial spirit which will add to the value of our own business. . . . We need suppliers to be sustainable [if they are] to be innovative. Diverse suppliers bring diverse ideas to move the needle in driving cost savings, reducing cycle time, coming up with the next big idea. It's going to be a game changer."[29]

Castore said that supplier diversity and sustainability at Sanofi are much more than compliance-driven initiatives, because they are "important to our patients; to our suppliers, who are our patients; to our customers, who are our patients—and all these constituents are just as diverse as the workforce diversity initiatives. They all have to be interconnected."[30]

I was impressed with Castore's passionate commitment to supplier diversity, which she summed up in her favorite quote from Albert Einstein, "Strive to be of value rather than a success." Castore is particularly proud of Sanofi's supplier mentor program—a program the company considers a best practice—in which people from Sanofi's corporate office volunteer to mentor minority, women, and other entrepreneurs. The mentor program is a structured, formal process with meetings and training sessions spanning one year to 18 months. Among the resources used in the program, said Castore, Diversity Alliance for Science (www.diver sityallianceforscience.com) is particularly valuable.

After running two consecutive cycles and personally mentoring three mentees' and their businesses, Castore considers the program a tremendous success for both the mentee and Sanofi and values the people she's worked with and met through the initiative: "Supplier diversity is a wonderful community to work with. People are very generous with their time, knowledge, and their background. The mentor learns just as much as the mentee. People are happy to help other people. When you ask people, they feel good about themselves."[31]

When I asked how the supplier diversity mentoring program helps build a culture for sustainability, Castore said that she works collaboratively with the suppliers to help them develop a sustainable business from every perspective, including the triple bottom line. "Our helping would-be suppliers be better helps our entire supply chain. We help them be more agile, provide better leadership, be more innovative, lower their costs, and reduce their overhead. Just like you have to invest in your employees, you have to invest in your suppliers," she said.[32]

Moving forward, Castore believes supplier diversity is an important area for investment. "It's not going away," she said, "and is only going to be getting more and more relevant to each and every corporation. Just like what happened with green. You don't have to know what it means to the nth degree, it's really about awareness and then about making a commitment to actions."[33]

Workforce Development

Workforce development is the third CSR priority under the People pillar. Sanofi has introduced a personalized training and development approach to maximize the contributions of its talent. Under this approach, each employee meets with her manager to identify needs and goals for her professional development. They formulate an action plan with a prioritized list of core and technical competencies to be honed, possible new assignments, additional training, and an associated timetable. The intention is to match specific local and regional needs as closely as possible and support Sanofi's increasing emphasis on consumer health care and emerging markets in particular.

Sanofi provides specialized pharmaceutical training at each of its industrial and R&D sites so that employees can keep up with new developments in the field and learn about regulatory requirements that may affect their jobs.

In addition to providing skills specific to the pharmaceutical sector, Sanofi has developed "support function academies" to provide training for support functions, including legal, health, safety, environment (HSE), communications, human resources, finance, and procurement. This training is designed to enable employees to develop new approaches to their work, with a major emphasis on learning how to forge better business relationships.

Leadership Development

To build a sustainable leadership bench, Sanofi promotes global talent development and offers several opportunities for international job rotation, which are coordinated at the corporate level. SEED (Sanofi Early Executive Development) is targeted at individuals who have at least five years of professional experience and graduated from leading colleges and universities. Over a two-year period, SEED participants rotate through four assignments in different countries and receive support from high-level mentors.

SWAP (Short Term Work Assignment) is designed to help Sanofi employees with less experience prepare themselves for the next step in their management careers. SWAP involves job rotations between emerging and mature markets, with each rotation lasting six months.

V.I.E., an international corporate volunteer program, is open to participants from the European Union and is sponsored by the French government in collaboration with schools and universities. Through V.I.E., Sanofi and Sanofi Pasteur offer students 12-to-24-month assignments abroad with their affiliates all over the world. In addition, they hire 15 to 20 people a year who have taken part in V.I.E. Sanofi is the largest V.I.E. recruiter in the health-care industry and uses this program as a significant source of new hires.

Environmental Defense Fund Climate Corps Fellowship Program

Sanofi's Genzyme business, discussed in detail later, partners with the Environmental Defense Fund (EDF) to provide a fellowship (edfcli matecorps.org/hire-fellow) for a student from one of the top business schools to work for 10 to 12 weeks over the summer on energy and GHG programs. These best and brightest students come to a Genzyme facility to make an impact with an emphasis on energy and sustainability. Jeff Holmes, principal engineer, environmental affairs, at Genzyme Corp. told me that he is extremely proud to be part of this program.[34]

Sustaining a Healthy Planet for Patients

Sanofi is committed to sustaining a healthy planet for patients. It reports that "thirteen million deaths can be prevented every year by safeguarding our environment."[35] Referring to the planet as "our shared home," Sanofi has established ambitious goals—based on its operations—to reduce its environmental impact, thereby protecting public health. The company has identified three overriding CSR priorities in its Planet pillar: water management, pharmaceuticals in the environment (PIE), and energy and carbon footprint.[36]

First and most important, Sanofi is concerned about climate change, because its effects on clean air, potable water, and food and shelter sufficiency affect people's health. Millions of otherwise avoidable deaths may be caused by climate-sensitive conditions. To illustrate, Sanofi reports that 2.2 million deaths per year result from climate-related gastrointestinal diseases. Three and a half million deaths are caused by malnutrition and 900,000 from malaria and dengue.[37] Sanofi believes that millions of these lives can be saved by decreasing GHG emissions, and more deaths can be averted by preventing such diseases from making incursions into new areas of the world.

Sanofi works to minimize its negative impact on climate change by shrinking its carbon footprint through reductions in its consumption of energy and in its GHG emissions. For example, in North America, Sanofi lowered its energy consumption and thereby decreased its direct and indirect CO_2 emissions by 7.6 and 19 percent, respectively, from 2010 to 2011. This was accomplished with lighting upgrades, use of renewable energy, van/carpooling, telecommuting, reduced HVAC, and repairs on air leaks.[38]

Genzyme

Founded as a biotechnology company in 1981, Genzyme Corp. (www .Genzyme.com) is known for having pioneered the development of treatments for very rare genetic diseases with patient populations numbering in the hundreds or thousands. Today, Genzyme continues its work on behalf of patients with rare diseases, and has expanded its focus into multiple sclerosis as well.

Green Buildings

When I interviewed Holmes by telephone from Genzyme's corporate headquarters in Cambridge, Massachusetts, he told me about the company's strong commitment to green buildings.[39] All new construction since 2005 at the Allston and Cambridge, Massachusetts, sites have received LEED (Leadership in Energy and Environmental Design) certification, and by summer 2012, Holmes reported, they had 13 certified build-

Photo 9.3   The Genzyme Corp. headquarters building, in Cambridge, Massachusetts, is certified LEED Platinum. (© 2013 Genzyme. Used with permission.)

ings, including two Platinum and several Gold and Silver. Stefan Behnisch, an architect from Stuttgart, Germany, who is known for his large imaginative projects—ranging from museums and spas to corporate headquarters—and his creative applications of sustainability principles, consulted with the leaders at Genzyme while designing the company's corporate headquarters (behnisch.com/projects/104). The Genzyme Center was one of the first LEED Platinum buildings and was voted one of the most important LEED buildings in the world by *Architectural Digest*. Holmes told me that he is most proud of the fact that Genzyme didn't make the overall decision just to get LEED certification or to go "point shopping" but has always made decisions in the best interest of each building and the communities in which Genzyme operates.

Genzyme installed a combined heat and power system at its Allston plant in 2011, saving $1.5 million per year in energy costs and reducing GHG emissions by 1,600 tons of CO_2. This produced Alternative

Portfolio Standard (APS)—a Massachusetts government standard—revenue valued at up to $200,000 per year.[40]

Sticker Program

Genzyme sites run a sticker program in which people put red (do not shut off), yellow (check with operator), and green (turn off when not in use) stickers on pieces of equipment. This results in dollar and carbon savings, is simple and inexpensive to institute, and engages employees.

Energy Sustainability Program

Holmes also told me about Genzyme's successful Energy Sustainability program to reduce energy consumption: a cross-functional team of representatives from procurement, engineering, and environmental groups collaborate to examine energy supply and demand and then develop ways to reduce energy demand and GHG emissions. He explained that the composition of the program provides an excellent basis for determining effective energy reduction policies because everyone comes with a different motivation: some people are interested in saving money, some efficiency, some reducing impact on climate. He reported that more than $2 million has been saved by energy-efficiency projects suggested by this group. Of Genzyme's global electricity use, 24 percent now comes from renewable sources, and it has reduced its carbon footprint by 40,000 metric tons.[41]

Preserving Water and Its Sources

Water scarcity is a key challenge and concern at Sanofi. The company notes that "available fresh water constitutes only about 1 percent of the water on the planet" and that "competing demands could lead to an estimated 40 percent global water supply shortage by 2030."[42] Because the company needs water to function—in its production processes, cooling systems used during manufacturing, fermentation, vaccine manufacturing, and cleaning processes—preserving it is a strategic imperative. Beyond that, as a global health-care provider, Sanofi is acutely aware of the importance of safe drinking water for the health of people around the world and is "committed to responsibly manage this vital resource in the interest of future generations and their continued access to water for years to come."[43]

In this context, Sanofi's policies are designed to create sustainable water-management systems and processes to preserve surface water availability and to curtail subsoil and groundwater contamination. To accomplish this, the company is improving discharge treatment systems and implementing quality controls for effluents. Several tools it uses are described later in this chapter under Frameworks, Tools, and Resources.

Sanofi's Merial headquarters site in Georgia instituted GreenSite, a program to reduce its water consumption. Some of the actions taken include a shift from standard landscaping to zeroscaping, doing preventative maintenance on interior plumbing, and training employees in ways to conserve water. The site has reduced its consumption by approximately 2 million gallons per year and decreased its water costs by 10 percent, despite a 300 percent rate increase by its water supplier.[44]

Challenges, Trade-Offs, and Conundrums

Here I summarize four significant challenges I gleaned from my interviews with company representatives and the ways in which Sanofi is addressing each. Two of the challenges are primarily due to external factors including Sanofi's being a global company operating in the United States: undervaluing of innovation in the United States and distrust about the clinical trial process. The other two challenges are primarily internal: too much to do in too little time and embedding CSR throughout the culture.

Undervaluing Innovation in the United States

Loupos described the undervaluing of innovation in the United States as a primary challenge faced by the company. He said that the United States is losing ground because it doesn't place enough priority on innovation. Contributing to this, he believes, is a lack of leadership that stresses the importance of innovation and legislative and educational factors. "People need to become more educated and support an environment where innovation can flourish," said Loupos.[45] To address these challenges, he cited Sanofi's efforts to support STEM and local community initiatives. In particular, he emphasized the value of providing resources including funding for science and young innovators.

Inherent Distrust about the Clinical Trial Process

As blockbuster drugs such as Ambien and Plavix go off patent, pharmaceutical companies face challenges to either replace them or find new ways to recoup the lost revenue. At the same time, pharmaceutical companies are confronted with a high degree of distrust regarding the clinical trial process, which is essential to maintaining their financial sustainability. And moreover, it is extremely costly for pharmaceutical companies to recruit and maintain people in their clinical trials.

Loupos provided an insightful analysis of this challenge and a recommendation for addressing it. Through increased patient presence, bringing them into the process of initiating new programs, the company is able to do better research and development and provide greater insights to scientists. "By bringing the patient voice into the clinical development process, researchers are better able to reflect the realities of what patients are living with," said Loupos.[46]

Reframing the Debate

Loupos explained that the life expectancy of a new compound—from the time it is created until it loses its patent—is typically only 15 years. Furthermore, the vast majority of the costs of pharmaceuticals stem from the research and development that goes into their creation, including the clinical trials mentioned earlier; the manufacturing of the drugs themselves represents only about 10 percent of the cost of the medication.

Given that the actual cost to bring a drug to market is typically over $1 billion, Loupos suggested that shifting the health-care debate from the cost of success toward an analysis of cost avoidance (i.e., how to reduce the cost of failure) would be a constructive step forward. Although the risk of failure will continue to be high, this might feed innovation and thus benefit everyone. "We're helping the patient, helping the family and caregivers, reducing health-care costs, improving quality of life and the environment and doing it in a more efficient way. If we're doing all this properly, everybody benefits all the way around," said Loupos.[47]

As I reflected on Loupos's comments, I began to think about the possibility of incorporating the precautionary principle into the drug-development process, identifying leading indicators and lagging indicators. This could potentially reduce the cost of failure by curtailing clinical trials and drug development earlier in the process, in those instances in which it becomes clear that either the chance of success is minimal or the risks associated with the drug are greater than current thresholds would allow.

Too Much to Do—Too Little Time

Given the drive toward financial sustainability and greater efficiency combined with constant pressure on costs, it is not surprising that almost everyone I spoke with at Sanofi talked about how constrained time and human capital were limiting everything they wanted to do. "The more resources I have available to me, the more we can move the dime," said Castore.[48]

Spitaletta spoke about the need to use resources more efficiently to allow employees to focus more externally when needed. Key here is the ability to constantly reflect and reevaluate priorities with the flexibility to navigate through constant changes and the agility to embrace change easily and quickly. "It's an evolutionary process. We want to change, but the barrier is perceiving obstacles and change as a negative. We need to learn how to reevaluate change and embrace change in a positive way," said Spitaletta.[49]

Embedding CSR throughout the Culture

Several people I interviewed spoke about the continuing cultural challenge of embedding CSR and sustainability throughout the company. One way Sanofi is making headway on this is by having passionate employee champions present at vice president and other leaders' staff meetings outside their own functions. This helps to ensure that the message is flowing across, up, and down, throughout the entire organization.

Lessons Learned

I invited each person I interviewed at Sanofi to reflect on his or her experiences working in CSR and building a culture of sustainability at Sanofi. I also invited each to share any lessons learned that may be helpful to others. Below I crystallize some of these lessons learned:

- Provide a solid foundation through a clear platform and align it strategically to your business. In the case of Sanofi, this is its four pillars: Patient, People, Ethics, and Planet.
- Look inside to see what you're already doing to communicate that you're on the journey to sustainability.
- Build awareness by helping people understand CSR in the context of their own mind-set and what it means to them personally to act in a sustainable way.
- Coordinate and bring your efforts together in an integrated approach.
- Garner leadership support at the top.
- Create a governing body to visibly highlight CSR-related issues.
- Develop and implement an education process for all employees. This is critical.

- Stick with it and don't give up. Persevere while believing that things can change and you can make a difference.
- Encourage diversity in your supply chain.
- Be aware that you can get a lot more traction through CSR than HR, because CSR speaks to people's hearts.
- Start small.
- Create a win-win for company and employee.
- Help employees take pride in the company. They are your best champions.
- Spread the message through peer-to-peer communications, the most powerful way to create buy-in across your entire organization.
- Don't just tell employees about CSR and what you're doing; find ways to help them experience it and feel personally involved.
- Share what didn't work; this is just as important as what did.
- Realize that change is an evolutionary process.
- Build strong bridges to the patient community. Try bringing patients into the conversations through social media platforms. This will help bridge the gap "from bench to bedside."
- Find areas of common interest and common concern across your employee base.
- Start locally.
- Help guide others with a "pay it forward mind-set" so everyone can grow together.
- Equip people with data and metrics to make the story credible.

Frameworks, Tools, and Resources

Sanofi's Four-Pillar Framework

As discussed throughout this chapter, Sanofi's four-pillar framework is the centerpiece and foundation for all its CSR strategic initiatives.

LEED Framework

As discussed earlier, Sanofi uses the LEED framework for its green buildings (www.usgbc.org/leed).

External Participation: Indexes

Sanofi participates in a wide array of CSR and sustainability projects and indexes. Among the indexes are

- The Dow Jones Sustainability Index (DJSI; www.sustainability-index .com). Sanofi was listed for the sixth consecutive year in 2012.
- FTSE4Good (www.ftse.com/Indices/FTSE4Good_Index_Series/ index.jsp)
- Ethibel Sustainability Excellence (forumethibel.org/).
- Vigeo Europe 120 and Vigeo France 20 indexes (www.vigeo.com); launched in 2012 with Sanofi on both.
- Access to Medicine Index; Sanofi is one of the top three companies listed on this index (www.accesstomedicineindex.org).
- Carbon Disclosure Project (CDP; www.cdp.org) is discussed in greater detail later. Sanofi reached a 93B score (93/100) for disclosure and B (on A–E scale) for performance in 2012.

External Participation: Memberships

Sanofi is an active member in the following organizations committed to fostering sustainability, CSR, and human rights:

- UN Global Compact (UNGC; www.unglobalcompact.org); Sanofi has been a member of UNGC since 2003.
- Business for Social Responsibility (www.bsr.org).
- The Institute for Sustainable Enterprise, Silberman College of Business, Fairleigh Dickinson University (www.fdu.edu/ise).
- The Center for Corporate Citizenship, Boston College (www.bcccc .net).

Furthermore, Sanofi's approach to human rights is in compliance with the "Guiding Principles on Business and Human Rights" endorsed by the United Nations in 2011. Each year the company issues "Communication on Progress," a report to the UN Secretary-General outlining its progress on human rights, labor rights, environmental protection, and fighting corruption. The document is signed by CEO Christopher A. Viehbacher.

Standards and Tools

Environmental-Management Systems: ISO 14001

ISO 14001 is an international environmental-management-system standard for managing environmental compliance, pollution, prevention, and continual improvement systems regarding site-specific issues. In our interview, Holmes explained that Genzyme instituted ISO 14001, which he highly recommends, so that all its manufacturing sites would conform to the same high standards. He said, "The system provides uniformity and consistency, forces you to look beyond compliance, beyond the scope of your buildings, and continually improve" and went on to explain that the system is not prescriptive; it is up to each site to decide how to use the information in a way that best fits it.[50] Holmes told me that although all European sites are certified using ISO 14001, the standard's use is not widespread in the United States.

Carbon Disclosure Project

As noted earlier, Sanofi participates in the CDP which primarily serves the investment community. For each company participating in the project, the CDP looks at emissions management, governance and carbon strategy, and risks and opportunities for carbon reduction and stakeholder engagement. Each company receives a disclosure score based on its level of transparency; companies are not ranked based on absolute emissions.

Scope 3 Emissions Inventory

Genzyme's Holmes told me about the company's commitment to reducing scope 3 emissions. According to the Greenhouse Gas Protocol, scope 3 emissions are "all indirect emissions (not included in scope 2) that occur in the value chain of the reporting company, including both upstream and downstream emissions."[51] Holmes described these as "huge." And Genzyme is one of the few pilot sites in the United States involved in the development of an inventory to identify scope 3 emissions and target areas for improvement.

Global Water Tool

Sanofi uses the World Business Council for Sustainable Development's (WBCSF) Global Water Tool[52] to identify its sites that are in water-scarce locations and then develop site-specific action plans. The company found that 42 percent of its sites are in areas of water scarcity or water stress and that these sites accounted for 65 percent of the company's total water consumption. As a result of its dedicated efforts to formulate and implement such action plans, the company successfully reduced its overall water consumption 25 percent between 2005 and 2011. Further, Sanofi reduced water consumption by its factories located in areas of water scarcity or water stress by 26 percent from 2010 to 2012.[53]

Conclusion

My hope is that Sanofi's holistic, strategic, and comprehensive approach to CSR and sustainability inspires others to move in a similar direction. I especially appreciate that the company puts the patient at the center of everything it does and is committed to engaging the hearts and minds of its 110,000 employees in addressing the greatest health and planetary challenges of our time.

CHAPTER 10

Wyndham Worldwide: Wyndham Green—One Goal. One Team. One Earth.

Doing the right thing is always right. Doing the wrong thing is never right.

—Eric Danziger, 2012

As a frequent traveler for more than 30 years—both in the United States and around the world—I have become increasingly sensitized to the variety of ways in which a hotel can exemplify its commitment to sustainability. For example, when I visited Australia to speak at the Tenth National Business Leaders Forum on Sustainable Development, in 2009, I noticed that all the bathrooms in that country had dual-flush toilets, which conserve water by providing two flushing options, one using less and one using more water. On the same trip, when I inadvertently left the faucet running too long in a public bathroom, a woman I was standing next to severely admonished me. But it was not until 2012, while researching Wyndham Worldwide (WW) and interviewing its leadership that I fully understood the magnitude, impact, and reach that a hospitality company that is truly committed to holistic sustainability can have on its franchisees, customers, suppliers, employees, shareholders, local communities, and ultimately on the sustainability of the planet itself.

WW's hospitality companies—with more than 100,000 locations in nearly 100 countries—employ 32,500 people in the United States and globally. The company is widely recognized as one of the most sustainable and greenest big companies in the United States. WW received *Newsweek*'s Green Ranking as one of the Top 100 Greenest Companies in America in 2011 and 2012, coming in first place in the hotel and restaurant sector, and it was one of the 2011 Carbon Disclosure Project's S&P 500 Carbon Leaders. At WW, corporate social responsibility (CSR) and sustainability are a way of working that embodies its vision, expresses its values, celebrates its diversity, and supports work–life balance. Understanding that its business activities affect the earth and its resources, the company is committed to developing environmental best practices in the areas of programs, products, and services, and it constantly updates and expands its tracking and measurement of key environmental, social, and governance metrics.

The company works actively to engage its employees, suppliers, owners, and local communities in minimizing their environmental impact, reducing energy consumption, tracking performance, lowering water use, decreasing waste, implementing sustainable procurement practices, and participating in local community environmental activities.

Wyndham Hotel Group (WHG) "is the world's largest and most diverse hotel company, with 7,340 hotels worldwide, featuring iconic brands and hotel choices in every category from upscale to economy," according to Faith Taylor, senior vice president, sustainability and innovation.[1] "Wyndham Exchange & Rentals is the world's largest member-based vacation exchange network with 3.7 million members and 4,000 affiliated resorts in more than 100 countries" and is "the world's largest professionally managed vacation rentals business with more than 100,000 properties in approximately 100 unique destinations worldwide," she added. Further, Wyndham Vacation Ownership (WVO) "is the world's largest vacation ownership business, as measured by the number of vacation ownership resorts, individual vacation ownership units, and owners of vacation ownership interests." This business "develops, markets, and sells vacation ownership interests and provides consumer financing to owners through its four primary consumer brands, Club Wyndham, WorldMark by Wyndham, Wyndham Vacation Resorts Asia Pacific, and Shell Vacations Club."[2]

This chapter explores the ways in which WW involves its employees in its key sustainability initiatives and looks at some of the impacts these initiatives have on its people, the environment, and the business as a whole. Key themes are the overriding importance of the company's values (captured eloquently in the chapter's opening quote by Eric Danziger, president and CEO, WHG); seizing on sustainability challenges as opportunities; managing through influence rather than control; creating a culture of collaboration and innovation; and holistically integrating all aspects of the enterprise to build awareness, educate, and provide helpful resources to employees, suppliers, customers, owners and franchisees, and local communities.

Building a Culture for Sustainability

WW is committed to holistically embedding sustainability in every facet and function of the company. During our interview, WW chairman, president, and CEO Stephen Holmes made this clear when he said,

> As one of the world's largest hospitality companies, sustainability is part of our culture, and how we operate every day in nearly 100 countries around the world. Our ongoing drive is the result of outstanding collaboration and innovation by our employees, franchisees, suppliers, [and] business and community partners. Through their combined efforts, talents, and dedication, we continue to take steps together as part of a larger journey, where we continually set our goals higher for our people, our company, and our planet.[3]

The company's strategic intent is to leverage its financial capital to conserve the earth's natural capital and improve the environment while leveraging its human capital for the benefit of all its stakeholders and communities. WW's CSR initiatives are centered on key internal and external strategic imperatives. Internally, the emphasis is on ensuring employee diversity, safety, and health and providing an outstanding environment in which employees can achieve their personal and professional goals. Externally, the company emphasizes education and training as a way of adding value to its partners and itself.

What Does a Culture for Sustainability Look Like?

I asked each of the 12 passionate leaders and managers from around the world whom I interviewed at WW to describe what a culture for sustainability looks like and how he or she goes about achieving it.

Taylor emphasized two essential components of a culture for sustainability: collaboration and innovation. The company is dedicated to developing new and different ways to implement its sustainability and green programs with a "less-is-more" mind-set. "Innovation and leveraging technology has been critical and then working together to make this happen across the enterprise is mandatory," she said.[4]

I asked how this innovative, less-is-more mind-set manifests itself in the employees' everyday behavior. Taylor explained: "What I'm particularly proud of is when our employees come forward with programs that they're developing on their own in their markets, because that shows it's an organic process where they can improve on their own, and I think that's where we need to be in this process, as opposed to us rolling out programs."[5] As an example, she cited the Caught Green Handed program, which was initiated by one of WW's business units, Wyndham Exchange & Rentals (WER), and then rolled out to the company's other business units. For Taylor, this kind of employee self-initiation is a sine qua non for a successful sustainability program. She believes that such programs are far more effective than those initiated by the company and that this kind of proactivity is "a reflection of a healthy initiative that's really taking hold as part of the culture."[6]

For Danziger, "It's all about engaging with people to create an infectious passion to combine doing good with doing well. Our job is to look for ways in which we can help our owners and employees do both those things—do good and do well—in everything we seek to do, and people will find ways to do it."[7]

Danziger believes that people too often confuse innovation with invention. He told me that people don't need to be the geniuses who invent completely new ways of doing things, but rather just need to "be the good apples who make things better."[8] His advice is to encourage employees to constantly ask, Is there a better way to do what we're doing? This is what he calls innovation.

Geoffrey Ballotti, president and chief executive officer, WER, described the culture in this way:

> It's a culture of pride, caring, planning, and embracing initiatives around green. A lot of cultures are so focused on profit and productivity, and frown on spending time on planning, corporate social responsibility initiatives, or working on a green council.
>
> But this culture embraces it. Managers, directors, leaders, business unit CEOs, our chairman and CEO all embrace the fact that I've gathered over a dozen of my best and brightest for hours at a time to talk about our sustainability practices, our planning, our building maintenance, things that don't necessarily drop to the bottom line or show any profit in the quarter or the short term.[9]

How to Get There

Wyndham Green

Faith Taylor started the Wyndham Green Sustainability Program (www .wyndhamgreen.com) seven years ago as a grassroots project, endorsed by CEO Holmes, when the company spun off from Cendant. Today, it is an integral part of the company's five-year strategic plan and one of WW's top strategic priorities, with a dedicated sustainability and innovation department and its own resources.

The company's carbon goal is to track and measure its carbon emissions and reduce them by 16 percent by 2016 and 20 percent by 2020. As of 2012, the company had reduced its carbon emissions by 11.7 percent globally. The 2012 global carbon footprint is 373,294 metric tons of CO_2e (carbon dioxide equivalent), a 6.3 percent reduction against the baseline in absolute terms, which calculates to an 11.7 percent reduction per square foot and 23.9 percent reduction per employee.

Make the Business Case Up Front and Center

For WW, the business case is as pragmatic as it is a no-brainer. WW's pragmatic approach is founded on the principle that going green works— plain and simple. Green buildings, those which are designed to use fewer resources and create a healthier environment for their inhabitants, reportedly use 30 percent less energy, 35 percent less carbon, and 30 to 50 percent less water and have a 50 to 90 percent reduction in waste cost.[10] The company works with a variety of strategic partners—U.S. Green Building Council (USGBC; www.usgbc.org) and its LEED (Leadership in Energy and Environmental Design) certification programs, the U.S. Environmental Protection Agency (EPA), the World Travel and Tourism Council, Energy Star, and many others—to realize these kinds of significant savings.[11] And, according to the USGBC, worldwide buildings account for 17 percent of freshwater withdrawals, 25 percent of wood harvests, 33 percent of CO_2 emissions, and 40 percent of material and energy use.[12]

WW works to build an "eco-learning culture" that continuously improves and sustains its positive results. The focal areas include reducing energy and tracking consumption, reducing water usage, improving air quality, minimizing waste, working with local communities, and educating employees to drive innovation.[13]

Embed Sustainability in Your Values and Strategic Priorities

WW's values are the central underpinning of the company's strategies. The company's core values are to "act with integrity, respect everyone everywhere, provide individual opportunity and accountability, improve customers' lives, and support our communities."[14] Its commitment to sustainability values is manifested primarily through Wyndham Green, which "is not just a program but a way of living and working based on our vision and values, enhancing our customers' lives by improving the environment, supporting our global and local communities, and developing sustainable programs that deliver economic benefits," said Holmes.[15]

The Wyndham Green Sustainability Policy (see sidebar) is the foundation for the company's global sustainability endeavors and is used to help the company deliver triple-bottom-line results for people, profits, and the planet.

Develop the Culture before You Develop the Program

Gary Hyde, senior vice president, operations, WVO, emphasized the importance of developing the culture for sustainability before thinking

---

WYNDHAM GREEN SUSTAINABILITY POLICY

Wyndham Worldwide is committed to sustainability, which by definition means meeting the needs of the present without compromising the ability of future generations to meet their own needs. We understand the impact our Company has on the natural resources of the earth. The core values at Wyndham Worldwide include our commitment to conserve resources, preserve natural habitats and prevent pollution, to act with integrity and improve our customers' lives, and to support the communities around the world in which we work, live and play.

Wyndham Green supports those values by delivering triple-bottom-line benefits by focusing on the following:

- **People (Human Capital):** Treating our associates and communities fairly, as well as saving the environment and improving health with clean air and water.
- **Profits (Financial Capital):** Implementing innovative programs and practices that reduce energy and in turn expenses, or generate new revenues from sustainable products and services.
- **Planet (Natural Capital):** Conserving the earth's resources and our natural environment by recycling, reusing and reducing the consumption of resources.

Source: © 2013 Wyndham Worldwide. Used with permission.

about developing the programs.[16] When I asked him how this is best accomplished, Hyde advised it is by developing and implementing operational best practices to engage and empower employees.

For starters, he recommended leaders spend significant time and effort up front to create the desired organizational culture through such means as a robust communications and participation plan that embraces all employees, enabling them to freely share their ideas and helping them develop and translate those ideas into a real opportunity for the organization. The critical factors here, said Hyde, are "it has to be real" and "it has to be an ongoing commitment at the core of the senior leadership team."[17]

Create Leeway through Financial Performance

Geoffrey Richards, chief operations officer, hospitality division, WVO, the world's largest developer and marketer of time-shares, supported this view when he said, "It really does boil down to the culture of the organization and what's important to the leaders and associates." (WW refers to its employees as associates.) He added this caveat:

> The business itself has to perform well financially to support the resource requirements necessary to implement these sustainability projects. If the business isn't performing well, people are more focused on hitting the numbers for the next quarter, so you can lose some of the momentum that's necessary for this fundamental aspect of the company. It's extremely important we do well so we do have that leeway.[18]

Richards drew an analogy to raising one's children: "If your children are getting all As and a couple of Bs, then you're giving them a whole lot of leeway with their free time. But if your children are coming in with Cs, Ds, and Fs, you're going to tell them what they're doing with their free time. You've got to come through with results, and that will allow you the flexibility to execute across every operation of the business."

Create Small Wins that Generate Long-Term Success

Almost everyone I spoke with at WW emphasized the importance of creating small wins, building on them over time, and eventually transforming them into long-term success. The intention is to find ways to reach and include *all* employees, which often requires the development of an array of vehicles both online and offline. Working closely with local teams to implement and roll out programs according to their specific market is crucial. And once the positive results start showing up, keep communicating the benefits over and over and over again.

Wrap It with Fun!

As we will see in many best practice examples below, having fun is key to engaging employees in sustainability programs at WW. And, as we'll also see, it's not that hard to do.

One intriguing aspect of Wyndham's culture is that it is very internally competitive and results oriented. Because everyone seems to like participating in contests, and people like to win, it is not surprising that many of the enjoyable activities supporting sustainability come in the form of internal competitions and contests.

Best Practices

In this section, I first describe WW's unique governance structure for sustainability, which I see as a key underpinning of its considerable success. I then briefly review just a few of the myriad best practices WW has successfully implemented on behalf of its employees, suppliers, customers, owners and franchisees, communities, and shareholders.

Governance: Creating a Workable Sustainability Structure

At WW, sustainability has a governance structure that is unique in three distinct ways.

Wyndham Green

First, Wyndham Green is placed as high as any strategic initiative could possibly be; it is coordinated by the highly placed Sustainability Leadership Council, which is part of the Wyndham Green Council I discuss below and has among its members key executive officers such as WW's chief human resources officer and the CEO of each of the company's three business units (WHG, WER, and WVO). Wyndham Green reports directly to the board of directors and executive officers of the corporation.

Wyndham Green Council

Second, the Wyndham Green Council acts as a board of directors for the sustainability and innovation department. This department and the senior vice president of sustainability work collaboratively with the company's three business units and oversee the development of policies and strategies. The department's roles are to "share best practices, facilitate and coordinate initiatives across the enterprise and build and develop internal and external resources."[19] In addition, the department steers the tracking and measurement of the company's carbon footprint, its legislative compliance, and communications and reporting about its many programs. I was especially impressed by the way in which WW links sustainability to innovation through this fully integrated department.

The company's Global Green Council—comprising more than 300 diverse, cross-functional members from across the business—spreads the sustainability message throughout the company. Its members are selected and appointed by the company's top leaders, with the explicit goals of being the champions for the company's sustainability programs and delivering triple-bottom-line results to the entire organization.

Alignment and Integration of Human Resources and Corporate Services

The third—and to me, the most interesting—way in which the WW sustainability structure is unique is that the sustainability and innovation department reports to the chief human resources officer. Because I had never seen this before in any other company, I was fascinated to learn how this reporting structure works.

Mary Falvey, executive vice president and chief human resources officer, explained that sustainability and innovation are aligned and integrated not only with the Human Resources (HR) department but with *all corporate services* under the human resources umbrella, including real estate, facilities, marketing and communications, security, and, of course, the HR department itself.[20]

Falvey and others I spoke with cited the many advantages of such a cross-functional approach to decision making and cross-fertilization of ideas. For example, when the company moved into its new corporate headquarters, a LEED Silver interior-certified building, the leaders took time to explain to the employees why they had decided to have a LEED building, what LEED certification means, and what the ramifications are of having such a building. Employees were also given green tours. "It helped get people engaged and bring them along," said Falvey. None of these things would have happened so effortlessly had the teams not been working closely and collaboratively all along. Falvey said, "It all works together when all facilities are using green cleaning products, all the functions are talking and working together, and it all crisscrosses."[21]

Equipping, Enabling, and Rewarding Employees

WW has successfully deployed many best practices that equip employees to go green and reward them when they do; the best practices then help the company and its stakeholders become more sustainable. I cover several of these best practices here: a recognition program known as Caught Green Handed; WW's online Sustainability 101, which has been viewed by nearly 70 percent of all employees; Count on Me!, which acknowledges instances of exceptional customer service; WW Green Day and related events; intranet-based Wyndham Nation; a group of employee-centered programs to promote wellness and reduce health disparities in the workforce; and the company's award-winning diversity initiatives.

Caught Green Handed

Caught Green Handed is a simple recognition program that acknowledges employees who are making contributions to sustainability practices at WW and producing triple-bottom-line benefits for the organization. Created and developed internally, it was initiated within a business unit in WER and was subsequently made available to the entire organization.

Sustainability 101

Sustainability 101 is an online learning module designed to educate all WW employees about sustainability, including the challenges of global warming, deforestation, energy, and water resources. After a high-level overview of these challenges, it delves into the basics of a carbon footprint, how it is calculated, and ways to attenuate it. The program was developed collaboratively by the training group in human resources, external vendors, and a green team. Offered in 10 languages, it provides highlights of proven sustainable business practices that have been implemented around the world by WW.

At the end of the online program, employees are asked to create a pledge by selecting two out of these six areas to work on: energy conservation,

I Got Caught Green Handed

Name Goes Here

Description Line 1
Description Line 2

Congratulations
and thanks for your
efforts to GO GREEN!

WYNDHAM
EXCHANGE & RENTALS

Printed on 100% post consumer recycled paper

Figure 10.1 Example of recognition certificate given to an employee who is "Caught Green Handed." (© 2013 Wyndham Worldwide. Used with permission.)

water conservation, recycling, education, community, and innovation. To seal this commitment, each employee prints a certificate indicating the two areas of attention she has chosen. As of 2012, the training program had reached almost 70 percent of the company's 32,500 employees.

Count On Me!

Count On Me! is a service culture, and awards are given internally to people who go above and beyond to serve the customer. It is seen as a way to build a culture of customer service at WW.

WW Green Day and Related Events

Once a year, WW celebrates WW Green Day throughout all its business units. Each event is locally planned to meet the needs of the employees and local community. Although the specifics might vary at each company location, typically the company brings in local green vendors and suppliers, and the local green team runs educational seminars for employees. These well-attended events have included placing a Smart Car in front of the office building and raffling off green products and services.

Additional green and sustainability education has been provided to more than 32,500 Wyndham employees on highly visible dates throughout the year. For example, seminars to build awareness about and inspire insights into sustainable business practices were run during events such as Earth Hour, Earth Day, Arbor Day, and WW Green Day. These sustainability and green themes are also covered in Wyndham's new-hire orientation.

Wyndham Nation

Sending a strong message of cohesiveness, the company's intranet is known as Wyndham Nation. It is a centralized idea center that drives all employees in the company to one common source. The site has a dedicated area called Wyndham Green, and employees can share best practices and ideas globally. Further, they can post pictures and recognize ongoing employee achievements.

Employee-Centered Programs

In synch with WW's holistic, triple-bottom-line approach to sustainability, the company provides a variety of programs targeted at ensuring its employees' health and well-being. Although space does not permit a detailed description of all these programs, I present a few highlights.

Be Well—Embracing a Healthy Lifestyle

WW is strongly committed to supporting employees' health and well-being. Because the company believes that "health and wellness invoke both professional and personal productivity, achievement and fulfillment," it offers Be Well—Embracing a Healthy Lifestyle to help its employees lead healthy lifestyles and balance their work and family responsibilities. It includes specific programs in such areas as "nutrition, exercise, lifestyle management, physical and emotional wellness, and financial health"[22]—for example, on-site fitness centers, on-site and virtual weight-management programs, and stress-reduction initiatives.

Similar to Sanofi's Health in Action, which I described in detail in chapter 9, WW's Know Your Numbers Campaign helps associates understand their blood pressure, cholesterol, and blood sugar levels through a biometric screening. Employees can earn "Be Well" credits toward the cost of their medical benefits by taking a health assessment and performing follow-up steps. This campaign has continued to evolve since its inception in 2012.

"Our culture at WW is based on our 'Count On Me!' service philosophy," said Bill Skrzat, senior vice president, compensation, benefits, and HRMS, WW, "and we take pride in our associates' knowing that they can count on WW to provide the support and resources they need to live healthier lives. Be Well may have started as a health program, but [it] quickly became part of how we do business around the world and continues to deliver great results for our associates as well as the company's bottom line."[23]

These results translated not only into tangible health improvements among its employees, but also into significant cost savings in medical benefits.[24] The program received the WW Chairman's Innovation Award in 2011 in corporate services. Additionally, on August 7, 2012, WW was recognized at the White House by the U.S. Department of Health and Human Services (HHS), in conjunction with the White House Business Council and the National Business Group on Health, for being a leading organization for innovation in reducing health-care disparities.

Wyndham Diversity Leadership and Training

Diversity is one of WW's strategic priorities. The company fosters diversity in its broadest definition—encompassing talent, thought, and experience—as well as with regard to the more traditional race, color, religion, gender, sexual orientation, and other protections established by laws and regulations around the world. Through the extensive reach and effectiveness of its diversity initiatives—for example, women represent 42.4 percent of its management positions—the company demonstrates its commitment to cultivating a diverse global company, inside and out. Believing diversity enriches the organization as a global hospitality provider, the company embraces a culture of diversity and inclusion that supports employees from all backgrounds.

"We are committed to providing a supportive environment that allows employees to have the awareness and confidence that they are valued as individuals in order to reach their full potential which speaks to the WW culture," said Patricia Lee, senior vice president, human resources and chief diversity officer, WW. "In a global marketplace, it is essential that we understand, value, and incorporate our people differences into our business operations as a leading workplace, and as one of the world's leading hospitality companies."[25]

WW's diversity and inclusion strategy extends to all its stakeholders: its employees, guests and customers, franchisees, developers, vendors, and suppliers (discussed in the next section). The company has long been a recognized leader in diversity and was named among the Top 50 Companies for Diversity by *DiversityInc* in 2013. It has also been listed in *Latina Style*'s Top 50 Companies, *Working Mother* magazine's Top 100 Companies, and the National Association of Female Executives' Top 50 Companies. Additionally, WW received a perfect score of 100 on the Human Rights Campaign's (HRC) annual Corporate Equality Index, and is recognized by the HRC as one of the "best places to work for lesbian, gay, bisexual, and transgender (LGBT) equality."

Additionally, WW sponsors several associate business groups (ABGs), in which associates with common interests share ideas and experiences and promote professional development, engagement, and inclusion throughout the company. Open to all associates, ABGs at WW currently include WYNPride (LGBT), ¡Fuerte! (Hispanic), Spectrum (African American), I-VOW (veterans), Women on Their Way (women in the workplace), Grupo de Jovenes (Generation Y), and AASK (administrative assistants).

Its award-winning diversity program is fueled by a broad array of internal and external alliances—including partnerships with the National Association of Black Hotel Owners, Operators, and Developers (NABHOOD); the Hispanic Association for Corporate Responsibility (HACR); the National Association of Black, Hispanic, Asian, and Women MBAs; Careers for the Disabled; and Veterans Across America.[26]

The company's diversity-education curriculum has offerings for employees at every level. These include the WW Diversity and Inclusion Leadership Workshop, a course called Is It Bias?, and a workshop focused on microinequities called Little Things Mean a Lot.

When it comes to recruiting a diverse workforce, WW has been, and continues to be strategic in its focus on attracting, retaining, and developing best-in-class employee talent. Diversity recruiting is an integral segment of the overall diversity and inclusion strategy, focusing on all the businesses. Using targeted marketing, WW partners with and reaches out to organizations, including college campus diversity groups and professional organizations such as the National Black MBA, the Hispanic MBA and the Asian MBA. In addition, outreach includes posting positions on job boards and in recruitment magazines such as *Diversity and Careers* and *Latina Style* magazine.

Creating a Sustainable Supply Chain

WW works diligently with its suppliers and vendors to build sustainable supply chains for its products and services. Paul Davis, senior vice president, strategic sourcing, WW, and the strategic sourcing department lead this effort in consultation with the sustainability team.[27] In this section, I highlight a number of best practices that show how WW encourages its numerous and diverse supply chains to become more sustainable and helps them in the process. Significantly, the company produces tangible change through influence rather than through control, because the vast majority of its hotels are independent franchisees.

Wyndham Green Supplier Program

Wyndham's strategic sourcing department strives to partner with suppliers and vendors who have a commitment to sustainability, protecting the environment, conserving resources, and preventing pollution. And it is expanding the number and array of sustainable products it offers customers. But, as Davis said, "It's not just about the green widget, but also how you make it."[28]

With this in mind, the company created the comprehensive Wyndham Green Supplier Survey, which all suppliers are required to complete. Managed by the sustainability and innovation group, the survey consists of more than 100 questions analyzing each supplier's environmental practices, its sustainability-related policies, and its methods for tracking, documenting, and reporting them.

Wyndham designates suppliers as "green" when they score 60 percent or higher in the survey. As of 2012, 25 percent of the company's total $1.2 billion spend was with such suppliers. The goal is to increase that number to 30 percent of the total supply chain spend by 2017.

Toward accomplishing this ambitious goal, the company recognizes green excellence by including green suppliers in requests for proposals whenever possible, reaching out to the green supplier community, and expanding its base of green suppliers internationally, especially in the United Kingdom and China.[29]

The company collects quarterly metrics from its key green suppliers to track sustainability performance for internal and external reporting purposes. Here are some of these green suppliers, the products Wyndham uses, and the savings to the planet, as reported in Wyndham's Global Reporting Initiative (GRI) report for 2011/2012 year-to-date product purchases:

- **Office Max Office Supplies.** More than 47,000 cases of recycled paper used.
- **Samsung Electronics, Inc.** More than 25,647 Hospitality LCD TVs supplied to WW's hotels and resorts. "The average LCD reduces power consumption, on average, by 40 percent compared to CRTs," according to WW.
- **Simmons.** Almost 40,000 mattresses purchased. Since 2007, when Simmons introduced its comprehensive recycling program, it has diverted more than 23 million pounds of materials from landfills. In addition, according to Wyndham, "these bedding products help reduce the need for energy-consuming machines in the manufacturing process."
- More than 188,000 compact fluorescent lightbulbs purchased, saving more than 86.3 million pounds of CO_2.
- **Ecolab.** Approximately 2,670 units of low-phosphate laundry detergent purchased, reducing water use and reducing plastic waste by more than 26,773 pounds.
- **Cascade and Georgia Pacific.** Bathroom tissue made from 100 percent virgin fibers and facial tissue made from 100 percent recycled fibers saved more than 2.3 million gallons of water and more than 621,000 pounds of CO_2 at the company's hotels, resorts, and corporate facilities.
- **Sobel.** A total of 247,991 WynRest soft goods (pillows, pads, inserts, etc.) were purchased in 2012. This is equivalent to recycling 4,463,488 20-ounce plastic bottles.
  Fewer chemical and heavy metals are used in the manufacturing of WynRest pillows and mattress pads, resulting in less environmental waste, and they have been screened for harmful substances, so they are better for consumers' health. The pillows, made from 100 percent recycled polyester microfiber, are hydrophobic—that is, they repel water—making the washing and drying process more efficient.[30]

In light of these noteworthy reductions in environmental impacts, Davis addressed the perception that sustainability and green products are more expensive. He cited TVs as a great example of how the gap is narrowing because their price is gradually coming down. Moreover, when the total cost of ownership (TCO) and the carbon footprint are taken into consideration, it should become a nonissue. "As companies are feeling pressure to compete either by being sustainable or by providing sustainable products, the cost differential disappears," he said.[31]

Next I present three specific examples of the creative ways Wyndham leverages its influence with suppliers and breaks new ground in sustainability in the process.

Cintas Front-Desk Suiting Made of Recycled Plastic Soda Bottles

Seeking to find innovative ways to use recyclable materials, Wyndham challenged its uniform company Cintas to create a green uniform for its staff. Stepping up to this challenge, Cintas created the two-piece Regeneration Suit, shown below, made from 100 percent post-consumer waste. Each suit is made out of approximately 25 recycled two-liter plastic bottles. According to Wyndham's 2011 GRI report, "apparel made from recycled materials uses 66 percent less energy compared to the manufacturing of polyester fiber, and the process reduces water usage by 90 percent."[32] These suits are worn by front desk staff in all the hotels in the WHG and WVO, and as of 2012, 66,468 front desk uniforms had been purchased.

Green Key Cards

Realizing the huge volume it consumes in plastic hotel key cards, Wyndham got its suppliers to create recycled key cards

Photo 10.1 Front-desk staff wear the eco-friendly Regeneration Suit, made entirely from post-consumer waste using 25 recycled two-liter plastic bottles. (© 2013 Cintas. Used with permission.)

for the doors in more than 90 percent of its 7,340 branded hotel properties. More than 4.1 million such key cards—made from 87 percent preconsumer recycled product—have been used, representing a reduction of more than 50,000 pounds of plastic waste as of 2012.[33]

Shade-Grown Coffee

Recognizing the environmental impact of coffee on rainforests, WVO switched to shade-grown coffee, and in the first two years—2010 and 2011—this has saved more than 52 million square feet of rainforest (the company purchases more than 250,000 pounds of shade-grown coffee a year for use in its hotels). "For every pound of coffee that we consume, we protect 103 square feet of rainforest," said Gary Hyde senior vice president, operations, WVO.[34]

Hyde recounted to me the story behind this decision, a story with elements ranging from biodiversity and local economy to history and the fate of the planet. "Coffee was genetically altered in the 1970s to be a sun-grown product," he explained, adding that in its natural state the coffee bush is a shade-grown plant. This genetic alteration paved the way for large coffee concerns to strip vast forest lands in Peru and Central America. The purchase of shade-grown coffee by WVO "provides an incentive for farmers [who live in the rainforest] to go back to natural growth in the undergrowth of the rainforests in these areas," said Hyde.[35] In some of the mountainous Peruvian locations that the Arbor Day Foundation (www.arborday.org/coffee) visited where shade-grown coffee is grown, its representatives were the first Anglo-Americans the local people had ever seen.

The shade-grown coffee that Wyndham buys is farmed by local cooperatives in Peru and has the Arbor Day and the Rainforest Alliance Certified PLUS designation. Hyde said this process adheres to the stringent guidelines of the Rainforest Alliance (www.rainforest-alliance.org).

In addition to helping save the rainforests and encouraging farmers to continue to live and farm on their land, buying shade-grown coffee helps the families in a variety of other ways. For instance, the buyer (in this case, WW) donates 10 percent of the proceeds back to the families to be used for education and health services.

Wyndham Supplier Diversity Program

During our interview, Taylor told me that one of WW's key priorities is to "try to seek out and grow diversity within our supply chain."[36]

And, according to WW's 2012 Sustainability Report, "diversity and inclusion are at the very heart of the WW culture . . . our corporate diversity strategy extends to the suppliers with whom we do business."[37]

August "Gus" Manz, senior manager, strategic sourcing, WW, said "sustainability and diversity need to become an integral part of the strategic sourcing process. You can't plug holes after the fact, but need to engage your stakeholders early and often, and be proactive versus reactive."[38] Because Wyndham is in the service business and supports an extremely diverse customer and supplier base, it is especially important that supplier diversity be a part of the fabric of the culture and manifested in the ways in which the company operates. "We firmly believe in our core values around diversity and sustainability, and also do it," said Davis.[39] "Our sourcing strategy is to have transparent and proactive inclusion of diverse suppliers and sustainable suppliers in every procurable activity, wherever we can have influence in supporting diversity."

Davis explained that when analyzing suppliers to determine whether to categorize them as sustainable, the company looks not only at whether they consider themselves green and meet specific thresholds or standards, but also at their diversity status. "If we're going to make this part of the core fabric of our employees and a requirement that our suppliers provide first and second tier reporting," he said, "then we needed to clarify how we are measuring it and put a focus on it."

When I asked how the company defined and calculates its "diverse spend," Davis explained that the first tier is suppliers that are 50.1 percent minority- or women-owned; the second tier comprises suppliers that provide diversity-related information about other companies they work with to get the goods they then sell to WW. The amount of that supplier diversity–related spend is the numerator; the denominator is the total procurable spend across all categories. Davis told me WW has increased its diverse spend from 1.8 to 15.2 percent in the past four years.[40]

As stated in the company's 2012 Sustainability Report, the five pillars of the company's supplier diversity initiative are as follows:

- Strong top management commitment
- Vibrant Supplier Diversity Council/Champion Structure
- Top-notch strategic sourcing commitment
- Stakeholder involvement and relationship building
- Proactive involvement in all aspects of supplier diversity[41]

Davis acknowledged Jose Nido, vice president, supplier diversity, for his work in challenging his team to get as many diverse suppliers as possible.

Davis explained that sometimes the company needs to go the extra mile to help its suppliers get up to speed. "We've had to bring some of them along, and that's why we ask for the information we do. We make it a requirement," he said. I was particularly impressed with his description of how the company responds to the three reasons for failure: "If they don't know, we'll educate them. If they can't do, we'll help them. If they don't care, we won't do business with them. It's also about mentoring. If they are the right supplier, we'll work with them to help them be more successful."[42]

Making Wishes Come True through Corporate Social Responsibility and Philanthropy

WW participates with the Committee Encouraging Corporate Philanthropy (CECP; www. cecp.co), a nonprofit organization that works with top executives in the business community to improve the level and quality of corporate philanthropy. As a result of its affiliation with CECP, WW began reviewing and advancing its philanthropic policies and practices in 2012, paying special attention to increased tracking and reporting.

In keeping with the company's long-standing commitment to making wishes come true, the company offers a vast array of CSR, volunteer, and philanthropic activities, with particular emphasis on those that involve its employees and support sustainability-related initiatives. Here are some highlights.

Wish Day

The company gives its employees in the United States and Canada one paid day off a year to volunteer with a community service project for a charity of their choice. All employees who work 20 hours or more a week are eligible.

Wishes by Wyndham Foundation

The Wishes by Wyndham Foundation, funded by WW, is the primary vehicle for the company's philanthropic activities. It focuses on three signature charities, each of which targets children in need: Christel House

International, SeriousFun Children's Network, and the Starlight Children's Foundation.

Founded in 1998 by Christel DeHaan, cofounder of WW-owned RCI, Christel House (www.christelhouse.org) builds and runs learning centers in poverty-stricken neighborhoods around the world. The goal is to create sustainable social and educational impact and improve the lives of impoverished children by providing them with education and job opportunities, and community support, health care, and counseling. The learning centers are located in India, Mexico, South Africa, Venezuela, and the United States, and today provide education, food, and other assistance to more than 3,000 children.

Ballotti spoke about DeHaan with great admiration, calling her "a saint" because of "the remarkable concept" she created. He explained that when DeHaan sold RCI to Cendant, she used the majority of the proceeds to form Christel House. These schools not only educate and feed people, he said, but transform their lives, and are an example of "giving back to the community in every way, shape, and form imaginable."[43]

SeriousFun (www.seriousfunnetwork.org) gives children with serious illnesses a variety of outdoor recreational activities and camp experiences that help build their resilience and self-confidence. Started in Connecticut in 1988 as the Hole in the Wall Gang Camp by legendary actor Paul Newman, the program is now a worldwide network of camps and programs that are offered free of charge to "help children and their families reach beyond illness to discover joy, confidence and a new world of possibilities," according to its website. Although the activities all involve fun and adventure, each is intended to provide therapeutic benefits for the children's health and quality of life.

The Starlight Children's Foundation (www.starlight.org) offers education, entertainment, and other activities for children suffering from life-altering injuries and chronic and serious illnesses. It helps these children cope "with the pain, fear, and isolation of prolonged illness."[44] Through this program, WHG recently donated about a dozen mobile entertainment "fun centers" to hospitals across the United States.

Million Tree Project

WVO invites owners and guests staying at the properties to plant trees at each WVO location as part of its partnership with the Arbor Day Foundation. In 2012, it expanded its tree initiatives by launching the Million Tree Project, with the goal of planting a million trees in U.S. forests that have been affected by beetles, fires, and natural blow-downs.

Wyndham donates a percentage of its overall sales to this project, as do its vendors and more than 5 million guests annually who are encouraged to participate in the initiative. When I asked why the company does this, Hyde explained, "We don't do it for profit. We do it because it's the right thing to do and believe we'll be rewarded accordingly. Do we capitalize on it from a marketing perspective? Sure, but it's the right thing to do, and we exploit that aspect. But we don't seek to derive revenues from that."[45]

Partnering with Universities, Governments, and NGOs

WW, through its sustainability department, partners with select academic organizations that are aligned with its business goals, direction, and sustainability goals. These include Cornell University, Fairleigh Dickinson University (FDU), Cambridge Climate Leaders, and Harvard University. The Cambridge Climate Leaders program provides leadership and educational offerings, including online resources on the science, economics, and technology of climate change (www.cpsl.cam.ac.uk). The Cambridge Corporate Leaders Group in 2012 presented the "Cancún Communiqué" at the United Nations Framework Conference on Climate Change. The group urged governments to accelerate their efforts to address climate change and called for a comprehensive international framework to accomplish this. More than 350 companies, including WW, were signatories to the Communiqué. Furthermore, WW's senior vice president, sustainability, was a delegate to and speaker at the Rio +20 Summit in Brazil.

In 2012, the company showcased the Wyndham Green program at the Clinton Global Initiative (CGI; www.clintonglobalinitiative.org). Also that year, the program was recognized at the White House by President Obama's Better Buildings Challenge (www4.eere.energy.gov/challenge/home).

At FDU's Institute for Sustainable Enterprise (www.fdu.edu/ise), the company participates in executive roundtables on topics such as building a culture for sustainability and sustainable supply chains and in monthly live educational seminars with sustainability and human resources thought leaders.

Arbor Day Foundation

The WVO resort team has been partnering with the Arbor Day Foundation for more than five years. As mentioned above, its resorts serve shade-grown coffee that was grown under the canopy of tropical rain-forests by local farm cooperatives in Peru and organize tree-planting events onsite. These activities educate Wyndham's employees and its guests about ways they can apply such commitments in their own personal lives and inspire them to do this.

Hyde lauded the Arbor Day Foundation for its commitment and the integrity with which it operates: "Arbor Day takes their foundation very seriously and is very particular about who they work with from a corporate perspective. They are very concerned with the legitimacy of their program; they document and certify it," said Hyde.[46]

Shifting Customer and Guest Mind-Sets and Behavior

Educating guests about the critical roles they can play in reducing environmental impacts during—and even after—their stays is critical to WW's comprehensive approach to sustainability. The company has found myriad creative ways to help its customers learn about sustainability and translate this knowledge into tangible results. I highlight a few of these here.

Ecologically Friendly Initiatives for Guests

EarthSmart, a guest linen reuse program to save resources and operational costs, and other "re-linen" programs are available in 90 percent of WHG's managed hotels and franchisees. The ecologically friendly guest room initiatives incorporate low-flow water practices, biodegradable guest laundry bags, and numerous recycling efforts including guest-room key cards made from recycled material as noted earlier.

Wyndham increasingly uses energy-efficient lights in guest rooms and corporate offices. Its literature points out that replacing just one incandescent bulb with an energy-efficient bulb equates to 1,000 fewer pounds of CO_2 emitted into the atmosphere over the bulb's lifetime.[47]

Wyndham Green's Programs for Kids

WW is dedicated to educating its stakeholder's children about the environment and the planet, increasing their awareness of the importance of sustainability, and showing them how they can make a difference by caring for the environment, community, and world. Toward this goal, the company has partnered with the EPA and Energy Star in the United States to create programs that teach children about Wyndham Green's six core strategies: energy conservation, water conservation, recycling/ reuse, education, innovation, and community service.

Through its Wyndham Green Kids program, announced in 2010, the company teaches children ages 3 to 14 about the environment, community, and world using a variety of workbook and hands-on activities arranged by local environmental organizations. Students learn how to use less energy at home, save water, recycle or reuse everything, teach their friends what they know about being green, find and implement creative ideas to support the environment, and volunteer at their local towns and parks.

The company has introduced a variety of novel and fun programs for children around the world ranging from self-guided activities like Winnie the Wallabee to programs in partnership with the Arbor Day Foundation. I describe a few of the most creative and successful ones here.

Wyndham Green Kids' Energy Adventure Scavenger Hunt

Wyndham Green Kids' Energy Adventure Scavenger Hunt teaches elementary school students about all aspects of energy—conservation, where energy is found, the different types of energy that exist. Ten stations are set up for the hunt, each with information that answers a different question about energy. The children are given an Energy Passport that includes the 10 questions from the stations. After they visit each station and answer all the questions, they receive a prize. Once they complete the scavenger hunt, and fill out their energy passport, they are designated an energy expert.

Winnie the Wallabee

Started at resorts in Tasmania, in Australia, and New Zealand, the Winnie the Wallabee program is spreading to eco-friendly locations around the world, said WVO's Richards.[48] The program's goal is to get kids to think about and learn about how they can make a positive impact on the environment while having fun on vacation.

When the children arrive at a resort, they receive an environmentally friendly backpack along with a coloring book with pictures of plants and nature that they might see while staying at the resort. By participating in the program throughout their vacation stay, the children gain direct experience with—and learn about—the natural environment where they are staying. At the end of their vacation, the children receive a prize in recognition of their participation in the program.

Fully Sustainable Bathroom Amenities

Another idea "taken from our friends down under," said Richards, is WVO's fully sustainable bathroom amenity program: all soaps, shampoos, conditioners, and their containers are made of completely biodegradable materials (i.e., they biodegrade completely in three years).[49] They are produced exclusively for the hospitality industry by the Australian company Earth Therapy. Richards said that WVO is the first and only hospitality company in North America to adopt such a program.

Instilling Sustainable Practices in Owners, Franchisees, and Time-share Owners

One of the most impressive things I discovered about WW is that it has been able to persuade its diverse customers to embrace its sustainability priorities, values, and strategies. This is a formidable challenge that requires crossing the chasm that exists between WW—or any company of this type—and its franchisees and time-share owners. It requires WW's exerting positive influence because such a company cannot exert direct control over its franchisees. In this section, I describe some of the sustainable best practices WW uses to do this with its owned hotels, franchisees, and time-share owners.

WVO Green Certification

Wyndham includes sustainable practices in the home owners' associations training and education initiatives it offers at time-share owners' annual meetings. Almost 100 percent of the WVO resorts have received the Wyndham Vacation Ownership Green Certification for their installation of energy-efficient lights, water-efficient fixtures, green cleaning supplies, and eco-friendly laundry detergents. The company has showcased its Green Certification program as a model to be emulated throughout the hospitality industry. As a result of this and other efforts to lead change, the first sustainability award in the industry, the ARDY Award, from the American Resort Development Association (ARDA), was presented to WVO for the Wyndham Green program and certification.

RCI's Green Award

RCI's Green Award for the owner base of RCI's 4,000 resorts is a highly effective means of influencing Wyndham's RCI independent time-share developer affiliates. Ballotti explained: "One thing I've learned in my career is that owners in any franchise community are very competitive. If you create an award for something, they all want to be recognized as the best."[50]

With this in mind, the company created the RCI Green Award, designating three levels of recognition, from the highest to lowest—Platinum, Gold, and Silver. The program was first piloted in Australia and was so "wildly successful" that the company implemented it globally. "The award represents a very important message and tool to promote both internally and externally," said Ballotti.[51] To maximize the impact of the award, the company announces the winners at the industry's annual conference.

Green Franchise Advisory Board

The WHG also influences by example. The Green Franchisee Advisory Board was formed in 2010 as a cross-brand team of 24 members in which brand owners and general managers showcase, test, and share best practices to advance sustainability in the WHG portfolio. The franchisees on this board represent the best examples of what some owners are doing at properties owned by Wingate by Wyndham, Hawthorn by Wyndham, Ramada Worldwide, Days Inn Worldwide, and Microtel by Wyndham, among other WHG franchises. As owners share what they do, other owners become passionate about the programs themselves.

Landal GreenParks

When I interviewed Thomas Heerkens, managing director, Landal GreenParks, I couldn't have been more inspired by what I came to see as one of the greenest and most sustainable groups of resorts in the world—Landal GreenParks (www.landal.com).[52] He explained the company's concept of engaged entrepreneurship, its commitment to being a regional player, and its offering of an exemplary sustainable experience to guests. Landal GreenParks has become my personal favorite, a standard-bearer for sustainable time-shares, resorts, and hotels.

Landal GreenParks, which was started in 1954, is one of Wyndham's oldest brands in Europe. Its more than 70 "chalet-parks" in the Netherlands, Germany, Belgium, Australia, Switzerland, Czech Republic, and Hungary offer almost 12,000 bungalows, villas, and apartments. Seven of the parks also offer campsites, with facilities for 1,500 tents. Sustainability is at the heart of this brand and a key element of its mission. The parks rely on renewable energy, and 30,000 megawatts are produced annually from waste. Energy-efficiency is everywhere, and select facilities have energy-efficient lighting, energy-efficient management systems, and gray-water management.

Landal GreenParks partners with Natuurmonumenten, an NGO, to maintain the biodiversity of more than 250,000 acres of wetlands and estates. Natuurmonumenten manages natural areas including forests, wetlands, mudflats, floodplains, and country estates that are located within visiting distance of Landal GreenParks. It helps organize and co-ordinate a wide range of outdoor activities throughout the year, such as a tour with a local park ranger, a trip in a covered wagon, a boat trip, and a children's party.[53] "One of the 'evergreens' is to go hiking with the forest ranger or with a nature guide to experience the woods and the dunes," said Heerkens).[54]

Landal GreenParks serves Puro fair-trade coffee and sustainably caught fish with the Marine Stewardship Council (MSC) Ecolabel at its locations, offers regional and local produce at its stores, and uses recycled glass bottles in its restaurants. It has low-energy lightbulbs in its facilities, LED lights in its pools, water-saving showerheads, and a 100-item green-savings checklist in its parks. It uses E-view, an online

Photo 10.2 Guests ride bicycles at a Landal GreenParks in the Netherlands. (© 2010 Landal GreenParks. Used with permission.)

monitoring system for managing energy use and costs, tracing leakage, and identifying excessive energy and gas use.

In its chalets, automated room thermostats respond to light and movement and switch automatically to lower temperatures when they do not sense either. The company uses geothermal heating—a sustainable energy source and environmentally friendly alternative to fossil fuels—in some of its locations in The Netherlands and Austria. How does this work? According to "Wyndham Green: Global Best Practices," "Using a geothermal heat pump the heat is extracted from underground. In the winter this geothermal heat is used for heating the accommodations. In the summer the heat is pumped into the ground, keeping the accommodations at a comfortable temperature. For other energy requirements, carbon neutral woodchips are used."[55]

Landal GreenParks has "eco-bungalows," which have solar panels on the roof, a southern-facing area made of glass, and an eastern-facing area without glass. The resorts use the highest standard of sustainable, cradle-to-cradle carpets and furniture. Heerkens told me that Landal is in the process of replacing all the cars in its parks with electric cars purchased in Europe from a French supplier; its housekeeping staff is already driving these.[56]

When I asked Heerkens to explain why the company does what it does at Landal GreenParks, he said, "You can do a lot of big things. Some of the big things we do are contracting with waste collection, investing in solar panels, and investing in new properties that don't use a lot of energy. . . . But the culture becomes an important element making everyone aware of the smaller things they can do themselves to reduce energy consumption." He pointed out that responsibility for most of the carbon footprint reduction rests with the guests, which requires educating and influencing thousands of people. "How do you do this?" I asked. "By talking about it and informing them," he answered.[57]

Despite the big things, Heerkens explained that "most of the power comes from a lot of small things. For example, shutting off lights at 10 P.M. instead of 12 midnight or having the lights go on when people arrive or are moving. There's a lot of wasted energy because everyone is always putting on light or heat when there's no one there. We must educate the staff to make them aware of what they can do themselves."[58] Another example of something that made a big difference is reorganizing Landal's logistics. Heerkens told me that when the company consolidated its distribution process so that all its inventory was in one warehouse and limited its deliveries to twice per week instead of once a day, it realized a very significant reduction in its carbon footprint.

There is an energy officer in each park who oversees energy-consumption and energy-reduction initiatives. Heerkens said the company is going to change this person's role to that of a green officer or sustainability officer who will focus more broadly on the regional—or community—aspect of Landal's strategy and its dedication to being a responsible partner in the area.

Corporate Social Responsibility

As part of WW's CSR priority to make wishes come true, Landal Green-Parks regularly offers stays at its parks free of charge to the Make-A-Wish Foundation Netherlands, the Cancer Center in Amsterdam, and Beyond the Moon, a Belgian wish foundation. In 2009, Landal's guest magazine, *Naturally,* asked readers to suggest people who deserved a free stay at the parks and explain why. It then granted 100 free stays to individuals based on the responses it received. Through a partnership with the National Children's Aid Foundation and the Asthma Foundation, Landal GreenParks grants free stays to vulnerable children and provides special accommodations for people with asthma, COPD, poor eyesight, and disabilities.

Heerkens told me about "a wonderful organization" called Right to Play (www.rightoplay.com)—a large organization based in Canada, with an office in the Netherlands—that collects donations and organizes programs to help children in Africa "through the transformative power of play." Founded in 2000 by former Norwegian Olympic speed skater and four-time Olympic gold medalist Johann Olav Koss, the organization is "all about [the] right to play sports, because if children don't learn to play at 12 or 13 years, and experience the positive benefits of competition and play, they make war," said Heerkens.[59] For nine weeks during summer holidays, Landal GreenParks brings together a variety of athletes to participate in such sports as field hockey, football, and cycling with its guests and conduct organized clinics in which they introduce guests to the purpose of the organization. In the process, they collected €45,000, all of which went to Right to Play.

Engaged Entrepreneurship

A core principle and building block of Landal GreenPark's business model, said Heerkens, is engaged entrepreneurship, which is finding ways for the resorts to team up with local entrepreneurs to make a combined offer for its guests.[60] In this way, the resorts actively cooperate with entrepreneurs in a region to build the local economy. Guests are encouraged to participate in a variety of local activities, including, for example, taking an excursion to a nearby cheese farm or picking and buying local produce and apples. One of the Landal GreenParks locations in Germany is in a wine-making region, so the company invites local vintners to the resort to explain to the guests how their wine is made and what is unique about the region. Guests can learn about the area while tasting wine, and they can buy the wine, thus supporting local entrepreneurs.

Heerkens spoke about the distinction between engaged entrepreneurship and ecotourism. He explained that the focus of engaged entrepreneurship is working with local entrepreneurs, which is not always the case with ecotourism.[61] All too often, tourists visit a beautiful, ecologically rich region, but the region doesn't benefit from their visits. Typically in tourism, or even ecotourism, people spend all their money at the resort (like Club Med) and do not do a lot of spending in the region.

Leading by Example with a Low-Car Diet

Heerkens told me he had gone on a "low-car diet," leaving his car at home for 10 days and taking public transportation (e.g., bus, train, tram) or riding a bicycle. This experiment had several positive ramifications for the resort and its employees. It showed a way for leaders to learn what it's like to have to rely on bikes and public transportation.

This had symbolic value to employees, guests, and staff, and the story of how committed the CEO is to sustainability spread, resulting in a tangible impact around the company. Employees were quite interested in knowing why and how he did this. This inspired the HR department to develop a sustainable mobility plan, which stimulates employees to choose more-sustainable transportation when going to and from work and when going to business appointments. The sustainable mobility plan includes such options as carpooling; using public transport, e-bikes, and plug-in hybrid company cars; and teleconferencing.

And ultimately, it could lead to smart design of resort locations—where no one needs a car but can still get to ecologically friendly sites to meet and buy from locals.

Challenges

Although WW is clearly a leader in sustainability and green within the hospitality sector, it continues to face some daunting challenges. Six key challenges are presented here, along with some of the actions the company is taking regarding them: influencing without control; dealing with global differences in standards; educating all employees; keeping up the momentum; addressing continual growth, including bringing new properties and new markets up to speed; and acknowledging resistance to green and sustainability among consumers.

Influencing without Control

I mentioned earlier the formidable challenge a company faces getting franchised hotels to embrace the company's values and priorities because the company has no actual control over its franchisees. WW has taken this challenge seriously and has made incredible progress educating its franchisees about the benefits of going green and becoming sustainable. Given WHG's heavily franchised model—WW has only 60 owned and managed properties and more than 7,200 franchisees—the company had to figure out a way to exert influence without control. Danziger explained this challenge: "In a franchise model, we can't be held responsible. I don't have my hand on the light switch. All we can do is encourage, lead, train, and guide that owner to do it themselves. We can't force them or control them in franchises."[62]

In its search for the effective ways to do this, Wyndham has found that understanding the franchisee's needs, building the business case, educating franchisees about the many advantages of going green, and working side-by-side with owners to enable them to be successful are key.

Danziger discussed the process: "First try to help them do better and do well. Saving money is very important to a mom-and-pop business like many of these franchisees. When people trust you, and see you're trying to help them, you get followers. If we can create passion around it and do well and do right, all at the same time, it's all good."[63] He pointed to the significant low-hanging fruit that helps save money and does right by the environment at the same time. Examples include changing lightbulbs, reducing water and energy use by not changing bedding and towels every day, and recycling soap.

"You know it is right because we've only got one planet, and there's no more water when the water's all gone, so they get it. But when you show them they can save money at the same time, they get excited. Doing the right thing is always right. Doing the wrong thing is never right. It is a huge value," said Danziger.[64] And then he proudly told me that the day before our interview one of the Ramada Worldwide hotels had received a zero electric bill. This was primarily driven by the owner's having installed a solar farm on his property.

Dealing with Global Differences in Standards

Several WW leaders identified the global challenges that stem from differences in—and lack of—standards in other countries, particularly in China and India where local laws vastly differ from those in the United States. Danziger characterized the rapid growth in China as both positive and a challenge. For example, in Shanghai only 20 years ago, thousands of people still rode bicycles and rickshaws. Because of its "unbelievable growth, Shanghai has gone from few or no cars to way too many cars," said Danziger.[65] This exacerbates the environmental and pollution problems affecting the 20 million people living there. On the other hand, Danziger lauded China's high-speed rail system. The point is, we have to find a way to support developing economies such as China and India without jeopardizing the environment.

Educating All Employees

As we have seen, WW is committed to educating all its employees in the hopes they will go green and use sustainable practices. Given that the company has 32,500 employees around the world, this is quite a challenge. And it is particularly difficult to find ways to reach the employees who do not have access to online tools at work—the housekeeping staff and other employees who do not work in an office setting. The company has developed alternative methods of education such as creating DVDs that employees can play on their own TVs, or implementing "train the trainer" programs for employees who do not have access to online solutions. The company continues to look for innovative ways to address this challenge.

Keeping up the Momentum

When a program such as Wyndham Green is so successful, sometimes it is challenging to find ways to keep up the momentum and go even further. Taylor said the company is determined to continue educating its employees about the Wyndham Green program, maintaining the momentum, and expanding its scope to include other key areas related to sustainability.[66]

Addressing Continual Growth

It seems ironic that growth itself would present challenges for a large, successful company like WW, but several people I spoke with said it brings with it significant challenges. Taylor said, "A key challenge is our growth in the U.S. and in new markets. When we add new properties and employees, we have to train and educate the employees about our sustainability program and quickly get them up to speed while simultaneously meeting our goals."[67]

This steady growth is particularly difficult because WW buys and assimilates other companies that are not as sophisticated as Wyndham and often have competing priorities. "There are always competing priorities for everybody in our personal lives and competing initiatives within the organization. How do you balance all of those, maintain the priorities within an organization, and keep moving forward? That's the biggest challenge for us," said Taylor.

Ballotti echoed this when he spoke about the need to communicate across the broad spectrum of the company's stakeholders. "We need to communicate across our entire stakeholder base. I'm talking about the thousands of owners who own our resorts and the hundreds of thousands of stakeholders who own the homes we rent. How we communicate is very important to our big initiatives."[68]

Acknowledging Resistance to Green and Sustainability among Consumers

A final challenge for the company stems from the wide range and varied nature of green consumers. Like any consumer or service organization, Wyndham has a number of different segments to address, some of whom do not understand or believe in the value of going green. "You have the very, very green (20 percent) to the moderates (about 60 percent) who are doing various things and the 20 percent who are not ever going to believe; they're not going to do anything. This is the case within any organization," said Taylor.[69]

Lessons Learned

Here I synthesize the primary lessons learned from the series of interviews I conducted with WW leaders and managers and from my examination of the company's GRI reports, and other documents. I believe these lessons are widely applicable not only to the retail, hospitality, and tourism industry, but to other industries as well.

- Focus and commit. Make sustainability a strategic priority. It has to be both bottom-up and supported and led by senior management.

People aren't going to embrace it unless everyone at the top is committed to it.

- Start with low-hanging fruit. Focus on small wins and build over time. It's a journey and an ongoing process of improvement. Small wins every day translate into long-term success for the organization.
- Create a multitiered strategy to address the needs of all your stakeholders, from top-down to grass roots. Work with local teams to roll out programs according to their market.
- Give employees opportunities to come forward, unleash innovation, collaboration, and education. Develop a variety of vehicles to reach employees both online and offline.
- Act with integrity, always. Let your values drive your actions.
- Keep communicating the benefits over and over and over again. Describe the kinds of successes you are having, cool things that are happening. Who is doing what? Make this nonstop. Consistency is key.
- Show everyone how they are contributing to a higher purpose through their work and how they make a difference every day. They want to belong and find meaning in their organizations. Bring the organization along with you. Do not get too far out in front in your eagerness to do so much. Take the time to communicate to others why what you're doing is important. You can't overemphasize communications; that's what gets people engaged and brings them along.
- Wrap it with fun! If you're not having fun with it, it's not worth doing it.

Frameworks, Tools, and Resources

WW employs numerous existing frameworks and global sustainability standards on sustainability. These include:

- Global Reporting Initiative (GRI). The company believes the annual GRI Sustainability Framework provides good guidelines and benchmarking inside and outside the industry.
- The Carbon Disclosure Project. WW views this as an excellent tool for investors.
- U.S. Green Building Council's LEED. WW's LEED-certified buildings include its LEED Silver interior certified corporate headquarters in Parsippany, New Jersey; a LEED Gold interior certification; and the Orlando-based Sea Harbor corporate office LEED certification.

WW's internally developed frameworks and tools include:

- The Hotel Carbon Measurement Initiative and the Wyndham Green Toolbox, which helps properties measure their carbon footprint
- A sustainability measurement framework for hotels, developed with Cornell University
- A TCO calculator, which is on its website

WW is active in industry associations such as the World Travel and Tourism Council, World Business Summit, International Tourism Partnership, American Hotel and Lodging Association (AH&LA), and Council on Hotel, Restaurant, and Institutional Education (CHRIE). It works with the Clinton Global Initiative, the U.S. EPA, and President Obama's Better Buildings Challenge.

Conclusion

In this chapter, I have tried to cover WW's deep dedication to the triple bottom line as manifested in the enormous breadth and depth of its sustainability initiatives and best practices. Here, I'd like to mention the fourth leg of that three-legged stool. That "fourth leg is all about passion and leadership," said Taylor.[70] I personally experienced this passion and leadership in everyone I interviewed at Wyndham. I hope that by my sharing their wisdom, which is fueled by their passion and leadership, it becomes contagious and ignites the sea change in mind-sets and behaviors necessary to create one green and sustainable earth.

CHAPTER 11

People, Planet, and Profits
in a New Green Economy

If building a sustainable enterprise was a fashionable trend five
years ago, today it is a business imperative. . . . And if done well, it
is a true competitive advantage.
                                    —Wharton Business School, 2011

I started this book on an optimistic, albeit soberly realistic, note of
hope and possibility, taking the position that we *can and will* find a
way to be and have *enough . . . for all . . . forever.* I conclude it with
concrete ideas, practical and inspirational recommendations, and action
steps to help us all move in that direction. But first, to provide a context
for these next steps, I distill and synthesize much of the information
presented in chapters 2 through 9.

I begin with best practices, introducing the appendix and the six interconnected categories I used to create the appendix, all of which must
be taken into account when an organization is creating a true culture for
sustainability. I also discuss how to prepare your company for implementing a best practice from another organization.

Next, I give an overview of lessons learned: Table 11.1a, "Lessons
Learned," offers topics to consider in the people, planet, and profit domains, and Table 11.1b, "Lessons Learned: Stepping-Stones on the Journey to Sustainability," provides examples from this book of the lessons
learned in those overlapping domains. I then review challenges that these
companies face and that they and others will continue to face.

After summarizing some of the best practices, lessons learned, and challenges from my research, I look more deeply into what this all means, or tells us. In Table 11.2, "Essential Elements of a Culture of Sustainability," I identify eight critical cultural dimensions and show how essential elements of these are manifested at either end of a continuum ranging from unsustainable to holistic-sustainable. In Table 11.3, "Sustainable Habits to Cultivate," I present 15 sustainability-inspired habits, or practices, and their counterposed unsustainable practices. I explain what the sustainable practices do (e.g., "promote self-awareness," "strengthens organization," and "motivate and inspire people") and how they work (e.g., "accomplished through suspension and redirecting patterns of thought" and "uses principles of positive psychology to motivate and inspire people") to help people in and out of organizations in their personal and organizational journeys. I end with some recommendations of my own to help companies build a culture for sustainability from a people, planet, and profits perspective.

Best Practices

How to Think About, Use, and Leverage Best Practices

I have presented a wide range of "best practices" throughout this book, and many will surely be generalizable and transferable not only to organizations in their industries and sectors but also to a wide range of other industries and types of organizations. But before implementing any best practice, it is always important to ask if it is a good fit for the specific context, organization, and need for which it will be applied. There are attendant risks to be considered when trying to implement a best practice in a context that is different from the one in which it was created. In addition, necessary support structures must be identified and put in place.

Be aware of key vulnerabilities such as inadequate levels of leadership buy-in and support, management capacity, employee and financial resources, and preexisting organizational structures and processes, and be prepared to address these before beginning. You may need to revamp entrenched organizational processes, reorganize your budget, and work with managers to ensure that they understand the best practice and have the time, passion, and staff to get behind it

In addition, when rolling out or piloting a new program, we often see what is commonly referred to as the Hawthorne effect: an immediate uptick in enthusiasm and other related favorable conditions that ultimately diminish or even fade over time.

In all cases when considering a best practice, it is important to develop realistic expectations, and test the waters before embarking on wholesale implementation. These caveats should not, however, prevent organizations and the people in them from learning from each other.

In the appendix, I offer some of the most intriguing best practices from throughout the book. For simplicity, I organized them into six overall categories: people, community, customers, planet, suppliers, and profit. Please be aware that these categories are interconnected, and a culture for sustainability cannot be achieved unless all are taken into account.

People Initiatives

People initiatives focus on inspiring and engaging people in sustainability-related initiatives through communications and social media, by providing opportunities for sustainability workforce development and training, and by recognizing and rewarding progress. Much of this is driven by organizations such as Ingersoll Rand's Center for Energy Efficiency and Sustainability (CEES), which has needed to learn how to exercise influence without authority.

The most sustainable companies find ways to leverage human resources on behalf of sustainability, including embedding sustainability in their leadership-development and talent-management programs and processes. Because of soaring numbers of baby-boomer retirements in the next few years, companies such as BASF have developed and implemented knowledge-transfer programs to ensure that the vast experience of its employees carries into the subsequent generations. A number of the companies endeavor to capture employees' hearts and minds through employee-centered initiatives organized around Earth Day and World Environment Day, and providing year-round, ongoing support for green teams.

Driving culture change around sustainability is explicitly emphasized, with a strong focus on fostering a culture of innovation, at companies such as BASF, Sanofi, Ingersoll Rand, and Wyndham Worldwide.

Ultimately, sustainability can only be achieved on a firm foundation of sustainable values (discussed in Recommendations, Essential Elements of a Culture for Sustainability). When approaching values, I found that companies focused on initiatives such as from home to workplace, a passion to help people, and incorporating sustainable values into the company's strategic priorities.

Because they have found that a healthy employee is a more productive employee, several companies' representatives spoke about the importance of making wellness programs available to ensure the health and well-being of their employees. Another common thread was the emphasis on promoting diversity and inclusion, and several outstanding examples of companies' programs are provided in the chapters on Alcatel-Lucent, Sanofi, and Wyndham Worldwide. Promoting greater work–life balance through flexible work arrangements and other policies also was a recurring theme in many of the companies.

Community Initiatives

Community outreach and involvement is an essential aspect of a culture for sustainability. Especially impressive is Alcoa's Community framework, which is at once comprehensive and empowering to all stakeholders. Local volunteerism efforts and employee-giving campaigns support communities' local economic development, address community social issues, and engage employees' hearts and hands all at the same time.

Throughout the book, I have highlighted effective ways companies collaborate across multiple stakeholders and industries. Examples are companies that work with nongovernmental organizations (NGOs) and governments to provide access to much-needed medicine for those who are otherwise not able to afford it and reduce health-care costs for the most vulnerable.

Corporate social responsibility and philanthropy is at its best when it brings together employees, the community, the people, and the planet as the ultimate beneficiaries.

Customer Initiatives

When addressing sustainability from the customer's perspective, the best practices involve leading by example, tying sustainability to innovation, creating and maintaining customer value, and shifting customer mind-sets and behavior. I found some of the most intriguing practices at Alcatel-Lucent, which makes breakthroughs in telecommunications and strives to close the digital divide; Ingersoll Rand, which deploys outcome-driven innovation (ODI) to address some of our most intractable sustainability challenges; and Sanofi, whose story exemplifies the evolution from environmentalism to social consciousness to innovation. Ingersoll Rand's focus on creating and sustaining customer value as it segments its marketplace and creates a green portfolio is instructive for companies of all sizes seeking to become more sustainable. Wyndham Worldwide's panoply of ecologically friendly initiatives for guests can become a role model for the hospitality industry. Particularly impressive is how the company has gone about instilling sustainable practices in its franchisees and time-share owners.

Planet Initiatives

As evidenced in the multitude of environmental best practices in every chapter of this book, all the companies profiled are passionately committed to respecting and restoring the planet.

Church & Dwight's dedication to the planet is manifested in its environmental and product stewardship, including full ingredient disclosure, and its management-systems-supporting programs, including responsible care, product care, and Business Impact Matrix.

BASF's leads the way in life-cycle thinking with its life-cycle assessment, environmental-management system, SEE Balance (social, environment, economic), SET (sustainability, eco-efficiency, traceability), AgBalance, Sustainability Check, eco-efficiency analysis, and materiality assessments.

Sanofi's energy sustainability programs and Global Water Tool demonstrate its commitment to reducing the use of energy and preserving water and its sources.

Notably, most all the companies find value in partnering across sectors with universities, government agencies, and NGOs to achieve their goals. In addition to the Institute for Sustainable Enterprise (ISE) at Fairleigh Dickinson University (FDU), frequently mentioned were the Environmental Defense Fund, the Clinton Global Initiative, and the Cambridge Climate Leaders.

Finding and using the right metrics came up repeatedly as a key component of change for sustainability. In particular, materiality assessments and total cost of ownership were often cited as helpful ways to make progress. Bureau Veritas described how they help customers through the use of materiality, assurances, and verification processes.

Regardless of industry, just about every company has made or is making green buildings a visible symbol of its commitment to sustainability and finding that these save money and create healthier work environments for their employees.

Supply Chain

Increasingly supply chain issues are coming to the fore of sustainability conversations, and this was true in almost all the companies I interviewed. Wyndham Worldwide spoke proudly about the Wyndham

Green Supplier Program, including its fully sustainable bathroom amenities, uniforms made out of 100 percent recycled plastic bottles, and more. A related recurrent theme was cultivating supplier diversity and linking it to sustainability, with many initiatives driving this desired dual outcome simultaneously, such as those at Sanofi and Wyndham Worldwide. Every company recognized the importance of instilling sustainable practices throughout the entire value chain. Particularly striking examples of this in practice are Ingersoll Rand's use of life-cycle thinking and its definition of what that means.

Profit Initiatives

A key way to create value is to incorporate sustainability into the company's governance structure, as Wyndham Worldwide has incorporated Wyndham Green and related sustainability policies into its governance structure. Shareholders benefit from each initiative described earlier and from the totality of these synergistic initiatives. Sustainability and Corporate Social Responsibility need to be fully integrated into the company's strategy if a company is to make genuine headway in its journey to sustainability. BASF's "Creating chemistry for a sustainable future" is a notable and impressive illustration of how this can be accomplished. Ingersoll Rand's explicit recognition of the inextricable link between sustainability and premier performance demonstrates how a company can effectively and strategically find ways to tie sustainability to the company's brand, promise, vision, and purpose. Ingersoll Rand's approach to translating sustainability into customer value is particularly worthy of note.

Lessons Learned

Each chapter in this book includes a summary of that company's unique lessons learned based on my interviews and my supplementary research into the company. Because I believe many of these lessons have great generalizability across the board, I have synthesized them into two overall high-level charts, based on the memorable acronym S.U.S.T.A.I.N.A.B.L.E. and the triple-bottom-line perspective of people, planet, and profits. In Table 11.1a, I present a wide range of topical areas for readers and organizations to consider when attempting to build a culture for sustainability. I strongly suggest that all companies and organizations think deeply about these topics and consider the associated descriptions in Table 11.1b important stepping stones as they strive to build their own unique cultures for sustainability.

It is important to note that the topic areas in Table 11.1a can be looked at in any number of ways, and the lessons learned in Table 11.1b are *examples* of significant takeaways from the companies in this book; they are not inclusive, and chapters 2 through 9 offer many more. I recommend that readers read all the "Lessons Learned" sections in this book (near the end of each chapter), paying particular attention to those in the companies that are most aligned with each reader's organization from an industry and/or size perspective.

Critical Issues and Challenges that Must Be Addressed

For a clear picture of the challenges and global risks we face today, please refer to *Global Risks Landscape 2013*,[1] which I referenced in the first chapter of this book. The risks most likely to "manifest" over the next 10 years based on a survey of 1,000 experts in industry, government, and academia and those perceived by the same 1,000 experts as the most likely to cause the greatest impacts on the global economy are virtually all related to sustainability. These include rising greenhouse gas emissions, water supply crises, food-shortage crises, chronic labor-market imbalance, mismanagement of population ageing, severe income disparity, persistent extreme weather, unsustainable population growth, failure of climate change adaptation, land-and-waterway-use mismanagement, mineral-resource-supply vulnerability, and extreme volatility in energy prices.

I believe all organizations regardless of their size, but especially corporations with a large global footprint, have a profound duty and moral responsibility to help address and resolve these, the defining challenges of the twenty-first century. In this context, I summarize the sustainability-related challenges the nine companies featured in this book continue to face in the areas of people, planet, and profits.

Company Conundrums in Addressing Sustainability-Related Challenges

People-Related Challenges

Although many companies have begun the process of putting together sustainability programs and establishing sustainability policies, research demonstrates that employees are not being engaged in these initiatives as much as they could be. Many companies are focusing solely, or primarily, on the environmental side of sustainability and missing the huge opportunity that the "people" side provides.

Volumes of research document strong linkages between employee engagement and higher organizational performance. At the same time, research shows that a sustainable company is a high-performing company. This suggests that involving employees in sustainability initiatives will greatly strengthen a corporation along all axes of the triple bottom line: It will boost employee engagement, increase sustainability, and expand the organization's financial bottom line.

Table 11.1a   Lessons Learned: Topical Areas for Readers and Organizations to Consider

These are distilled from the lessons learned during my research into the nine companies featured in this book.

	People	Planet	Profits
S	Stakeholders	Stewardship; Sound science	Strategic Sustainability filter
U	Understanding	Undoing harm	Urgency
S	Safety	Sustainable supply chain	Standards
T	Top-down and bottom-up; Teams	Transparency	Timing
A	Authenticity	Attention	Alignment
I	Involvement; Inclusion	Install a process; Integrate	Innovation
N	Network	Neutralize	Say "no" to unsustainable things
A	Awareness	Appreciate	Apply and activate
B	Behaviors	Balance	Branding
L	Leadership; Leading by example	Local	Legacy
E	Educate and equip	Ethics	Evolutionary

Table 11.1b Lessons Learned: Stepping Stones on the Journey to Sustainability

S	Using *sound science* and a *strategic sustainability filter,* find creative ways to engage all your *stakeholders* in conversations for sustainable prosperity as you work steadfastly to become better *stewards* of the planet and people. Own responsibility for legacy issues and the entire life cycle of your products, including end-of-life. Minimize use and control impact of products and ingredients that are harmful.
U	Develop *understanding* in your employees, suppliers, and communities of the importance of *undoing harm* to the planet. Do this *urgently* and comprehensively.
S	Ensure the *safety* of your people, the planet, and your products. Raise minimum *standards* for products and use influence to develop diversity and life-cycle consciousness in your *supply chain.* Use best practices in sustainable supply chain management, implement carbon-neutrality strategies, and conduct supplier assessments for environmental and social responsibility.
T	Take a *top-down and bottom-up* approach as you translate sustainable behavior into business practices. Have middle management be accountable for sustainable business objectives, and create cross-functional *teams* to implement them. Recognize that it takes *time.* Be *transparent:* Go public with your successes and your failures. Report the bad with the good.
A	With *authenticity,* gradually build awareness among your employees, leveraging existing resources and learning from others. *Align* everything with sustainability, making it a strategic priority and paying *attention* to the impact of all your decisions and actions on the planet.
I	Tie sustainability to *innovation.* Give all employees opportunities to be *included* and *involved* as you unleash their creativity and collaboration on behalf of *innovation. Install a process* that fully *integrates* sustainability into your business plan. The process starts with having a goal, making a commitment, and setting milestones and targets. Stick with your commitment no matter what.
N	Cultivate wide online and face-to-face *networks* because the future will be networks of people working together to address seemingly intractable problems. *Neutralize* any harm you are doing to the planet. *Say no* to unsustainable actions and decisions; stopping doing unsustainable things is as important as starting doing sustainable things.
A	Develop *awareness* of global needs and ways to address them through ongoing education that reaches all employees. Inspire employees to *apply* their passion and talent to finding answers and solving problems.

(Continued)

Table 11.1b   (*Continued*)

	Activate them by engaging their hearts, minds, and hands. Show *appreciation* and respect for all people, healthy living, and the planet.
B	Review the priorities of your entire enterprise and find a new *balance*. Know that changing mind-sets and *behavior* is a long-term process. Help employees take pride in the sustainability of your company. Focus on *branding* that promotes sustainability to attract the kinds of employees and customers you want and need.
L	*Lead by example,* guiding others with a "pay it forward" mind-set and listening to people along the way. Involve the *local* community. Build on your company's *legacy* by tying it to sustainability.
E	*Educate and equip* people with valid data and metrics that supports your story and makes it credible. Take responsibility for your actions and don't ever compromise on *ethics*. Be committed and intentional, and persevere through every step in the *evolutionary* process that is sustainability.

© 2013 Jeana Wirtenberg and Transitioning to Green

Companies undertake employee engagement for sustainability initiatives for many reasons: to attract and retain top talent, enhance employee loyalty and community trust, involve employees in problem solving and innovation, increase employee productivity, and reduce costs. However, there is still significant opportunity for improvement. Gallup estimates that the "engagement gap" costs United States businesses about $300 billion in lost productivity each year.[2]

Joel Makower and his GreenBiz colleagues propose that sustainability may be the key to closing that employee engagement gap. It could well provide employees with the "reason, opportunity, freedom and knowledge" to participant in meaningful and purpose-driven work that simultaneously addresses the most significant risks described earlier.[3] So what's keeping companies stuck and preventing them from moving forward in this direction? The challenges still facing the leading-edge companies featured in this book may hold a clue.

Changing Mind-Sets and Behavior

Every company encounters challenges regarding changing the entrenched mind-sets and behavior in its leaders and its employees. In the Recommendations section later, I provide two frameworks I've created specifically for this book in response to these challenges: Table 11.2 describes the eight essential dimensions of a culture for sustainability and numerous elements within each that I believe must be present for it to be sustainable, and Table 11.3 recommends sustainability-inspired habits that need to be cultivated if a culture for sustainability is to thrive. As Steve Fromkin said in chapter 3, "These are difficult nuts to crack because you need to change people's habits."

Filling the Pipeline from STEM Disciplines

The STEM (science, technology, engineering, and mathematics) education gap and shortage of talent in the United States is widely experienced by most of the companies featured in this book. The ability to attract and retain young people from these technical fields will be essential if the United States is to maintain its competitiveness. I believe this challenge is interwoven with the undervaluing of innovation and that both must be addressed simultaneously. Tying sustainability to innovation drives prosperity, creates jobs, and addresses intractable problems.

Overwhelming Workloads and Competing Priorities

Today's almost ubiquitous "do more with less" organizational culture cuts too far into the muscle. Many companies are sitting on mountains of cash but not investing in their people, jobs, and the future. Sustainability initiatives frequently get "stuck in the middle" as they vie for managers' limited time and attention. All too often, managers wearily view these initiatives as just one more thing to do on an already overflowing plate. This is resulting in burn-out, stress, and disengaged employees who are waiting for the opportunity to leave their jobs at the earliest possible opportunity.

HR Needs to Step Up to the Plate

In all too many companies, the Human Resources (HR) function has yet to fully embrace sustainability.[4] The sustainability leaders I interviewed want HR to become an advocate for embedding sustainability in everyone's goals and objectives, which would be a great first step. HR could be a lever that when pulled generates a "multiplier effect," which would embed sustainability in myriad HR strategies and key initiatives including those that

- Maximize employee engagement
- Optimize talent-management systems and processes (e.g., attraction, recruitment, performance management, and compensation)

- Ensure diversity and inclusion in a global, multicultural context
- Promote ethics and transparency
- Incorporate sustainability in workplace policies

Yet at many companies, including several featured in this book, HR hasn't fully incorporated sustainability into its work and needs to step up and play a much larger role.

Planet

Consumer Perceptions that Green Costs More, and Finding a Workable Trade-Off

The jury is still out on how to best shift consumer mind-sets to a triple-bottom-line vision, so they see the big picture and consciously choose sustainable products, voting with their pocketbooks. What is not contestable is that a large segment of the consumer population believes that green costs more and doesn't work as well, and this is a serious challenge for corporations. The various companies that mentioned this problem had different approaches to addressing it: some were using market segmentation that targets consumers according to their shade of green; others were based on innovation and technology solutions; and still others on educating consumers in the importance of the total-cost-of-ownership perspective.

Being Sustainable versus Touting It

The challenge "being sustainable versus touting it" is highlighted by Lowry and Ryan in the foreword to Jacquelyn Ottman's 2011 book *The New Rules of Green Marketing:* "The recent explosion of green media, products, services, and green marketing has brought with it a sea of confusion and a lack of trust, all of which risk undermining the entire green movement and returning us to an era of consumer apathy." As Ottman's book went to press, "some of the world's largest polluters also rank high as some of the most 'environmental' companies, according to consumer perception."[5]

This misalignment between public perception and true environmental impact is amply documented by TerraChoice, in its "Seven Sins of Greenwashing":

- Hidden trade-off
- No proof

- Vagueness
- Irrelevance
- Lesser of two evils
- Fibbing
- Worshiping false labels[6]

This presents a profound challenge to all companies that are authentically seeking to go green and market their products and services as such.

Tree Hugging, Cutting Edge, or Bleeding Edge?

Many people I interviewed acknowledged significant levels of resistance to green and sustainability among consumers. They were struggling to meet customers where they are in light of ever-changing marketplace expectations while at the same time educating them about the value of green and sustainable products and prodding them to see the value of purchasing such products. These sustainability champions have a strong personal commitment to environmental sustainability, and often an altruistic desire to do good, but it is a challenge for them (and their companies) not to be seen as "tree huggers" or too "bleeding edge." In responding to this challenge, I was especially impressed with Church & Dwight's strategy of "being actively prepared," as it pressed itself to constantly look ahead to prepare now for potential changes that likely are coming down the pike.

Profits

Measuring ROI of Sustainability Initiatives

All the companies profiled in this book face the challenge of finding ways to manage and measure the return on investment (ROI) of sustainability initiatives for their shareholders. They must ask the question, How does the financial bottom line improve when we focus simultaneously on leveraging the talents of our people and mitigating our impact on the environment (e.g., in terms of savings from energy efficiency, waste reduction, and so forth).

The key to measuring ROI from sustainability initiatives is determining how to calculate cost savings and financial benefits that accrue from a focus on the triple bottom line.

Where sustainability's ROI gets tricky to measure is when looking at key performance indicators (KPIs) such as employee engagement, community involvement, stakeholder engagement, and public relations (PR) and branding. In order to see what these areas are actually contributing, companies may need to figure out how to develop new gauges of successful outcomes that incorporate these broader dimensions of the triple bottom line.

Importantly, companies need to account for "externalities." Externalities are real costs of doing business that are not included in the balance sheet of a company. Right now, this accounting sleight of hand leaves companies free to make decisions that increase their short-term profits by laying off costs (usually related to people and planet) to the public in general, costs whose payments are most often deferred to the future. These are both direct monetary costs and more-broad social and environmental costs. In addition to artificially inflating its bottom line by not including the real costs of doing business, the company exposes itself to significant additional risks.

Externalities are the "black swans" of the economy that contain the potential to devastate not only individual companies but also whole industries. "Universal Ownership: Why Environmental Externalities Matter to Institutional Investors," a 2010 report published by the United Nations Environment Programme (UNEP), asserts that "externalities can affect shareholder value because they lead to a more uncertain, rapidly-changing economic environment and greater systemic risks."[7] It also estimates the 2008 cost of environmental damage caused by the world's 3,000 largest publicly listed companies to be $2.15 trillion. Were companies to have to pay for the damage they cause, their revenues would be substantially reduced.

The challenge and the opportunity is to develop sustainability strategies that optimize a company's ability to reduce its operating costs, costs of goods sold, and ecological and carbon footprints while enhancing employee productivity, revenues, and market share growth through strategic investments in product and business model innovations. One of the critical gates that companies need to go through to achieve this is getting buy-in for total cost of ownership and life-cycle costing.

Dealing with Short-Termism

Publicly held companies are especially challenged to meet or exceed Wall Street expectations for each quarter; often forcing them to remain myopically focused on keeping profits high or increasing them in the coming few months.

Unfortunately, this all too often leads companies to make decisions that are counterproductive, such as laying off the people who can help the company become more sustainable in the long term.

Working with Different Measurement Systems
and Methods around the Globe

Global companies face the significant challenge of needing to work with many different sets of standards, measurement systems, and methods related to sustainability depending on which countries they are working in. While writing this book, I learned that many countries have their own measurement systems for carbon, waste, water, paper, and energy. A company must be nimble enough to learn these quickly if it is to be able to customize its measurement system for use in other regions and countries. Supporting standards, such as ISO14001, that are global yet allow for maximum local autonomy in implementation is a good first step in addressing this challenge.

Recommendations

> You cannot solve a systems problem by an analysis of its parts.
> —Russell L. Ackoff

As we have seen, changing organizational culture is very hard but not impossible. Ed Schein's classic model of organizational culture sheds light on its complexity and shows how it operates at three levels of depth. At the most visible, or surface, level are what Schein calls artifacts—the organizational structures, processes, and behaviors we can readily observe. At the next level are the "espoused beliefs and values," which include the organization's strategies, goals, and philosophies. And at the deepest level are the "organizational assumptions," which are "the unconscious, taken-for-granted beliefs and values" that "determine [the] behavior, perceptions, thought, and feelings" of the people within the organization.[8]

Because I strongly believe building a culture for sustainability must mindfully address all three levels (artifacts, espoused beliefs and values, and underlying assumptions), my recommendations below are both broad and deep.

Examine and Explore the Eight Dimensions
of a Culture for Sustainability

Creating an authentic culture for sustainability takes a lot more than words or proclamations. Table 11.2 presents eight critical cultural dimensions that I believe are the underpinnings of a culture for sustainability: values; mind-set; leadership; transformational change process; employee engagement; learning; diversity, inclusion and social justice; and intelligence. Within each dimension, I present several elements that fall at either end of a continuum from unsustainable to holistic-sustainable. For instance, unsustainable manifestations and elements in the *values dimension* include "lack of caring for people and planet"; those in the *mind-set dimension* include "either/or"; and in the *leadership dimension,* "command-and-control."

Table 11.2   Essential Elements of a Culture for Sustainability

Dimension of Culture	Unsustainable	Holistic-Sustainable
Values	• Overly self-absorbed/disconnected • Attached to being right • Values money and "having" over all else • Lack of integrity • "Do what I say, not what I do" • Lack of caring for people and planet • Values are espoused but not demonstrated in practice	• Sees self and organization in context of community, society, and earth • Understands that sustainable values (people, planet, profits) are the underpinning of everything—from the way business is done to how decisions are made to the way in which the business relates to the various systems of which it is a part. • Values intangibles and things that are difficult to measure • Values triple-bottom-line prosperity • Committed to personal growth, new learning, and opportunities • Seeks ways to contribute • Values and acts with integrity • Genuinely connects with others to collaboratively create the will and consequent actions; acts with mutuality • Demonstrates respect for all people and precious natural resources • Exhibits no difference between espoused values and values-in-use; i.e., values are authentic

Dimension of Culture	Unsustainable	Holistic-Sustainable
Mind-set	• Stopped by fear • Scarcity • Separation • Either/or • Taking • Viewing people as objects, instruments for your own benefit • Holding on tightly to what you have	• Actions are consistent with values; not stopped by fear • Possibility thinking • Appreciative • Abundance • Systems thinking • Both-and • Global, inclusive • Hopeful • Service • Giving; generous (with everything—time, money, ideas, information, empathy, compassion)
Leadership	• Command-and-control • Suppresses peoples' energy • Stifles creativity • Operates in functional silos • Focuses on value extraction • Compliance • Risk-averse • Withholds information	• Leads with purpose • Builds "leaderful" teams and organizations • Authentic • Sees organization as living system • Inspirational: expands people's energy • Enables self-organizing, cross-functional teams • Unleashes creativity and innovation • Shares information • Works collaboratively to address big challenges • Focuses on value creation • Thinks and leads strategically • Servant leadership; asks "How can I help?" • Courageous
Transformational change process	• Fixated on problems • Reactive, tactical • Tells people what to do	• Visionary; balances short term and long term • Envisions the future we want to create

(Continued)

Table 11.2   (*Continued*)

Dimension of Culture	Unsustainable	Holistic-Sustainable
		• Values emerging possibilities • Asks, listens, and appreciates what people have to say • Dances with the realities of life • Fluid and dynamic
Employee engagement	• Hierarchical • Tells • Stressful and overly demanding • Tedious: lacking in meaning • Aggressively competitive	• Includes • Asks • Builds flexibility, agility, resilience • Engages imagination; fun • Uses games and creative, team-oriented competition • Contributes value
Learning	• Believing you must have the answers • Know it all • Linear • Single disciplines; siloed thinking • Sustainability as bolt-on • Doesn't translate data and information into usable knowledge • Expert model • Insular	• Inquiring: frames and asks profound questions • Listens deeply and generously • Connects the dots: pattern recognition • Multidisciplinary • Open to new possibilities • Embeds sustainability throughout learning and development • Usable knowledge, wisdom • Searches outside organization for innovative ideas • Transparent
Diversity, inclusion, social justice	• Compliance • Politically correct; marketing • Tokenism • Homogeneity • Unaware of, doesn't understand, or is resistant to seeing historical and sociological patterns that contribute to present problems	• Corporate social responsibility • Cultural sensitivity • Multicultural • Transgenerational • Plurality • Simultaneity; intersectionality • Inclusive • Deep caring for all people

Dimension of Culture	Unsustainable	Holistic-Sustainable
Intelligence	• Narrowly defined • Elitist • Super-rational	• Appreciative • Emotional • Social • Ecological • Values, gains, and applies knowledge • Wisdom • Versatile, multifaceted, creative, and innovative • Appeals to both sides of the brain

© 2013 Jeana Wirtenberg and Transitioning to Green

At the other end of the continuum, holistic-sustainable elements of the *transformational change dimension* include "fluid and dynamic"; the *employee engagement dimension* includes "engages imagination"; and the *learning dimension* includes "inquiring."

I recommend that all my readers, from every size organization and corporation, examine and explore the elements of holistic sustainability and find ways to adopt them, customizing them so you can make them your own.

Cultivate Sustainability-Inspired Habits and Practices

Taking this a step deeper, to become truly sustainable, we need to change our automatic, unexamined behaviors, or *habits*. In his book *The Power of Habits*, Charles Duhigg provides a framework for understanding how habits work and guiding principles for how to change them.[9] Habits make up a good portion of the functions people perform every day, and changing them takes both intention and attention.

To achieve the greatest results with the least amount of effort, I recommend that individuals and organizations focus on changing what Duhigg calls keystone habits—small wins that require moderate effort. He captured the essence of these habits in the following quote: "The habits that matter most are the ones that, when they start to shift, dislodge and remake other patterns."[10] Shifting these habits begins to create a structure that encourages other related habits to begin to shift and ultimately to flourish. This works by creating a microculture of the individual and the people around them. Changing such habits encourages widespread and deep cultural change, which will in the end lead to a more sustainable culture.

Table 11.3   **Sustainability-Inspired Practices**

Unsustainable Practices	Sustainable Culture Practices (SCP)	How Each SCP Works
Telling; lecturing; dominating through power and control	Silent reflection	Promotes self-awareness and contemplative habits.
Inflexibility; holding onto one's previous or single point of view	Reframing, versatility	Allows for letting go of the past and for different perspectives to enter; accomplished through suspension and redirecting patterns of thought.
Closed-minded	Appreciative inquiry	Inclusive; open; curious; builds capacity for learning and understanding.
Ego-driven; self-centered	Mindfulness; presence	Leads to self-knowledge and discovery, acute awareness, and strength of mind.
Dogmatic; holier than thou	Listening generously; opening mind to others' perspectives; empathy	Strengthens organization. Builds collective capacity and wisdom over long term.
Either/or	Both-and; ambicultural	Demonstrates respect for opposing viewpoints. Allows for new possibilities to emerge and finding common ground in the integration of opposites.
Excessive focus on consumption and having	Being, satisfaction	Leads from inside out. Cultivates inner strength, resilience, and peace.
Domination; seeing people as objects or instruments for one's own benefit	Caring; Compassion and service; partnership	Connects to deeper level of humanity at individual and organizational level.
Command-and-control	Involvement	Mobilizes engagement of whole person. Provides meaning.

Unsustainable Practices	Sustainable Culture Practices (SCP)	How Each SCP Works
Self-aggrandizing; narcissistic	Positive leadership; humility	Infuses positive energy.
Sees glass half full or empty	Culture of abundance	Speaks to heart and head.
Overly critical	Gratitude	Uses principles of positive psychology to motivate and inspire people.
Excessive internal competition	Collaboration	Takes relationships into account. Broadens boundaries and approaches.
Top-down	Self-organizing; emergent	Encourages cocreation. Seeing and acting from the whole system.
Consumption = happiness	Balance (neither asceticism nor hedonism)	Creates flourishing today and over the long term.

© 2013 Jeana Wirtenberg and Transitioning to Green

With this in mind, Table 11.3 presents 15 sustainability-inspired habits, or practices, that need to be cultivated to help build a culture for sustainability.

Taken together, these habits will promote a new, more caring way of being toward people, planet, and profits that will significantly increase the possibility that the vision of the sustainable world of 2050 that I presented in chapter 1 will become a reality.

Create a Holistic Business Sustainability Roadmap and Plan

Most companies and organizations today still largely function by separating people, planet, and profits into different buckets, as depicted in "People, Planet, and Profits in a New Green Economy." The challenge and the opportunity is how best to encourage and help every company and organization, regardless of where it is now, to make the leap as rapidly as possible to the other side of the figure where people, planet,

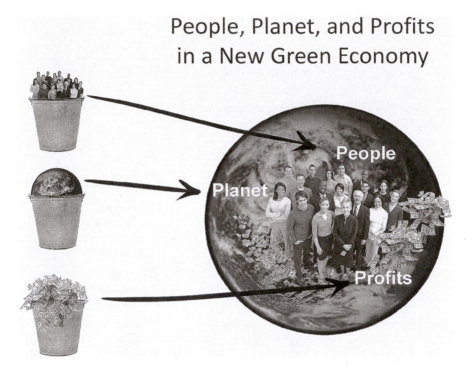

Figure 11.1   © 2013 Transitioning to Green.

and profits all interconnect synergistically in a new green economy. This is the triple bottom line, in which organizations *simultaneously*

- Bring out the best in their employees
- Help serve the local and regional communities and economies in which they live and work
- restore and regenerate the planet
- Thrive and prosper financially

In the vision presented in "People, Planet, and Profits in a New Green Economy," people in every organization live, work, and manage their organizations sustainably, working collaboratively to solve complex business and societal problems, capitalizing on opportunities in ways that simultaneously enhance their societal, environmental, and economic vitality.

Where do we begin? A holistic business sustainability roadmap and plan can help companies begin to make the shift to the triple bottom line by refocusing their business on products, processes, and services that add value to the organizations and are beneficial to people and the planet. A big picture roadmap and a more granular plan for your unique organization can help guide you in taking a strategically integrated view of your company, aligning your business goals and capabilities, and creating a structured process that will allow for nimble adaptation to the inevitable changes that will continually move the goal.

The following is a high-level four-phase process for making this shift.

Phase I. Discovery: Conduct a Comprehensive Company or Organization Self-Evaluation

The discovery phase will help you create a business sustainability roadmap to get you started on your journey. The process of building a roadmap begins from the *inside-out,* looking at your company or organization through a triple-bottom-line lens to take stock of where you are now, and from the *outside-in,* understanding how your organization fits into the larger ecosystem in which it exists from a systems perspective.

Inside-Out: Diagnose Your Current Situation from an Integrated Triple-Bottom-Line Perspective

Early in the process, it is important to look inside and self-evaluate where you are now on the journey to sustainability. Conduct a robust and honest self-evaluation, which at minimum includes these steps (all in relationship to the integrated triple bottom line of people, planet, and profits):

- Examine current business strategy, products and services, and plans.
- Inventory ongoing activities.
- Cocreate baseline performance measures and benchmarks.

For many companies that are just starting out or are at an early stage in the shift to an integrated triple-bottom-line perspective, the process comes to life with the CEO, key functional senior leaders, and managers from many functions, including at a minimum human resources, finance, and operations, getting together to examine where the company is now relative to people, planet, and profits. This might include an examination across three broad categories:

- *Eco-efficiency opportunities,* including energy, materials, water, and waste

- *Employee policies, practices, and opportunities,* including productivity, engagement, talent management, attraction and retention, development and training, and so forth
- *Innovation and growth opportunities,* including revenue and growth

Get HR Actively Involved Early On

As we have seen, because the people and cultural aspects are so integral to sustainability, HR needs to get actively involved early on and stay actively involved throughout the entire process of discovering, designing, developing, and deploying your business sustainability roadmap and plan. Areas in which HR needs to proactively provide its expertise to help companies move forward on their journeys to sustainability include leadership and management development and training; embedding sustainability into all functional areas (e.g., sustainable supply chain and procurement, green accounting, green marketing); managing the transformational change process; fostering collaboration and teamwork; creating and inculcating values; and supporting health and safety initiatives. HR needs to find ways to educate all employees, from the most senior executives to middle management to the factory workers and even the young summer interns who are still in college and just beginning to think about starting their careers. Everyone's voice needs to be heard and included; everyone has something to contribute. And it all starts with awareness and education.

Outside-In: Who Can You Learn From?

Take the time to look outside and learn from others. At minimum:

- Research sustainability-related trends and risks affecting your industry.
- Conduct stakeholder analysis and develop key stakeholder lists inside and outside your company or organization.
- Review industry standards and best practice examples.
- Gather marketplace and competitive intelligence.

Phase II. Design Your Future: Cocreate Your Sustainability Vision and Desired Culture

Your holistic business sustainability roadmap and plan continues with Phase II in which a broad cross section of people from every function get together to cocreate a shared vision that everyone can stand behind and rally around. It includes your sustainable business vision—a description of your future as a sustainable enterprise—and a clear picture of your desired culture in light of the dimensions described earlier. Importantly, it is informed by, but not limited to, your current context and culture. It needs to inspire, engage, and motivate your corporate leaders, managers, and employees as they collaborate to discover together what holistic sustainability can mean to the future of your company.

Find Your Higher Purpose

For some organizations, including several in this book, the process involves creating a long-term future vision and then standing in that vision, looking back at where you are today to help figure out how to get where you want to go. This can be revisited frequently as companies and organizations seek to discover their higher purpose in the context of the unfolding megatrends that affect sustainability and the triple bottom line. An explicit commitment to addressing important sustainability-related problems and the evolving understanding of the higher purpose of your organization and its potential contributions to the world can inform this vision as it evolves.

In addition, organizations may want to look through the lens that Jim Collins and Jerry Porras, in their seminal book *Built to Last*,[11] famously called a BHAG (big hairy audacious goal). Throughout this book are examples of companies establishing such goals: Alcatel-Lucent's commitment to closing the digital divide, Sanofi's commitment to making critically needed medicines available to solve the most challenging health issues around the world, and Ingersoll Rand's focus on addressing climate change through innovations in renewable technology and energy.

Seek first to discover what's important to the world and how to address those needs in a way that *simultaneously* helps address the sustainability BHAG or problem, supercharges your people to get their creative juices flowing, and helps you create a truly purpose-driven business or organization.

Phase III. Develop Your Plan

When you have a basic understanding of your company from a triple-bottom-line perspective and have begun to design a shared vision of your future, it's time to establish a working strategy and business plan for achieving your sustainability objectives. You can begin to get traction with your plan by methodically working through the following streams of activities:

- Create a high-level outline of your company's business sustainability plan and roadmap
- Select critical performance measures to assess success of different opportunities
- Screen, evaluate, and prioritize major opportunities
- Analyze risks; assess and document financial and nonfinancial risks associated with your strategy
- Create an implementation and integrated tactical plan for stakeholders and employee engagement
- Codevelop and practice presenting next-step recommendations and action plans

Phase IV. Deploy Your Plan

Now you're ready to deploy your plan. Don't delay just because all the *i*'s are not dotted and *t*'s are not yet crossed. Those finishing touches can be put in place only by actively working in those areas. Your plan might begin with low-hanging fruit for cost-saving initiatives or things that, in your company's self-evaluation, you noticed are urgently needed. In many cases, the savings from these sorts of incremental improvements, made in the context of your overall business sustainability plan, can provide valuable sources of funding for future programs. Ultimately, there will be a snowball effect, as incremental improvements multiply, synergize, and lead to the desired goal of systemic innovation. So get started today! And if this is too daunting or overwhelming, know that there are lots of organizations and people ready to help you get going on your journey.

Conclusion

We have come a long way, but have much further to go to get on a path toward a sustainable world. Bringing about a world we can only begin to envision starts with each person's individually and collectively acknowledging that we have created and are perpetuating the world we have today. When we collectively accept ownership not only of the problems but also of the creative resources we have to address them, we build the capacity and take the responsibility necessary to create a new future for us all. We need to develop the wherewithal to reframe every horror and devastation that occurs not as a sign that we are failing, but as a giant wake up call to spring us into action.

Who Can and Will Guide Us There?

The leaders of tomorrow's sustainable enterprises must be created and supported today. These are those talented members of the organization—who may come from *any function* and *any level*—who exhibit the leadership potential necessary to meet unforeseen challenges and manifest the capacity to transform present-day success into a very different future.

But an organization cannot rely on a small set of leaders to build and carry on its culture for sustainability. A truly sustainable culture exists and lives on in perpetuity far beyond any current set of leaders or individuals. So creating a *leaderful* organization, one in which every person in the organization takes responsibility for leading it into the future, is a central component of building a culture for sustainability.

Today we stand at a crossroads. The choices each of us make with respect to people, planet, and profits will determine the kind of future we have. What will we choose? What can each of us do to help move us toward a sustainable future, with *enough . . . for all . . . forever . . . ?*

Appendix: Best Practices for Building a Culture for Sustainability

People	Chapter	Examples
Learning to influence without authority	7. Ingersoll Rand 10. Wyndham Worldwide	• Center for Energy Efficiency and Sustainability (CEES) • Influencing without control
Inspiring people through Communications and social media	2. Alcatel-Lucent 4. BASF 10. Wyndham Worldwide	• Engage • We Create Chemistry World Tour • Simply Dare! • Wyndham Nation
Recognizing progress	3. Alcoa 10. Wyndham Worldwide	• Applause • Caught Green Handed
Investing in people to build an engaged Workforce	3. Alcoa 7. Ingersoll Rand 9. Sanofi 10. Wyndham Worldwide	• Four E's and a P • One STEP Forward • Connecting with employees in every function • Create small wins that generate long-term success • Wrap it with fun!

(*Continued*)

People	Chapter	Examples
Leveraging human resources	4. BASF	• Three-prong global people strategy: excellent people; excellent place to work; excellent leaders • Development centers • Market customer focus teams
	10. Wyndham Worldwide	• Alignment and integration with Human Resources and Corporate Services
Leadership development	8. Pfizer	• Global Health Fellows Program • Measuring leadership-development value
	9. Sanofi	• CSR Ambassador Program • Sanofi Early Executive Development (SEED) • Short Term Work Assignment (SWAP) • International volunteer program (V.I.E.)
Knowledge transfer	4. BASF	• Transitions at work • Sustainability Knowledge Verbund
Managing culture change	4. BASF	• Becoming better version of who we already are
	9. Sanofi	• Fostering a culture of innovation
	7. Ingersoll Rand	• Driving outcome-driven innovation • Taking a strengths-based approach and developing new capabilities
Capturing employees' hearts and minds through employee-centered initiatives	5. Bureau Veritas	• World Environment Day
	6. Church & Dwight	• Celebrating Earth Day • Pay the Piggy

People	Chapter	Examples
	7. Ingersoll Rand	• Green Teams —Green Team Certification —Green Team Advisory Council
	10. Wyndham Worldwide	• Wyndham Worldwide Green Day and related events
Focusing on values	7. Ingersoll Rand	• Values: from home to workplace
	9. Sanofi	• A passion to help people
	10. Wyndham Worldwide	• Embedding sustainability in values and strategic priorities
Workforce development and training	4. BASF	• Core spotlight behaviors
	7. Ingersoll Rand	• Sustainability champions • Sustainability workshop
	9. Sanofi	• Connecting with employees in every function • Workforce development is one of CSR12 priorities under People pillar
	10. Wyndham Worldwide	• Sustainability 101
Wellness programs	9. Sanofi	• Health in Action
	10. Wyndham Worldwide	• Be Well
Diversity and inclusion initiatives	2. Alcatel-Lucent	• StrongHer • Hiring and working across generations • ConnectEd
	9. Sanofi	• Mosaic of ERGs
	10. Wyndham Worldwide	• Wyndham diversity leadership and training

(Continued)

People	Chapter	Examples
Providing recognition, awards, and certifications	3. Alcoa 7. Ingersoll Rand	• Gotcha! • Green Team Certification
Promoting work–life balance	2. Alcatel-Lucent	• Flexible work arrangements

Community		
Supporting community outreach and involvement	3. Alcoa	• Alcoa Community Framework • Alcoa community advisory board • Keystone Institute for Teacher Education
	5. Bureau Veritas	• Community Involvement
	9. Sanofi	• Local volunteerism and community outreach
Employee giving and local Volunteerism	3. Alcoa	• Worldwide Month of Service • Bravo! • ACTION • GreenWorks • Earthwatch Institute Partnership • Makean Impact • Alcoans in Motion
	6. Church & Dwight	• Employee Giving Fund • Volunteerism
Collaborating across stakeholders and Industries	9. Sanofi	• Providing access to medicines and reducing health-care costs • Partners in Patient Health
Corporate social responsibility and Philanthropy	8. Pfizer 9. Sanofi 10. Wyndham Worldwide	• Global Health Fellows Program • The story of Josh • Making wishes come true

Community

		—WishDay —Wishes by Wyndham Foundation —Million Tree Project • Landal GreenParks —Engaged Entrepreneurship

Customers

Leading by example	5. Bureau Veritas 10. Wyndham Worldwide	• Walking the talk • Count on Me! • Landal GreenParks's low-car diet
Tying sustainability to innovation	2. Alcatel-Lucent	• lightRadio • Green Touch • Smartgrid • Smarthouse
	7. Ingersoll Rand	• Outcome-driven innovation (ODI) • Applying ODI to sustainability challenges
	9. Sanofi	• Evolving from environmentalism to social consciousness to innovation
Creating and sustaining customer value	7. Ingersoll Rand	• Segmenting the marketplace • Creating a green portfolio
	10. Wyndham Worldwide	• Landal GreenParks
Shifting customer mind-sets and Behavior	7. Ingersoll Rand 10. Wyndham Worldwide	• Open innovation • Ecologically friendly initiatives for guests • Wyndham Green's programs for kids • Wyndham Green Kid's Energy Adventure Scavenger Hunt

(Continued)

Customers

		• Winnie the Wallabee • Instilling sustainable practices in owners, franchisees, and time-share owners —WVO Certification —RCI Green Award —Green Franchise Advisory Board

Planet	Chapter	Examples
Becoming environmental and product stewards	3. Alcoa	• Composting • Particulates • Water
	6. Church & Dwight	• Material Safety Data Sheet • Full ingredient disclosure • Animal-testing policy • Reducing waste, energy, and water
	9. Sanofi	• Sustaining a healthy planet for patients
Life-cycle thinking	4. BASF	• Life-cycle assessment (LCA) • Environmental management system • SEE Balance (social, environment, economic) • SET (sustainability, eco-efficiency, traceability) • AgBalance • Sustainability check • Eco-efficiency analysis • Materiality assessment
	7. Ingersoll Rand	• LCA
Management-systems-support programs	3. Alcoa	• Creating accountability with metrics • A3 Process
	5. Bureau Veritas	• BV Carbon • Vericert • Veriperf • Standards

Planet	Chapter	Examples
	6. Church & Dwight	• Responsible Care • Product Care • Business Impact Matrix
	9. Sanofi	• Genzyme sticker program • Genzyme energy sustainability program • Preserving water and its sources • Global Water Tool
Partnering with universities, governments, and NGOs	3. Alcoa	• Earthwatch Institute Partnership • Keystone Institute for Teacher Education
	6. Church & Dwight	• Partnerships with NGOs: World Wildlife Fund (WWF) and the Nature Conservancy
	8. Pfizer	• Managing and aligning partnership
	9. Sanofi	• Environmental Defense Fund Climate Corps Fellowship Program
	10. Wyndham Worldwide	• Clinton Global Initiative • Cambridge Climate Leaders • Institute for Sustainable Enterprise (ISE), Fairleigh Dickinson University (FDU)
Metrics that matter	4. BASF	• Materiality assessment • Total cost of ownership
	5. Bureau Veritas	• Materiality • Assurances • Verification
Green buildings	8. Sanofi	• Genzyme Corporate Headquarters • Green buildings

(*Continued*)

Supply Chain	Chapter	
Creating a sustainable supply chain	10. Wyndham Worldwide	• Wyndham Green Supplier Program • Fully sustainable bathroom amenities
Cultivating supplier diversity and sustainability	9. Sanofi	• Supplier diversity and sustainability initiatives
	10. Wyndham Worldwide	• Wyndham supplier diversity program
Instilling sustainable practices throughout the value chain	7. Ingersoll Rand	• Life-cycle thinking • LCA

Profit	Chapter	
Governance: creating a workable sustainability structure	10. Wyndham Worldwide	• Wyndham Green • Wyndham Green Sustainability Policy
Incorporating sustainability fully into company strategy	4. BASF	• Creating chemistry for a sustainable future
	7. Ingersoll Rand	• Recognizing the inextricable link between sustainability and premier performance • Tying sustainability to company's brand, promise, vision, and purpose • Translating sustainability into customer value
Managing and measuring return on investment	8. Pfizer	• Global Health Fellows Program: Measuring return on investment

Notes

Chapter 1

1. John Elkington, *Cannibals with Forks: The Triple Bottom Line of 21st Century Business* (Gabriola Island, BC, Canada: New Society Publishers, 1998).

2. World Economic Forum, *Global Risks 2013*. 8th ed. (Geneva, Switzerland: World Economic Forum, 2013).

3. Richard Wells, "To Build Long Term Sustainability, Envision the Future First," GreenBiz Blog, June 21, 2013. http://www.greenbiz.com/blog/2013/06/21/creating-scenarios-sustainable-competitiveness. Used with permission.

4. Accenture, "A New Era of Sustainability: UN Global Compact–Accenture CEO Study 2010." http://www.unglobalcompact.org/docs/news_events/8.1/UNGC_Accenture_CEO_Study_2010.pdf.

5. Jeana Wirtenberg, William G. Russell, and David Lipsky, eds., *The Sustainable Enterprise Fieldbook: When It All Comes Together* (Sheffield, United Kingdom: Greenleaf Publishing, 2008), 283.

Chapter 2

1. Barry Dambach, Presentation for Fairleigh Dickinson University's Institute for Sustainable Enterprise (ISE) Corporate Partner Roundtable Series on Creating a Culture for Sustainability. Held at Ingersoll Rand, Piscataway, NJ, January 13, 2011.

2. Alcatel-Lucent, Corporate Responsibility Report 2011, 4. http://alcatel-lucent.publispeak.com/corporate-responsibility-report-2011/.

3. Barry Dambach, Personal interview, March 1, 2012.

4. Alcatel-Lucent, Corporate Responsibility Report 2011, 70.

5. Ibid., 121.

6. Richard Goode, Personal interview, April 24, 2012.

7. Dambach, Presentation for Fairleigh Dickinson University's Institute for Sustainable Enterprise (ISE).

8. Alcatel-Lucent, Corporate Responsibility Report 2011, 121.

9. Christine Diamente, Personal interviews, March 29, 2012; March 6, 2013.

10. Alcatel-Lucent, Corporate Responsibility Report 2011, 1.

11. Ibid., 4.

12. www3.alcatel-lucent.com/sustainability/recognition.html.

13. Diamente, Personal interview, March 29, 2012.

14. Elisabeth Eude, Personal interview, March 6, 2013.

15. Ibid.

16. Alcatel-Lucent, Corporate Responsibility Report 2011, 119.

17. Diamente, Personal interview, March 29, 2012.

18. Alcatel-Lucent, Corporate Responsibility Report 2011, 4.

19. Goode, Personal interview.

20. Ibid.

21. Ibid.

22. Diamente, Personal interview, March 6, 2013.

Chapter 3

1. Steve Fromkin, Personal Interview, April 16, 2012.

2. Alcoa Inc., Alcoa at a Glance (PowerPoint presentation). 2012.

3. Alcoa Inc., "Alcoa Named to the Dow Jones Sustainability Indexes: World and North America." (Press release). 2012. http://www.alcoa.com/global/en/news/news_detail.asp?pageID=20120913006628en&newsYear=2012.

Wirtenberg, Jeana, Joel Harmon, William G. Russell, and Kent Fairfield, "HR's Role in Building a Sustainable Enterprise," *Human Resource Planning* 30(1) (2007): 10–20.

4. Laurie Roy, Personal interview, April 13, 2012.

5. Alcoa Inc., Alcoa at a Glance (PowerPoint presentation). 2012.

6. Roy, Personal interview.

7. Fromkin, Personal interview.

8. Laura Carpenter, Personal interview, April 17, 2012.

9. Janice Maffei and Joanne Spigner, *vision·in·a·box Leader's Guide* (Madison, NJ: VisionFirst, 2000), 1.

10. Fromkin, Personal interview.

11. Ibid.

12. Ibid.

13. Roy, Personal interview.

14. Jamie Horst. Employee Engagement. Alcoa Foundation 2012.

15. Ibid.

16. Roy, Personal interview.

17. Ibid.

18. Horst, Employee Engagement.

19. Ibid.

20. Ed Barker and Laurie Roy, "Using Partnerships to Enhance Sustainability Outcomes." Presentation. Held at Fairleigh Dickinson University's Institute for Sustainable Enterprise, Madison, NJ. June 18, 2010.

21. Horst, Employee Engagement.

22. Ibid.

23. Carpenter, Personal interview.

24. Make an Impact Program. Press Release, 2012. http://www.c2es.org/newsroom/releases/mai-schools-challenge-2012.

25. Roy, Personal interview.

26. Kent Fairfield, "Case 4. Environmental, Health & Safety Issues at Alcoa Howmet," in *The Sustainable Enterprise Fieldbook: When It All Comes Together,* ed. Jeana Wirtenberg, William G. Russell, and David Lipsky (Sheffield, United Kingdom: Greenleaf, 2009), 156–157.

27. Roy, Personal interview.

28. Fromkin, Personal interview.

29. Ibid.

30. Roy, Personal interview.

31. Alcoa Community Framework. 2012. http://www.alcoa.com/sustainability/en/info_page/community_stakeholder.asp#comm_engage.

32. Carpenter, Personal interview.

33. Fromkin, Personal interview.

Chapter 4

1. Hans Engel, "We Create Chemistry for a Sustainable Future." Presentation to Rothman Institute of Entrepreneurship's 2012 Innovation Summit "Sustainability through Innovation." Held at Fairleigh Dickinson University, Madison, NJ. October 3, 2012.

2. Charlene Wall, Personal interview, November 20, 2012.

3. Engel, "We Create Chemistry for a Sustainable Future."

4. Ibid.

5. Edward Madzy, Personal interview, November 16, 2012.

6. James Bero, Personal interview, October 24, 2012.

7. Engel, "We Create Chemistry for a Sustainable Future."

8. Footprint Network. 2013, "World Footprint: Do We Fit on the Planet." http://www.footprintnetwork.org/en/index.php/gfn/page/world_footprint/.

9. Wall, Personal interview.

10. www.basf.com.

11. Charlene Wall. "Creating Chemistry for a Sustainable Future." Presentation. Held at Fairleigh Dickinson University's Institute for Sustainable Enterprise, Madison, NJ. December 17, 2010.

12. Wall, Personal interview.

13. Engel, "We Create Chemistry for a Sustainable Future."

14. Wall, Personal interview.

15. BASF. Strategic Business Tools: Improving Performance through Sustainability. 2012.

16. www.basf-admixtures.com.

17. Wall, Personal interview.

18. Ibid.

19. Judy Zagorski, Personal interview, November 27, 2012.

20. Ibid.

21. Ibid.

22. Andreas Meier, Personal interview, November 14, 2012.

23. Wall, Personal interview.

24. Zagorski, Personal interview.

25. Bero, Personal interview.

26. Ibid.

27. Zagorski, Personal interview.

28. Bero, Personal interview.

29. Ibid.

30. Wall, Personal interview.

31. Bero, Personal interview.

32. Madzy, Personal interview.

33. Ibid.

34. Bero, Personal interview.

35. Madzy, Personal interview.

36. Robin Rotenberg, Personal interview, October 24, 2012.

37. Ibid.

38. Meier, Personal interview.

39. Ibid.

40. Ibid.

41. Zagorski, Personal interview.

42. Ibid.

43. Ibid.

44. Ibid.

45. Patricia Rossman, Personal interview, November 13, 2012.

46. Zagorski, Personal interview.

47. Rossman, Personal interview.

48. Zagorski, Personal interview.

49. Ibid.

50. Caitlin Harmon, Personal interview, January 10, 2013.

51. Ibid.

52. Zagorski, Personal interview.

53. Environmental Leader, "BASF Debuts Compostable Snack Bag at Seattle Mariners Game." September 6, 2012.

54. Ibid.

55. Zagorski, Personal interview.

56. Bero, Personal interview.

57. William Pagano. Written interview. May, 2013.

58. www.nsf.org/business/eco-efficiency.

59. Zagorski, Personal interview.

60. Rotenberg, Personal interview.

61. Rossman, Personal interview.

62. Ibid.

63. Ibid.

64. Ibid.

65. Pagano, Written interview.

66. BASF. BASF in North America Report 2011. http://www.basf.com/group/corporate/en/function/conversions:/publish/content/about-basf/facts-reports/reports/2011/BASF_in_North_America_2011.pdf, 35.

67. Chris Groff, Personal interview, February 19, 2013.

68. Wall, Personal interview.

69. Ibid.

70. Ibid.

Chapter 5

1. Jyoti Agarwal and Laurie Lane. Presentation for Fairleigh Dickinson University's Institute for Sustainable Enterprise (ISE) Corporate Partner Roundtable Series on Creating a Culture for Sustainability. Held at Sheraton Raritan Center, Edison, NJ. April 14, 2011.

2. Ibid.

3. John Stangline. Presentation for Fairleigh Dickinson University's Institute for Sustainable Enterprise Corporate Partner Roundtable Series on Sustainable Supply Chains. Held at BASF, Florham Park, NJ. July 24, 2012.

4. Ibid., 20.

5. Ibid.

6. Lisa Barnes, Personal interview, August 27, 2012.

7. Charlotte Breuil, Personal interview, August 28, 2012.

8. Murray Sayce, Personal interview, August 20, 2012.

9. Barnes, Personal interview.

10. Ibid.

11. Breuil, Personal interview.

12. Kah Yin Chan, Personal interview, August 29, 2012.

13. Joshua Choong, Personal interview, August 29, 2012.

14. Ibid.

15. Ibid.

16. Bureau Veritas. 2012 United Nations World Environment Day at Bureau Veritas Group. June 15, 2012, 2.

17. Ibid.

18. Bureau Veritas. 2010. Bureau Veritas-WED 2010 EN.pdf

19. Bureau Veritas. 2011. Bureau Veritas-WED 2011 EN.pdf, 6.

20. Choong, Personal interview.

21. Bureau Veritas, Bureau Veritas-WED 2011, 4.

22. Bureau Veritas. HSE in Bureau Veritas: Package for tenders. May, 2012, 7.

23. Bureau Veritas, HSE in Bureau Veritas, 13.

24. Janet Peterson, Personal interview, August 24, 2012.

25. Breuil, Personal interview.

26. Sayce, Personal interview.

27. Ibid.

Chapter 6

1. Robert Coleman, Personal interview, August 10, 2012.

2. Matthew Wasserman, Personal interview, May 1, 2012.

3. Church & Dwight Co., Inc., 2011 Sustainability Report. http://www
.churchdwight.com/company/our-values-and-vision/sustainability.aspx.

4. Coleman, Personal interview.

5. Michael Buczynski, Personal interview, August 10, 2012.

6. Coleman, Personal interview.

7. Ibid.

8. Buczynski, Personal interview.

9. Coleman, Personal interview.

10. Ibid.

11. Ibid.

12. Ibid.

13. Ibid.

14. Church & Dwight, Sustainability Report.

15. Ibid.

16. Ibid., 13.

17. Ibid.

18. Michael Buczynski. Office of Sustainable Development and Product
Stewardship (internal document). 2012.

19. Buczynski, Personal interview.

20. www.churchdwight.com/brands-and-products/product-safety-overview
.aspx.

21. Ibid.

22. Church & Dwight, Sustainability Report.

23. Coleman, Personal interview.

24. Ibid.

25. TerraChoice (part of the UL Global Network), "The Sins of Greenwashing: Home and Family Edition 2010" (report on environmental claims made in
the North American consumer market). http://www.terrachoice.com.

26. Wasserman, Personal interview.

27. Ibid.

28. Coleman, Personal interview.

29. Wasserman, Personal interview.

30. Buczynski, Personal interview.

31. Wasserman, Personal interview.

32. Ibid.

33. Buczynski, Personal interview.

34. Church & Dwight, Sustainability Report, 13.

35. Ibid., 18.

36. Wasserman, Personal interview.

37. Johnson & Johnson. Sustainable Energy Best Practices (JNJ Energy Tool for CHD). 2007.

38. Ibid.

39. Ibid.

40. Church & Dwight, Sustainability Report, 20.

41. Ibid., 32–33.

42. Ibid., 32.

43. Coleman, Personal interview.

Chapter 7

1. Scott W. Tew, Personal interview, July 19, 2012.

2. Ingersoll Rand. Delivering Results. 2012 Annual Report. 2012, 6.

3. Ibid.

4. Ibid.

5. Scott W. Tew. "Journey to Sustainability." Presentation. Held at Fairleigh Dickinson University's Institute for Sustainable Enterprise, Madison, NJ. October 19, 2012.

6. Ibid.

7. Ingersoll Rand. Delivering Results. 2012 Annual Report, 18.

8. Christopher Tessier, Personal interview, July 19, 2012.

9. Paul Camuti, Personal interview, July 19, 2012.

10. Ingersoll Rand. Delivering Results. 2012 Annual Report, 18.

11. Camuti, Personal interview.

12. Ibid.

13. Ibid.

14. Ibid.

15. Gretchen Digby, Personal interview, July 20, 2012.

16. Katie Pogue, "Step Up to Sustainability" (white paper). Ingersoll Rand. May 2012. http://www.cees.ingersollrand.com/CEES_documents/GreenInitiatives_Whitepaper_Final.pdf, 1.

17. Ingersoll Rand. Delivering Results. 2012 Annual Report, 15.

18. Gretchen Digby. Written statement. July 29, 2013.

19. Ibid.

20. Ingersoll Rand. Certified Green Teams Brochure. 2012. http://www
.cees.ingersollrand.com/CEES_documents/GreenTeamsCertification_Brochure_
Final.pdf, 3.

21. Digby, Personal interview.

22. Ibid.

23. Ingersoll Rand. One STEP Forward Public Announcement. 2012.

24. Digby, Personal interview.

25. Ingersoll Rand. One STEP Forward Public Announcement.

26. Digby, Personal interview.

27. Deborah Kalish, Personal interview, July 19, 2012.

28. Digby, Personal interview.

29. Ibid.

30. Ingersoll Rand. One STEP Forward Public Announcement.

31. Digby, Personal interview.

32. Ingersoll Rand. One STEP Forward Public Announcement.

33. Digby, Personal interview.

34. Kalish, Personal interview.

35. Ibid.

36. Ibid.

37. Tew, Personal interview.

38. Clayton Christensen and Michael E. Raynor, *The Innovator's Solution*
(Boston: Harvard Business Review Press, 2003).

39. Jeff Dyer, Hal Gregersen, and Clayton Christensen, *The Innovator's
DNA* (Boston: Harvard Business Review Press, 2011).

40. Tew, Personal interview.

41. Christensen and Raynor, *The Innovator's Solution*.

42. Ibid., 78.

43. Tew, Personal interview.

44. Ibid.

45. Ibid.

46. Ibid.

47. Ibid.

48. Anthony W. Ulwick, "What Is Outcome-Driven Innovation (ODI)?"
(white paper). (San Francisco: Strategyn, 2013), 3.

49. Ibid., 1.

50. Ibid.

51. Tew, Personal interview.

52. Ibid.

53. Ingersoll Rand. Delivering Results. 2012 Sustainability Supplement.
2012, 42.

54. Ibid.

55. Ibid., 37.

56. hpb.trane.com/high-performance-buildings/global/en/trane-intelligent-services.html.

57. Tew, Personal interview.

58. www.trane.com/high-performance-buildings/global/en/about-high-performance-buildings.html.

59. Ingersoll Rand, Delivering Results. 2012 Sustainability Supplement, 14.

60. Ibid., 15.

61. Camuti, Personal interview.

62. Ibid.

63. Ibid.

64. Ibid.

65. E. Jefferson (Jeff) Hynds, Personal interview, July 19, 2012.

66. Ibid.

67. Camuti, Personal interview.

68. Ibid.

69. Hynds, Personal interview.

70. Camuti, Personal interview.

71. Ibid.

72. Hynds, Personal interview.

73. Joe Wolfsberger, Personal interview, July 20, 2012.

Chapter 8

1. Pfizer, Inc., Letter to Stakeholders in Pfizer 2012 Annual Review. February 2013. http://www.pfizer.com/investors/financial_reports/annual_reports/2012/letter.jsp.

2. Oonagh Puglisi, Personal interview, March 27, 2012.

3. Ibid.

4. Ibid.

5. Ibid.

6. Ibid.

7. Pfizer-m2m Case Study Kit, March 2012.

8. Michael Benigno, Personal interview, May 9, 2012.

9. It is noteworthy that the intellectual property generated by this project and other GHF programs does not belong to Pfizer; it is publicly owned and widely shared. As such, all of the metrics and methods developed in Benigno's assignment are nonproprietary and are openly used by researchers.

10. Benigno, Personal interview.

11. Ibid.

12. Karen Stegman, Personal interview, May 23, 2012.

13. Ibid.

14. Ibid.

15. Ibid.

16. Ibid.

17. Ibid.

Chapter 9

1. Sanofi. Corporate Social Responsibility: 2012 Report. 2012, 4.
2. John Spinnato, Personal interview, June 25, 2012.
3. Peter Loupos, Personal interview, June 26, 2012.
4. Ibid.
5. Ibid.
6. Christopher Viehbacher. Senior Management Interview in Sanofi, Corporate Social Responsibility: 2012 Report. 2012, 3.
7. Ibid.
8. Sanofi, Corporate Social Responsibility, 14.
9. Ibid., 13.
10. Ibid., 16.
11. Ibid., 26.
12. Sabrina Spitaletta, Personal interview, June 26, 2012.
13. Loupos, Personal interview.
14. Ibid.
15. Sanofi. Providing Hope. Corporate Social Responsibility North America 2012.
16. Ellyn Schindler, Personal interview, June 25, 2012.
17. Ibid.
18. Ibid.
19. Ibid.
20. Ibid.
21. Nuala Culleton, Personal interview, June 25, 2012.
22. Sanofi, Corporate Social Responsibility, 60.
23. RedBrick. Your Guide to RedBrick Health (PDF document). 2012.
24. RedBrick. Health in Action: Programs and Services (PDF document). 2012, 2.
25. Sanofi, Corporate Social Responsibility, 61.
26. Ibid.
27. Lara Jones, Personal interview, June 26, 2012.
28. Ibid.
29. Kathleen Castore, Personal interview, June 18, 2012.
30. Ibid.
31. Ibid.
32. Ibid.
33. Ibid.
34. Jeff Holmes, Personal interview, June 26, 2012.
35. Sanofi, Providing Hope, 3.
36. Sanofi, Corporate Social Responsibility, 6.

37. Sanofi, Providing Hope, 11.

38. Ibid.

39. Holmes, Personal interview.

40. Sanofi, Providing Hope, 11.

41. Holmes, Personal interview.

42. Sanofi, Corporate Social Responsibility, 78.

43. Ibid.

44. Sanofi, Providing Hope.

45. Loupos, Personal interview.

46. Ibid.

47. Ibid.

48. Castore, Personal interview.

49. Spitaletta, Personal interview.

50. Holmes, Personal interview.

51. www.ghgprotocol.org/files/ghgp/public/FAQ.pdf.

52. www.wbcsd.org/work-program/sectorprojects/water/global-water-tool
.aspx.

53. Sanofi, Corporate Social Responsibility, 78.

Chapter 10

1. Faith Taylor, Personal interview, October 3, 2012.

2. Ibid.

3. Stephen Holmes, Personal interview, February 20, 2013.

4. Taylor, Personal interview.

5. Ibid.

6. Ibid.

7. Eric Danziger, Personal interview, November 13, 2012.

8. Ibid.

9. Geoffrey Ballotti, Personal interview, November 19, 2012.

10. Faith Taylor, "One: Goal. Team. Earth." Presentation. Held at Fairleigh Dickinson University's Institute for Sustainable Enterprise, Madison, NJ. May 21, 2010.

11. Ibid.

12. Ibid.

13. Wyndham Worldwide (WW). Wyndham Worldwide Sustainability Report. May 2012.

14. Ibid., 21.

15. Ibid., 3.

16. Gary Hyde, Personal interview, November 6, 2012.

17. Ibid.

18. Geoffrey Richards, Personal interview, November 6, 2012.

19. WW, Sustainability Report, 16.

20. Mary Falvey, Personal interview, November 19, 2012.

21. Ibid.
22. WW, Sustainability Report, 52.
23. William Skrzat. Written communication. July 9, 2013.
24. WW, Sustainability Report, 51.
25. Patricia Lee. Written communication. July 9, 2013.
26. WW, Sustainability Report, 57.
27. Paul Davis, Personal interview, November 5, 2012.
28. Ibid.
29. WW, Sustainability Report, 43.
30. Ibid., 47, 48.
31. Davis, Personal interview.
32. WW, Sustainability Report, 45.
33. Ibid.
34. Hyde, Personal interview.
35. Ibid.
36. Taylor, Personal interview.
37. WW, Sustainability Report, 36.
38. August Manz, Personal interview, November 5, 2012.
39. Davis, Personal interview.
40. Ibid.
41. WW, Sustainability Report, 59.
42. Davis, Personal interview.
43. Ballotti, Personal interview.
44. WW, Sustainability Report, 63.
45. Hyde, Personal interview.
46. Ibid.
47. Wyndham Worldwide (WW). Wyndham Green: Global Best Practices. 2010, 11.
48. Richards, Personal interview.
49. Ibid.
50. Ballotti, Personal interview.
51. Ibid.
52. Thomas Heerkens, Personal interview, December 3, 2012.
53. WW, Wyndham Green, 31.
54. Heerkens, Personal interview.
55. WW, Wyndham Green, 32.
56. Heerkens, Personal interview.
57. Ibid.
58. Ibid.
59. Ibid.
60. Ibid.
61. Ibid.
62. Danziger, Personal interview.
63. Ibid.

64. Ibid.
65. Ibid.
66. Taylor, Personal interview.
67. Ibid.
68. Ballotti, Personal interview.
69. Taylor, Personal interview.
70. Ibid.

Chapter 11

1. World Economic Forum, *Global Risks 2013*. 8th ed. (Geneva, Switzerland: World Economic Forum, 2013).

2. businessjournal.gallup.com/content/439/what-your-disaffected-workers-cost.aspx.

3. Richard Matthews, "Workshop: Employee Engagement for Sustainability," *Before It's News,* April 12, 2013.

4. Joel Harmon, Kent Fairfield, and Jeana Wirtenberg, "Missing an Opportunity: HR Leadership and Sustainability," *People & Strategy* 33(1) (2010): 16–21.

5. Adam Lowry and Eric Ryan, Foreword to *The New Rules of Green Marketing,* by Jacquelyn A. Ottman (Sheffield, United Kingdom: Greenleaf Publishing; San Francisco: Berrett Koehler Publishers, 2011), xi–xii.

6. TerraChoice (part of the UL Global Network), "The Sins of Greenwashing: Home and Family Edition 2010" (report on environmental claims made in the North American consumer market). http://www.terrachoice.com.

7. United Nations Environment Programme (UNEP), *Universal Ownership: Why Environmental Externalities Matter to Institutional Investors,* 2010.

8. Edgar H. Schein, *Organizational Culture and Leadership* (San Francisco: John Wiley & Sons, Inc., 2010), 24.

9. Charles Duhigg, *The Power of Habit* (New York: Random House, 2012).

10. Ibid.

11. James C. Collins and Jerry I. Porras, *Built to Last: Successful Habits of Visionary Companies* (New York: Harper Business, 1994).

Index

About the Author

JEANA WIRTENBERG, PhD, is president and CEO, Transitioning to Green, and cofounder/senior advisor, Institute for Sustainable Enterprise, Fairleigh Dickinson University, Madison, New Jersey. Her published works include "Sustainable Enterprise for the 21st Century" in Praeger's *The Business of Sustainability: Trends, Policies, Practices, and Stories of Success;* "Transitioning to the Green Economy," a special issue of *People & Strategy;* and "Unleashing Talent for a Sustainable Future" in *The Talent Management Handbook: Creating a Sustainable Competitive Advantage by Selecting, Developing, and Promoting the Best People.* She was lead editor of *The Sustainable Enterprise Fieldbook: When It All Comes Together.* For several years, Wirtenberg wrote a weekly newsletter on sustainability for the *Wall Street Journal.* She teaches in the MBA in Sustainability program at Bard College. Wirtenberg holds a doctorate in psychology from the University of California at Los Angeles.